Downsizing

Strategies for Success in the Modern Computer World

Downsizing

Strategies for Success in the Modern Computer World

Dan Trimmer

ADDISON-WESLEY
PUBLISHING
COMPANY

Wokingham, England · Reading, Massachusetts · Menlo Park, California · New York
Don Mills, Ontario · Amsterdam · Bonn · Sydney · Singapore
Tokyo · Madrid · San Juan · Milan · Paris · Mexico City · Seoul · Taipei

Cover designed by Chris Eley
and printed by The Riverside Printing Co. (Reading) Ltd.
Typeset by Colset Private Limited, Singapore
in 11½/13 point Baskerville.
Printed and bound in Great Britain at the University Press, Cambridge

First printed 1993.

ISBN 0-201-62409-5

British Library Cataloguing-in-Publication Data
A catalogue record for this book is available from the British Library.

Library of Congress Cataloging-in-Publication Data is available

'Much learning does not teach common sense'

Heraclitus

Contents

Preface

The purpose of this book is twofold. First, it aims to convince the reader that, in current times, the downsizing and distributing of computer systems away from the central mainframe represents the best option for the vast majority of organizations. Second, it aims to show how the downsizing exercise can be accomplished most effectively.

Hardware and software technologies surrounding the downsized system are undergoing exceptionally rapid rates of change. These changes are of profound importance. However, much success with downsizing depends upon such non-technical factors as management sensitivity and determination. There is in fact a long history behind downsizing as we know it today, and many lessons can be applied to current situations. Unfortunately, too often these lessons are ignored, leading either to failure or to only partial success of the downsizing effort.

The bulk of this book aims to provide a practical, complete and relatively non-technical guide to downsizing. To that end, it follows a top-down approach, looking at the technological base and broad organizational needs before delving into the minutiae of product strategies, design methods and the various human factors relevant to the subject. By avoiding the most obvious traps, and by optimizing the combination of technology, user and IT skills, the reader should be able to attain a higher degree of success with his downsizing efforts than otherwise might be the case.

Because a wide spectrum of readers is being addressed, some suggestions as to how to use this book are in order. Managers whose responsibilities lie outside computing, but whose departments will use downsized systems, might focus most of their attention on the less technical chapters. These include the introductory sections (Chapters 1 to 16) and those dealing with organizational matters (Chapters 9 to 11). For those concerned with management information applications,

Chapter 17 is relevant, and the case studies (Chapter 24) provide a practical perspective.

Readers from the IT side of the equation, on the other hand, should pay at least as much attention to the organizational matters as to the more technical subjects, as in downsizing most opportunities and dangers reside outside territory that is strictly technical. Also, those readers with a particular technical specialization might read the sections dealing with technologies other than their own. Such topics as database (Chapter 13), and communications (Chapter 14), aim to bring out major points (as opposed to technical detail) which will determine the success or otherwise of the downsizing effort. Technicians from other territories might thus gain useful insights where they need to acquire a broad view of a downsizing project.

Much of this book stresses the need for simplicity. While the 'keep it simple' school of IT implementation has been around for decades, it has been widely ignored. Part of the problem is that managers have been unable to draw on practical techniques which enforce simplicity. Throughout the book, we try to offer suggestions as to how simplicity can be maintained. In particular, Chapter 10 (on organizational topologies) and Chapters 15, 16 and 20 (on design-related topics), try to present ways of achieving and maintaining application simplicity.

Other pointers to simplifying the overall downsized environment are contained in discussions of system platform selection, mainly in Chapter 21 (hardware) and Chapter 22 (software). Simplicity in personnel structures is covered mainly in Chapter 23.

The majority of readers of this book will already be aware of some aspects of downsizing. Many arguments are put forward not only for the reader's benefit, but also to help him advance valid downsizing views to others. In most organizations, downsizing has been carried out only to a very limited extent, and much progress remains to take place. In order to maximize both the pace and success of further downsizing, we hope to illustrate a variety of perspectives which will help to consolidate the reader's own knowledge and also to enable him to present constructive and practical plans to his colleagues.

While the main readership of this book is intended to be among users of computers, a word or two are in order to the supplier side of the industry. Many providers of hardware, software and services are having even more trouble with downsizing than are user organizations. Typically, suppliers understand the technology behind downsizing well enough. The usual problem is that they may not be sufficiently aware of how to apply it, or how to advise users in configuring downsizing plans. The several chapters on organization, applications and management topics may help suppliers as well as users to make the most of the downsizing revolution.

1

The organizational imperative

For well over three decades, most organizations of any size have had a computer department of one sort or another. In many situations – perhaps the majority – the relationship between what is now called the IT (for Information Technology) department and the rest of the business has not been a particularly happy one. Partial successes have been offset by slow applications development on the one hand and cost overruns on the other. In many cases, the application presented has been out of date by the time it was delivered, or was otherwise not what the user had in mind.

Until recently, advances in computer technology have not noticeably eased this stalemate between IT staff and the rest of the organization. Indeed, advanced technology has often added to the suspicion and discredit already suffered by IT. Some computer professionals, especially if they feel threatened and defensive, may unwittingly allow new products to be oversold in their eagerness to please their users. They may be encouraged in this overselling by computer manufacturers who are themselves under great pressures as markets approach saturation point.

Because this cycle of exaggerated expectations followed by only moderate gains has been going on for many years, end users and general management have become cynical about the whole process. Even where some improvements in applications do appear, they are often counterbalanced by higher hardware costs or by a larger and even more complicated IT department than existed before.

Problems of the centralized system

Many of IT's problems have been caused by the character of the large mainframe, where the latter is placed in a centralized environment, remote from the end user. This type of machine is not only very expensive when compared to alternatives, it is also much more difficult to work with. It is further insulated from the business by the large numbers of specialized technicians who are required to operate such systems.

It is of utmost importance for mainframe users to recognize this link between technical product complexity and the inevitable bureaucracy which must accompany it. It means, among other things, that mainframe concepts may be defended by those whose main experience is in this area and who see their positions threatened. Many such people will genuinely be unaware of alternative solutions. They will be backed by those suppliers who remain overly committed to mainframe designs, having failed to perceive shifts in the market that have been occurring steadily over the past thirty years.

Another point arising from the above is that arguments against centralization can be successfully directed at general, non-technical management. This writer has frequently used the often chaotic per-

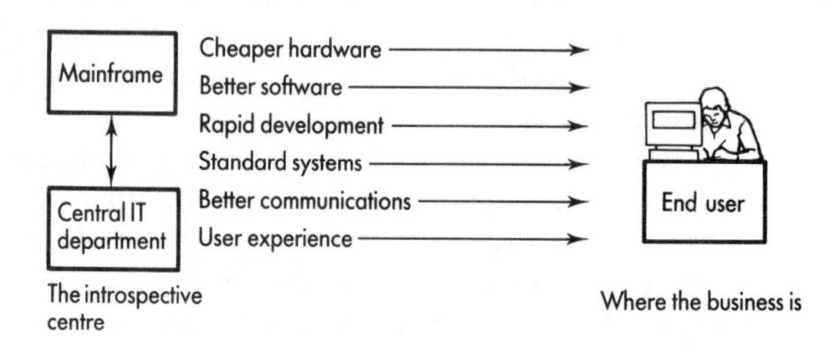

Figure 1.1 Trends toward the end user.

A number of related developments are drawing the computer world away from the traditional in-house computer establishment. The developments have been steadily progressing for over thirty years, yet they surprise many even within the industry. The developments and their implications are fundamental and are very unlikely to be reversed.

sonnel structure within IT to show that, whatever the machinery may do, such a human system could never produce results quickly. Managers most receptive to this line of argument are often in non-technical areas such as the public sector. There, one has to squeeze results out of low-level staff and therefore has to organize them well. Many managers, public-sector or private-sector, appreciate such a non-technical discussion of administrative principles. In other words, just because a manager may appear technically naive, IT managers should not assume he need remain uninvolved in the downsizing argument. When problems are explained in terms they can understand, such people often become the most enthusiastic allies of the downsizing effort. They are able to see that, leaving technical factors aside, downsizing is simply a much better solution to administrative questions.

Downsizing as today's solution

The movement which is now called 'downsizing' has been proceeding for a good couple of decades. The term gained currency in the late 1980s, when technology improved suddenly in parallel with other developments, notably user maturity. The concept of downsizing today is a comprehensive one, and represents much more than just using the occasional PC (Personal Computer) or other small machine to do odd jobs that the mainframe cannot address. In the early 1990s, a number of broadly related advances in both hardware and software have conspired to render downsizing solutions far more feasible for corporate-wide computing than they were in the past. While the detail of these developments will be discussed in subsequent chapters, the point to be made here is that a major threshold has been crossed, such that many large organizations over time will be able to dispense with mainframe computing entirely. To the business at large, this implies vastly reduced hardware, software and personnel costs. For a business funded by shareholder equity, this can mean several percentage points added to the return on that equity, or a percent added to turnover, or perhaps five percent added to profits. To a public-sector or charitable concern, the savings are equally meaningful. Most such organizations are hard pressed to show results to taxpayers or donors in

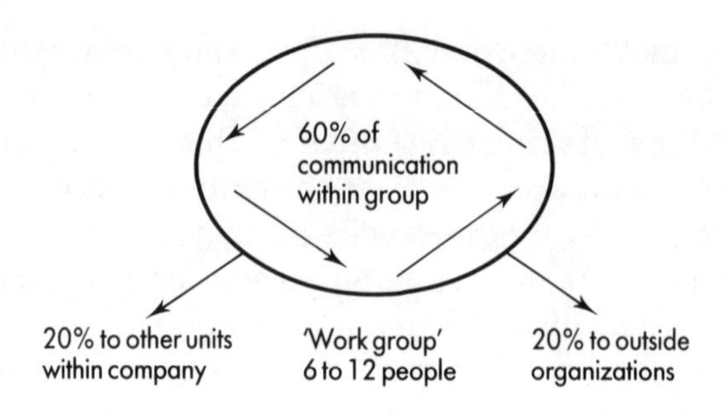

Figure 1.2 Downsizing theory.

Work group theory is fundamental to much downsizing. Though there is much variation depending upon the work group's role, on average the majority of communication of all types takes place within the group. Much of the model was established by Mr J.H. Bair while doing research for Xerox and the Stanford Research Institute. The model says, above all other things, that such groups need their own local machine facilities, and that such facilities must include good communications links.

today's strict financial climate. Any significant amount of money that can be diverted to the real purpose of the organization will be exceptionally welcome.

Direct cost savings are but part of the downsizing equation. Other benefits, obviously more difficult to quantify but nevertheless there, include a higher quality of application, in the sense that software can be made to fit the end user's needs more precisely. Downsized applications can be developed in less time than would be the case on a mainframe, and so will bring their benefits more quickly. They are less likely to be out of date on delivery, and to be more easily modified when changes are required. Users generally feel more motivated using an application in the development of which they have participated, which is the usual case with a downsized or distributed application. Overall user productivity is more easily maximized because of the combination of the above items.

The threat to jobs

Though a number of people within a given IT department are probably aware of downsizing's potential, many will simply view it as a threat to jobs or as a de-skilling exercise that may limit career prospects. In the past, it has been customary to reassure existing staff that, when a new item of technology is introduced, there will be no threat to existing jobs and roles. It was assumed that any manpower saved by the new productivity-increasing product would be used to shorten long development backlogs. In the event, the new item inevitably turned out to be overrated, so in reality there rarely was a threat to computer staff.

With downsizing, this is no longer the case. When an organization downsizes comprehensively, both application developers and product-specific technicians supporting the mainframe's operating software are threatened in varying degrees. As substantial staff reductions are part of the rationale behind downsizing, one can no longer lull everyone in sight with bland promises of job security. Where trade unions are involved, the lowering of staff levels as well as the redeployment or regrading of staff will undoubtedly pose formidable problems. While suggestions will be made later on how staff redeployment can best be handled, the point here is recognize that it is a major issue and should therefore be factored into any initial thoughts on downsizing.

The credibility problem

Aside from the threats seen in downsizing, much of the resistance is due to genuine disbelief, caused by a variety of factors. Despite the publicity given to downsizing, most people are still unaware of what the technology can do. Few IT people have the time to read regularly or systematically. Even those who do may feel swamped by the volume of trivial verbiage which afflicts the computer press. Most widely-circulated computer periodicals are not up-to-date on downsizing matters, and typically present many issues pertaining to it inaccurately.

IT professionals who do recognize the potential of downsizing should therefore be prepared from square one to spend reasonable amounts of time politely educating their own colleagues. Those requiring the most education are generally the most specialized technicians, and a certain percentage of these may be very resistant to new technologies. One's strategy here is, if possible, not to offend them and create even more resistance, but instead to circumvent them by talking to more friendly faces. Over time, at least some of the more resistant technicians may come over, especially if the new items can justifiably be presented in a non-threatening manner. It helps to point out from time to time that the business purpose of the organization can be met by a variety of machine types, and that in some cases these are complementary to the mainframe, not a direct or immediate replacement.

The non-technical issues

It is vital to convince both IT personnel and business managers that success with downsizing is mostly a non-technical matter. This will increase confidence and will encourage participation, thus lowering risks on two counts. This is not to say that technology itself is unimportant. We have already made the point that the whole base of downsizing rests upon recent strides in the technical world. However, many of these developments are those which help to simplify and de-mystify technology. Parallel developments have cut costs drastically of what are straightforward and well-established components. In other words, for both IT departments and end users, there is less need to understand technical complexity and to speak in jargon.

A basic goal in the downsizing project should be to decide early on what areas of technology can either be ignored outright or at least summarized. Although they mean well, some technicians, if given excessive leeway, will invent needlessly complicated systems in the downsized world just as they may have in the more traditional one. They may also delay evaluations and implementations with unnecessary investigations. It remains crucially important to choose the right suppliers and products, but these selections can be done with a relatively short, economical and semi-technical effort.

Success with downsizing comes from dealing accurately and swiftly with a multitude of organizational issues. IT departments in large concerns may not always be at home in such territory. Those within IT who are to carry forward the downsizing banner must therefore be chosen with care, and will need some conditioning before being let loose upon their management and users. A rapidly descending top-down approach is one of the keys to downsizing success. In other words, analysts must be encouraged to spend only limited time looking at high-level corporate goals and the way the business is structured, though obviously the perceptions arrived at must be accurate. Proportionally more time needs to be spent on issues that are theoretically lower down - meaning the characteristics of the end-user department and the details of the actual application to be implemented.

These are not theoretical points, but are based on experience. The corporate scene over the last twenty years has contained many examples where large IT departments have, doubtlessly with good intentions, clung to older methods while trying to install newer technologies. Many of these older methods are characterized by their consumption of excessive human resources and elapsed time.

The IT department's traditional lack of success with small machines often leads both IT and general management to an incorrect conclusion. That is, if big machines are a nuisance, smaller ones are a positive danger. The question rarely occurs that, if ordinary people can operate small machines, why cannot IT professionals? Those examining downsizing must be alert for the negative small-machine reference, especially if in one's own organization. Most large companies have a failed small machine somewhere in the woodwork, unloved and unused because some elementary mistake was made in its selection or installation. It behoves one to try to identify such cases in advance, and to find out the real reasons for the failure, so preempting the inference from IT traditionalists that downsizing is necessarily a disaster.

The risk issue

This leads logically to what is undoubtedly downsizing's greatest obstacle: it is perceived as a risky proposition. This *perception* of risk is fair enough, as far as it goes, and must be faced squarely. We have just noted that small machines do not always go in successfully, especially in the hands of those perceived inaccurately as experts. It is therefore important to look objectively at risks, and to look at earlier unsuccessful situations where risks were not identified or measured. Otherwise, those who doubt the effectiveness of downsizing may be tempted to use the risk issue to cripple the effort.

Risk is such an important aspect of downsizing - or of any computer implementation - that we devote Chapter 6 to the issue. Suffice it to say here that there are plenty of risks inherent in traditional styles of computing. Risk is rarely estimated with any precision in any environment - in most cases simply because the attempt is not made. Also, one needs a method whereby risks can be traded off against known deficiencies in existing systems. What may be a low-risk system, in other words, may still be a highly undesirable one.

Downsizing's changing definitions

Because of the advance of technology, as well as altering user perceptions, the notion of downsizing is altering as time progresses. As with all supposedly standard industry buzzwords, different parties offer different definitions of the subject, generally to suit their existing positions. The term 'downsizing' came into fairly wide use when the mainframe market was seen to be stagnating and when people were looking for alternatives. Such alternatives included relatively powerful minicomputers and subset-mainframe products such as IBM's AS/400 business-oriented computer. These newer systems were seen as alternatives to the mainframe, but for generally similar types of application.

This initial definition of downsizing, then, meant the replacement of applications running on the mainframe by essentially similar (but perhaps simpler) program sets running on a cheaper and easier-to-use machine. The rationale was to save both acquisition costs and personnel. Another major benefit was a more responsive installation, able to react quickly to changed circumstances, as downsized systems are less time consuming to change. Such benefits as lower space costs because of smaller machine footprints and fewer staff also meant meaningful savings, particularly in crowded, high rent districts.

Initial concepts of downsizing left aside non-traditional types of work such as office automation. Much of this had already been taken over by PCs in the early and mid-1980s. Highly numeric computing and small units of commercial work such as distributed order processing were not thought of as within the definition.

Downsizing, in most peoples' minds, therefore means something like the following:

> 'The comprehensive replacement of mainframe functions by cheaper - and possibly smaller and distributed - types of machine, for both existing and new applications.'

The definition in Table 1.1 leaves open the question whether the mainframe is to be completely replaced, though in many situations in the 1980s and early 1990s this was in fact the assumption. For a medium-sized organization (say with an annual IT budget of up to $2 million or so), this complete replacement by alternative technology

Table 1.1 Degrees of downsizing.

Centralized solutions	0	Do nothing.
	1	Alter mainframe usage.
	2	Outsource mainframe services or use facilities management.
	3	Substitute cheap box centrally.
Distributed solutions	4	Nodal medium-to-large minicomputers linked to mainframe.
	5	Smaller, highly distributed minis, linked to each other.
	6	Client/server, with PCs or UNIX workstations linked to mini server.
	7	Client/server, using and PCs and PC-compatible technology on server.

There are several steps along the path to full downsizing. The gradations by no means imply that it is safer to take small, slow steps away from the centre - quite the reverse is true. In order to maximize downsizing's effectiveness, one should move to as high a number in the above scheme as is consistent with application needs, user characteristics and technological potential.

is feasible, and over quite a short time-scale (12 to 18 months if the organization really wants to get on with it). In the majority of such cases, not a great deal of distribution of processing took place. The old mainframe might have been replaced by a fast UNIX box, or by a small number of VAXs or AS/400s.

For very large organizations, this sudden dropping of the mainframe is generally not feasible because of simple logistics. In either medium or large situations, it is not likely that a high degree of distribution could take place throughout the organization within the short time-scales mentioned. For such situations one needs to realise that downsizing may need to be a longer-term policy, allowing the mainframe to atrophy over a few years rather than killing it stone-dead with one blow. In some cases, the mainframe may have to remain for quite a long time, either to allow for very intricate conversions or to allow downsized technology to catch up with the very heavy workloads that might be required.

One of the more interesting shortcomings of our downsizing definition is that it does not cater for the downsizing of the mainframe itself. As we will show in our discussion of mainframe technology, this can in fact be done. The mainframe product itself represents only part of what is wrong with the old IT world. The changing of values and processes which surround the machinery is equally, if not more, important. So far as the mainframe system itself goes, it can be configured and managed to run as productively in human terms as can most minicomputers, though neither mainframe nor mini can approach client/server systems in terms of overall operating economy or application spread.

Downsizing's definition bears upon a number of complementary or even contradictory notions currently circulating. 'Rightsizing' is a term used by many vendors, but generally by those who are nervous that downsizing is proceeding too quickly and therefore threatening the sales of existing (overpriced) product lines. Rightsizing in theory means picking the right size of machine for a particular job. The definition is a needless one, because that is what downsizing implies – does one deliberately embark upon a product selection exercise with the objective of buying a machine too small for the job? Presumably the proponents of 'rightsizing' also spend their time worrying that the rest of the population is deliberately buying off-the-rack clothing several sizes too small just so they can benefit from the price scales applying to children's wear.

As if rightsizing were not enough, 'upsizing' has now entered the IT vocabulary. At first sight it conflicts squarely with downsizing, suggesting that the latter is not the best strategy after all. In fact, what upsizing usually refers to is the PC world. Many PC advocates – among both users and IT staff – initially became overly enthusiastic about the PC's potential. While this fervour is a tribute to both the PC and its people, it often gets carried to undue lengths.

Upsizing has now arisen because some of the more objective PC enthusiasts now recognize that the PC cannot do everything. Upsizing can mean attaching a server to a network, or allowing the PC to communicate with a larger machine such as a minicomputer or a mainframe. The irony of upsizing is that the term is coming into usage just as PC technology is progressing at such a rate that it really can do (almost) everything. As with rightsizing, upsizing does not really conflict with the basics of downsizing, and in any case one does not require a concept that is 180 degrees out of phase with the real world.

The history of downsizing

If the definitions of downsizing and related concepts are a bit fluid, at least its past is not. The history of downsizing is eminently worth looking at, because there are many lessons to be learned. Unfortunately, because of pressures and other concerns, very few people were able to understand earlier downsizing events as they were happening, so perhaps the perspective offered by history can give a better view.

Downsizing in fact goes back to 1959, and was invented by IBM and Digital Equipment Corporation (DEC). Both companies recognized the shortcomings implicit in large mainframe design (though IBM could not admit this too openly, as to do so would have scuppered the robust mainframe profits of that era). Both organizations introduced quite reasonable alternatives, given the technology of the times. The IBM offering was conceptually a subset mainframe (the 1401 series) and was targeted on small commercial (meaning record-handling) situations. DEC's PDP-1, launched a year later in 1960, was an inexpensive interactive machine targeted on numeric computing for engineers and scientists. Both types of machine have their direct descendants today: the AS/400 on the IBM side, and DEC's VAX range. The point behind the two exercises is important, and is with us today: with downsizing we are talking about different *types* of machine, not just different sizes. In the 1970s, when powerful minicomputers began to challenge the mainframe, a pertinent saying gained currency:

> 'A minicomputer is different from a mainframe in every respect except size.'

The saying is still accurate, and versions of it might apply to the AS/400 and PC client/server systems also. While a mainframe is designed to perform all types of work, more specific designs are targeted to their own envisaged environments. Not only are AS/400 and VAX, for example, different from the general-purpose mainframe, they are also different from each other. The newly emerging client/server architectures, as might be expected, are different in character from all previous machine types, and have different design needs and performance characteristics.

As small-machine types evolved, becoming more functional, easier to use and more powerful, they were increasingly used for specific application niches, both by small companies and by large ones. Despite its alleged wealth of IT skills, it was often the large company, an existing mainframe user, that failed to exploit the small machine properly.

These early small-machine disasters by supposed experts provide valuable lessons for downsizers today, as do the many successes with unsophisticated new users of such technology. In other words, downsizing and its use of different technology represent in many ways a

Table 1.2 The history of downsizing.

1960	Cheap subset-mainframes (IBM 1401)
	First minicomputers
1970	Small, easy-to-use computers, reasonably powerful and cheap (DEC PDP-11, IBM System/3)
	Larger minicomputers (VAX, System/38)
1980	PCs (Apple, IBM)
	Generic PC packages (spreadsheet, word processing)
	Relational databases and program generators
	Open systems, standard communications
1990	Windowing
	High-capacity servers
	Network management

Downsizing technology was initially centred on minicomputers and minicomputer-like 'subset-mainframes' such as the IBM System/3x family and AS/400. Over the last decade the star of the show has been the PC, with software playing perhaps an even more significant role than hardware in advancing the product type.

new world. While some skills are common to both areas, many of those on the management and design sides are not. The downsizer will encounter many situations where it is better to train either new or adaptable junior people rather than to try to re-orient those overly wedded to the mainframe's way of doing things.

The introduction of the IBM PC in 1981 gave an enormous boost to downsizing, and in several ways. It provided cheap and reasonably usable technology on the user's desktop, so giving him both useful function and IT training into the bargain. It also gave users a healthier, if sceptical, attitude towards their own IT department. People began to ask why it took IT so long to do things and at such high cost, if they, the users, could accomplish so much so quickly on a cheap, simple machine. Though such comparisons are drastically over-simplified, they are legitimate up to a point. Users in large companies could equally have looked at much smaller companies using such items as IBM's System/3x range of computers or DEC's PDP-11 or VAX, and might have come up with similar conclusions. Again, they would not have been comparing like with like, though the degree of likeness would have been much higher than the esconced IT department would have liked to admit.

The PC effectively flanked the orderly progression of downsizing, both speeding up the movement and offering a new type of

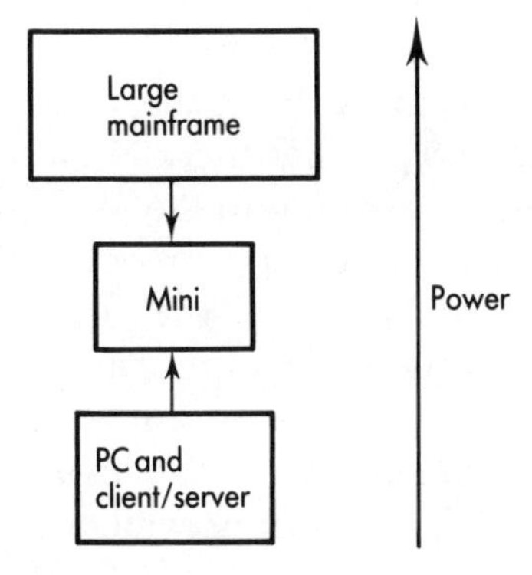

Figure 1.3 The mini squeeze.

The PC both accelerated and disrupted the formerly staid pace of the downsizing marketplace. It effectively outflanked the minicomputer by being not only much cheaper but actually superior in many respects. The continuing growth of the PC and the PC-compatible multi-user server is causing severe problems for suppliers of aging and overpriced minis, a large number of whom have already effectively gone out of business.

technology. Today, thanks to technological developments in PC architectures and software, that flanking movement is largely complete. Not only the mainframe, but also the traditional minicomputer (including many running on UNIX) are under severe threat from this relative upstart. Downsizing history is still being made, and at a high rate. This may turn out to be too exciting for some downsizing prospects, and doubtlessly some will decide to wait until some of the dust settles (which it will - on them, and they will be well behind those competitors who had the energy and courage to encounter the new technology).

The new and the old

The downsizing movement contains a mix of new and older technology and methods. Partly to minimize risk, and partly to avoid being taken for a high-priced ride by salesmen, one should keep clear in one's mind which is which. Established products and methods can be used with confidence, especially if one is using them broadly within their intended application areas and within known performance limits.

A problem with downsizing today, and mainly for the more ambitious user, is that there are a number of very significant product developments hanging in the air. Two new and hopefully very powerful chips are due to appear on the market during late 1992 or 1993 (Intel's P5 - also called the 'Pentium' - and Digital's Alpha). The Intel chip is the most significant, as it should drive down prices and up the power of PC products (including large servers and multiprocessors based on PC basics). On the software side, Microsoft's Windows (NT) operating system is arguably the most important software development of the decade. If it is successful, it will give an enormous lift to PC and client/server technology, especially if it runs well on some of the faster chips at which it is aiming (the Mips R4000 and DEC's Alpha, as well as Intel's). If this happens, then PC and similar technology, already very attractive, will be boosted against UNIX, and will help, with UNIX, to kill off virtually all proprietary systems.

The newer items in the downsizing kitbag which have not quite settled revolve primarily around the Windows environment.

Microsoft's Windows 3.1, the current release, has yet to be absorbed by designers and complementary software organizations. While one can use the product itself with confidence, one should exercise care in choosing complementary items and in both windows and application task design. Very few non-generic applications yet use windows. Those that do often make only token usage, effectively wrapping a front end window or two around older (and extremely ugly) screens.

When one turns to the question of old and new methods related to downsizing, it is fair enough to say that there is a reasonable amount of design skill related to common small-machine types. Such mid-range items as AS/400, VAX and UNIX products all are established enough in third-party markets to represent safe solutions - so long as one knows which designers to choose. Regrettably, the mid-range market is low-cost in orientation and fragmented, meaning that there is a very wide quality spectrum. As always, you do not necessarily get what you pay for - this writer has seen some of the supposedly best and most expensive consultancies produce some of the worst results.

The shortage in implementation skills includes those in the windowing arena, as suggested above. Client/server systems are also new enough such that the third-party markets have not been able to adapt enough to new design and implementation methods. With client/server, as with windows, one sees a number of older products partly adapted. In both areas, however, progress is much more rapid than has been the case with UNIX and proprietary systems, as there are high incentives to learn quickly.

Convincing the corporation

As downsizing's benefits become increasingly known, and as its opposite, the installed mainframe, is clearly going nowhere, there is much greater acceptance among general organizational staff and managers that alternatives exist to the traditional world. However, downsizing advocates should not be complacent here, nor underestimate the amount of salesmanship and public relations necessary to establish the credibility of the exercise. There is a virtuous circle involved in this type of initial marketing: the more that people believe in the systems, the better job they will make of installing and subsequently running them. Convincing general users and managers also provides a valuable hedge against one's own IT department, and gives them less room for manoeuvre. The convincing exercise should begin right at the beginning of any downsizing study, in order to gain as long an exposure as possible and to maximize absorption of the issues. The expected benefits should be stated clearly, and as time progresses they should be larded with examples of specific interest to the organization. Users are tired of hearing only conceptual arguments from salespeople, whether internal or external, and they welcome down to earth discussions that will actually make them more successful in their own enterprises.

One should not underestimate the body of discontent with computing in an organization, though it is easy to do so because much of it is repressed for political reasons or otherwise understated because some users still do not feel competent to discuss the issues. One has to be careful, as some of this discontent can operate against downsizing. Some people will initially see it as just another computer gimmick designed to consume money and build empires without delivering much of a concrete nature. One therefore needs to have good reference stories about downsizing.

PC usage will normally be one such topic, and there may be others within an organization or in like organizations (competitors are obviously watched with interest, especially if it is feared they might be getting ahead with a particularly technology). Small machines or areas of the information centre might be pointed to as examples of what can be done with some distribution. One can thus represent downsizing as an extension of already proven technology, and one with which the business is already reasonably comfortable.

Key issues

- Downsizing's social and political, as well as technological, aspects must be recognized.
- The movement is a long-term one, and there are no developments on the horizon that mitigate against it continuing.

- Cost savings are only part of downsizing's benefits package; one should also anticipate significant improvements in system quality.
- Risks apply to any change, and the ones inherent in downsizing should be identified and skirted.

2

The technological base

We have already established that some elements of downsizing have a history of over thirty years, and that progress over that time has been reasonably consistent. The history of computing is full of examples where a sudden change in emphasis occurs. There is considerable evidence that, so far as downsizing is concerned, we are now in such a period. In such times, progress becomes very rapid, and markets suffer a high degree of dislocation as new suppliers gain share at the expense of older ones.

These breakthroughs occur because a number of market and technical factors suddenly coalesce, even if the threads of the developments have been in existence for some years. While most of the excitement has been on the PC side of the industry, there have been movements in the UNIX and proprietary mini areas as well. The broad upshot is to make downsizing much more attractive than it used to be and in several dimensions:

- Lower costs
- Less risk
- Wider choice of products
- Easier use and more flexibility

The technological developments that have pushed the downsizing market ahead lie in several areas:

- Much lower costs for existing components. For example, the Intel 486 chip, which started life at around $1000, now sells for less than $100. Memory and disks are also becoming substantially more cost-effective.
- Faster components, notably chips (by Intel, Mips, IBM and

Sun primarily), but also input/output buses, disk drives and communications lines.

- The settling in of components announced earlier. These include local networks such as Novell, Ethernet and Token Ring, and windowing technology.
- The exponential growth in the number of software packages. Over the main four sectors of the downsized market (UNIX, PC, VAX and AS/400), there are many tens of thousands of packages available, with dozens being announced daily.

The technical developments have some indirect results that prospective users should also appreciate. Where hardware is concerned, fast individual components make more feasible the 'single-component' system. In other words, if one can design a system using one central processor chip, one input/output bus, one disk controller, and so on, then it becomes much cheaper to design, build and support than in the alternative case where several units of a given type have to be

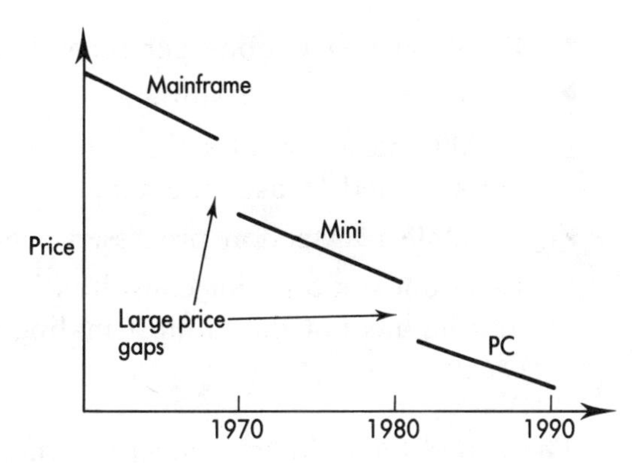

Figure 2.1 Discontinuous development.

Two major hardware developments have advanced downsizing's momentum considerably. In each case, the advance took a long time to absorb because of the market's fundamental inertia. Users who were able to embrace the new, more cost-effective technology normally profited doubly, in that they also enjoyed much greater ease of use. Because of more rapid development rates, the newer technologies matured more rapidly than their predecessors. This leads to the interesting speculation that the mainframe and the traditional mini may have become geriatric before they became mature.

interconnected to give adequate power. It also makes it easier to write operating software for the system.

It should be noted that the hardware about which we are talking is relatively un-innovative. Nearly all downsized systems (including the PC) rely on minicomputer-like components that have been around for decades. There are very few unknowns, and therefore few risks, in buying a well-made PC from a reputable constructor. Even when one looks to new generations of these components, the risk is relatively low. Items like Intel chips, input/output buses, memory and disk drives generally use established methods and designs, and are merely speeded up by conservative margins. Even if an oddity occurred, one could either run the system slightly slower than intended, or else revert to the previous generation of technology which would be broadly compatible. Little disruption would occur to the actual application programs and to the user community.

Because the early 1990s appear to be in the midst of a high-speed revolution, it is apparent that the fast rate of change will continue for some years. Aside from faster chips entering the market, much cheaper memory is becoming available. If one wants to think of what $1.00 will buy in 1995, the following choice might raise a few eyebrows:

- 1 million instructions per second (mips) at chip level.
- 1 megabyte of disk storage.
- 64 000 characters of solid-state memory, and much more of the so-called 'Flash' memory.
- 1 simple transaction processed every 15 minutes.
- 10 seconds of a senior consultant's commentary, establishing that he has not the faintest inkling what any of it implies in practice.

The computer industry concept of the 'threshold of acceptance' has been demonstrated many times over, confirming that, when prices drop substantially, user demand grows disproportionately. The acceptance of the PC, the minicomputer, office automation and local communications all rested upon a combination of price falls, maturing technology and perceived user needs, such that the right solution almost automatically fell into place at the right price and at the right time.

Standard and open systems

2

Aside from technical issues in their narrower sense, a great accelerator of the downsized market has been the emergence of a number of widely used systems that effectively represent standards of various types. The largest and most established of such standards is the PC, with Intel chips and Microsoft's DOS and Windows operating software ruling the roost. Second in importance is the UNIX marketplace. Some widely used proprietary systems might also be thought of as standards of sorts, though in both conceptual 'openness' and in market size they cannot compete with either of the two leaders.

There is a great deal of confusion in users' minds as to both the generalities and the specifics of the open systems area, and it has not been helped by the setting up of too many standards bodies that overlap, squabble and procrastinate. The great plus of the PC market is that there are few standards bodies involved. Most of the standards involved are *de facto* ones: Intel designs the chips; Microsoft, Lotus, Oracle and a few others provide the software; and Novell links the boxes together. The presence of several bickering committees, each member defending his own profit margins and only secondarily thinking of the customer, would slow the process tenfold.

At the moment there are two main standards bodies looking after UNIX and a number of others bearing upon the subject. There is a conceptual overlap between so-called official standards bodies and looser consortia. Neither type of organization is necessarily stable, as both membership and policies may change. The intentions of most standards bodies in theory are unarguable enough. But because committees, even if enlightened and charitable, are slow moving and often confused about objectives and how to achieve them, a fast moving market will catch them out. This is exactly what happened when the PC market began squeezing UNIX.

UNIX would become more credible if the two leading standards bodies were to merge, as there is no justification for having both UNIX International and Open Software Foundation trying to set standards for what is supposed to be the same product. The two organizations do cooperate on occasion, and sometimes accept each other's technology. It is also true that one can sometimes port applications from one type of UNIX to the other with little difficulty.

Aside from the PC and UNIX markets, at least two proprietary

Table 2.1 Who's where in open systems.

Open Software Foundation (OSF)
IBM
Digital Equipment (DEC)
Siemens
Hewlett-Packard
Bull
UNIX International
AT&T/NCR
Fujitsu/ICL
Unisys
Sun

In 1988, the formation of the Open Software Foundation (OSF) split the UNIX portion of the open systems movement. The major players in each camp are shown above, there being a host of minor companies in each group as well. Though the two groups do sometimes exchange technology, the split annoyed and confused users. This jockeying for position reflects the mixed motivations of suppliers in entering such alliances, as for them openness can mean more competitiveness and lower profits. Most of the major suppliers are still pushing proprietary (and generally expensive) offerings as well as open ones, which adds further muddle to a market which needs less of it, not more.

systems are widely enough dispersed in the market to qualify as standard systems, though they are not very open. IBM's AS/400, on the commercial side, and DEC's VAX, mainly for technical and scientific users, each have sold in the hundreds of thousands of units. This is a wide enough base to bring in many complementary hardware suppliers as well as a large number of application package providers. In rough numbers, around 10 000 applications exist for each machine. Large numbers of people know the machines and can provide tuning, maintenance and management services for them.

A couple of older standard and partly open systems are still in the market, though they are being eclipsed by newer developments. The Pick system and MUMPS are both long-established items for smaller machines. The two have some similarities, being a combined operating system and database, making them easy to use and providing good performance – but in both cases only for very simple applications. Both of these systems can now be run atop a UNIX system. One should normally do so to take advantage of an application package or to keep existing applications running, not to undertake any new long-term developments.

The packaged downsized environment

2

Aside from the technical items, one aspect that separates the new downsized market from both mainframe and earlier minicomputer efforts is the role of the packaged system. This is effectively part of our 'threshold' argument, advanced above. When the technology, prices and user attitudes are right, suppliers enter the market with items that are effectively well wrapped packages. This makes solution identification that much easier in the user's eyes, and it adds much to the usability of the items.

More traditional machine types (for example, the IBM mainframe, the DEC VAX mini) are very much bits-and-pieces assemblies, much like a Lego set (with no discourtesy intended to that system supplier). One can put the bits together all sorts of ways, and sometimes indeed an impressive construction will result. But it takes a long time to do it, requires specialist expertise, and is not at all easy to change quickly once put together. This approach suits complex systems that are very stable to the point of being inert – not exactly the real business world most of us face today.

The market over the past twenty years has seen some very good packaging exercises, yet a large segment of the industry appears to have learned nothing from them. It is all the more irritating when a supplier puts together a good package and then appears to forget the lessons learned. Good packages have certain very important common features:

- They hit a defined target, and one which the user recognizes as important.
- They do not try to do everything.
- They are inexpensive for what they are.
- They are much easier to use than would be the bits and pieces of technology which comprise them.

The package means, among other things, that users accept it readily, hastening its advance into the marketplace and creating interest from complementary or competitive organizations. The nature of the large standard market means that these surrounding items can be developed and marketed quickly, as a supplier needs only a small percentage acceptance initially to get a product started. Even if the package supplier is not very good at direct marketing (many in fact are terrible), a good package is still a good indicator of a more fundamental level of marketing skill. In other words, somebody has thought both of what the customer needs and of how to meet that need in a simple, attractive fashion. In the longer-term, the more traditional style of computer marketing (sell the solution, then look for the problem when no one has anything better to do) will mercifully become more rare.

Product complexity and application development

The growth of packages of various types, from those for specific applications down to generic items such as word processing and database, is one of the most important threads in the downsized world. It is all the more important because of a countervailing trend: that of a growth in overall complexity of systems. Despite the notion of small, simple machines (accurate enough as far as it goes), the maturing of computer technology implies a vast range of diverse items which, even with careful selection, cannot be avoided by most users. While some of these items are well packaged, this is still a relative concept. Such items as networking software and windowing products, however packaged, can be very troublesome to deal with because of their inherent complexity.

While products vary in their complexity, fragmentation poses a separate but conceptually related issue as both fragmentation and complexity result in an intricate picture in the user's eyes. There is a wide choice of programming languages, databases, windowing tools and other types of program generator. Some of these items, such as the C and C++ languages, are complicated in their own right. Some products work better in certain combinations than others. Many downsized users are rightfully reluctant to perform traditional programming at all, especially where windowing products with their 700 or so separate calls are involved. Instead, many look for 'packages of packages' – combinations of high-level products often from different suppliers but which nevertheless work well together.

Other types of user organization – generally the smaller and less technical ones – will forego application development altogether. They

Table 2.2 The user-supplier software split.

Users	*Software suppliers*
Package use and adaptation	Provide:
Simple coding (if any)	Generic packages
Use of program generators	Industry-specific packages
	Tailored systems
	Middleware (database, program generators)
	Outsourcing and facilities management
Few highly technical staff	Many highly technical staff

As downsizing progresses and overall systems become much more complicated, users are increasingly less willing to engage in highly technical activities, as they have better things to do with their time. The result is that the software scene is becoming more polarized, with most technical emphasis being within the supplier sector. Even where users are willing to do some programming, they will progressively migrate to high-productivity tools rather than coding in such low-level languages as COBOL, BASIC, RPG and C.

will merely use bespoke packages, perhaps with a few adaptations or by complementing them with generic packages for management reporting purposes. Increasingly larger organizations will be willing to abandon any attempts at in-house development, perhaps not maintaining any program coders or systems analysts in their traditional roles on the payroll. The very large user, especially if he runs a mainframe installation as well as a downsized network, will need to keep traditional development staff employed for many years to come.

This does not mean that technical skills will face a declining market; far from it. The point is important from a variety of viewpoints. Technical staff, observing the developments in downsizing and the consequent packaging of systems, often feel under threat. Though in specific instances they may feel threatened, in the more general sense they need not be. A market growing in overall complexity, and requiring ever more new types of development and support organization, will provide jobs for many technicians for many years into the future. What we are seeing is a split in the IT scene, with most users becoming less concerned with the details of development, and with a growing services side taking up the slack. Aside from software package development and support, such areas as facilities management, outsourcing and new concepts such as desktop support (providing support services for PCs and their related local networks) all evidence this growth.

Downsizing in the late 1990s

If we combine the above technical and service issues, one can envisage how the downsized environment will look near the end of the decade. For a start, it is fairly difficult to see much of interest aside from downsizing. Certainly, many large mainframes will still be in place, some for legitimate reasons but many simply because of user inertia backed by vendor selling pressure (pressuring users to be inert may sound inconsistent, but it is a tried and true account protection tactic).

It is likely that most transaction processing will take place on a customer service point basis, meaning that a single operator or a small group will look after a given set of customers. What is called the complex transaction, using windowing technology on a PC, will be the interface between most sales personnel of whatever type and their computer system. High-capacity servers will store both customer and product/service distribution information. Despite supplier hype, it is not probable that so-called multimedia applications will be widespread for some years. While the technology for multimedia is more or less ready now, the perceived business needs of the vast majority of users are some distance away from what are seen as costly concepts.

The vast array of application packages should make the writing of one's own code superfluous in 95% of cases. Better window- and program-generator tools will be used to write most applications even within the package supplier environment, meaning that the packages can be modified at low cost should a given user require adaptations.

Hardware issues for downsizing

We have already touched on some of the hardware technology available in today's market. A feature of most downsized systems currently is their broad similarity in design. Both PCs and minicomputers (including most UNIX products) are essentially an outgrowth of the early minicomputer designs pioneered by Digital in the late 1960s.

The major feature of such a design is its simplicity. The central processor performs most general functions, needing only relatively simple add-on processors (normally on cards to be slotted into the chassis) to perform extra or non-standard functions such as communications, higher-speed numeric processing or specialised graphics. The input/output bus acts as a general data highway within the machine, passing all data between the central processor, main memory and the various peripheral devices such as disks and communications lines. Extra devices can easily be added, and non-standard types of work can be handled with relatively small modifications to the basic machine. Examples of this include retail point-of-sale terminals, which may require special scanners and coin handlers, and small robots for manufacturing assembly work.

When developments occur at high speed, it is interesting to note what is not happening. For some time various pundits have been predicting the emergence of the intelligent machine, where very complex hardware would take over some of the duties now performed by software. Such predictions stem from a well justified desire to see less software in the computer, as current sizes of programs are very large and growing larger. PCs and UNIX workstations now require something like 10 to 12 megabytes of main memory if they are going to incorporate the latest operating system (OS/2, Windows (NT) or UNIX) plus windowing software, communications and a few applications.

The problem with very large amounts of software is not necessarily the cost of the hardware to run it, as this is falling rapidly enough to accommodate very large programs economically. The real

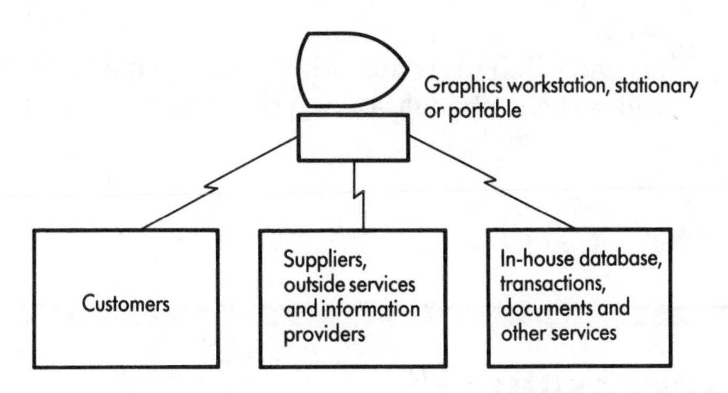

Figure 2.2 Downsizing's logical end.

From the user's point of view, the goal of downsizing should be the provision of a single desktop or portable device that can send and receive any information which he needs to accomplish his daily work. The type of technology used below this interface and where it is located are irrelevant to this user, so long as basic constraints of cost, response time and reliability are adhered to.

issue is the reliability of such software, and the limits one might encounter on this score. A large software product may contain millions of lines of code, as it is dealing with a very unintelligent machine and needs to specify every action in terms of very detailed machine steps. Most new releases of software contain numerous faults, either actual bugs or performance bottlenecks, and so place user installations at risk and inconvenience. The product may refuse to work fully or rapidly or, worse, it could propagate errors in vital data such that the business itself is jeopardized. It is a point which users should keep in mind, especially if they plan to use several items of large software. The industry needs intelligent computers, but none seems to be forthcoming.

Among mid-sized machines such as servers and minicomputers, an area of rapid progress is in disk input/output systems. So-called 'RAID' technology (for Redundant Arrays of Inexpensive Disks) is now with us, and provides low-cost disk storage which also has security and recovery features, should data become mechanically corrupted.

Aside from becoming cheaper and more robust, disk systems are becoming more performance conscious. One of the main limits of earlier small machines has been very limited input/output capability. While, compared to the larger mainframes, meaningful limits will apply, small systems are nevertheless improving. Disk performance is particularly relevant to commercial record-handling applications, as perhaps 20 to 30 disk accesses need to take place for each transaction of medium complexity. A system performing 10 such transactions per second would therefore need to handle 200 to 300 disk accesses per second. This is now within the capability of many minicomputers and servers, though a few years ago it would have stretched many.

The successful PC

By a wide margin, the PC has been downsizing's most successful product to date (though it is typical of some industry analysts that they may not even include the product in their definitions of downsizing –

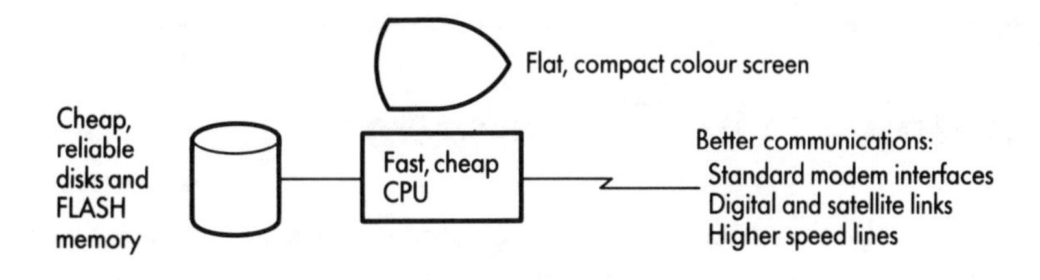

Figure 2.3 Computer portability.

Portability is an important aspect of downsizing, as it enables many types of end user to participate in computing. Anyone who works from home or whose job involves mobility can now use reasonable computing power on location and can still communicate when required to do so. Improving communications plus rapidly falling PC prices indicate a high growth rate in portable business computing.

it is not expensive or awkward enough to look like a 'professional' item). Depending upon what one calls a PC, close to a hundred million such products have been sold, though only a minority of these are in what might be called corporate environments.

To appreciate the role of the PC, one can only look at other types of technology to draw some parallels. When we make a telephone call, we use the 'telephone', our mental image being the handset. When we watch television, again we have in our minds the set in our home. In neither case do we worry much about what is behind the consumer commodity. The windows-driven PC is assuming a very similar role in the eyes of the end user. 'The computer' will be what he sees before him. The services he chooses to access (data, messaging, particular applications) will be conceptually right there for his use. The faded and inscrutable empires of mainframe and mini enthusiasts will be of no concern to this user, even if they exist down the wires somewhere.

To call the PC the centre or the focal point of the downsizing movement is probably worth doing simply because it will alarm so many IT traditionalists. This view of the PC is worth having on other counts as well. It wakes people up to the realities of downsizing; that computers are there to advance the business purposes of end users, and for no other reason. It is also an accurate enough view, so long as the professional keeps in mind that it is up to him alone to provide the technology and logistics needed to support that end-user service.

Windows: the fundamentals

The sudden appearance and acceptance of windowing environments on the PC and other workstations poses a fundamental issue to the downsizer. The importance of this technology in the user's eyes is beyond doubt. To anyone who has worked in a windowing environment then been forced to revert to traditional screens, the differences between the two worlds are profound. Non-windowing systems look plain, colourless, primitive and boring. The point bears emphasizing because there are still defenders of the dumb terminal and the earlier screens (DOS layouts on the PC and a variety of soporific products from dumb terminal suppliers). Some major users are planning to bring systems up in several years' time with no use of windowing. Anyone with the most basic notions of media, communications, absorption of information and ergonomics will instantly grasp the superiority of the windowing environment.

Windowing, along with cheap and powerful hardware and the multiplicity of good applications, is one of the major forces pushing the focus of computing out to the workstation itself. Anyone who ignores this shift of gravity will only have to make up the lost ground later. It is a painful issue for traditional IT types, immersed in the increasingly irrelevant minutiae of mainframe obscurity, to have to admit that old skills are *passé* and that they have not the faintest notion of how to design and install a windows system.

The shift of emphasis to the workstation automatically promotes closely related concepts. Servers based on local-area networks suddenly become more important. Servers can be constructed using components compatible with the PC itself (Intel chips, OS/2 or NetWare, similar disk systems and communications connectivity), and so can be built cheaply. As the PC grows in power, the main complement needed is a system for communicating and sharing large amounts of data. This is what servers provide; to furnish much more would in most cases be redundant, and would add needless complexity and cost to the overall system. Exit both mainframe and mini, except in those cases (increasingly few) where the server cannot provide the local function needed. The recent (and somewhat unexpected) acceptance of IBM's OS/2 version 2.0 is a reflection of this growing server market, as many copies of the software will be installed on servers in corporate environments (common press articles knocking OS/2 often forget this corporate-server targeting).

Broad software issues

2

As with the hardware and communications technology, much software used in downsizing has been around for some time (the main exceptions being windowing software). Major components such as operating systems, databases, local network drivers and remote communications packages have all adapted themselves to small-machine situations with relatively little trouble.

Competition and relatively open markets act to keep software prices moderate, especially in the PC arena. This is something to keep uppermost in mind, as the tendency in distributed environments is to use many separate items of software because of the diverse application mix covered (much wider than on more central machines). Even on the PC, a few products on each machine at a few hundred dollars add up quickly, though costs should still be lower than the same offerings on alternative machine types.

One should always remember that in downsized environments, where many copies of a given software item may be bought, negotiation over pricing is an eminently worthwhile activity. In these recessionary times, even vendors of popular PC items may be willing to talk about large cuts for high-volume purchases, particularly if little or no support is required for most of the extra copies (support, like price, should always be a major feature in discussions).

Probably the most rapidly developing area in downsizing software is development tools for Microsoft's Windows 3.1 (3.1 being better than earlier releases because of its implementation of true drag-and-drop capabilities). Other meaningful developments are the emergence of object-oriented programming languages (mainly C++ and SmallTalk). Effectively, object-oriented languages improve coding efficiency and enable better management of the development process to take place. As noted earlier, these languages are expected to be mainly of interest to software development companies, as the overheads in programming for the windowing environment are beyond most users' reach.

The end user's comprehension of IT

If IT professionals are now having a great deal of trouble understanding not only the detail of new developments but also their implications, one might turn one's attention to the end user and his view of such matters. While users have undoubtedly improved their grasp of matters technical over the past few years (thanks in part to the PC), there is still a vast gap between their thoughts and that of an IT professional. Notions that the downsizing movement can be run largely by end users are futile, though users can and do play major roles in both developing and operating small systems.

Even users with substantial experience tend to have problems with many of the more abstract areas of computing. They understand what they see, but may have only vague ideas as to how underlying data is stored and how processes manipulate information. Database structures, metadata (meaning definitions of data, which are of course themselves data) and distinctions between actual stored data and derived information such as summaries and totals, all generally cause bafflement. To the average user, things are simply in the computer, and his main task is just to decide which bits to look at.

There has been much theoretical discussion by media experts as to whether the windowing environment will increase or decrease the user's understanding of computer internals. The 'television rots the brain' school of thought draws analogies to the superficial aspects of the television image, suggesting that overly vivid and trouble free presentation of information effectively discourages further investigation. A slightly more charitable interpretation of this view might suggest that, if information is easy to get at and is understandable, the end user will have more mental energy to spare in carrying out the organizational functions for which he was employed.

Other commentators think that, the more usable and attractive computer systems become, the more they will encourage at least some understanding of the basics. This will be a gradual process, and great differences will exist between users. Given the great variety of user types, the two views of windowing's impact may not be incompatible. The main issue to bear in mind is that one should be careful in assuming that users might either understand or care about the technology that so enthuses the rest of us. In the downsized environment, one will encounter a very wide spectrum of interest as well as ability. All gradations along this spectrum must be handled in a constructive and expeditious fashion.

Key issues

- Rapid reductions in the prices of downsized items should continue over the next few years, enabling the movement to maintain its pace.
- Standard and more formally 'open' systems are of key importance.
- Large and very competitive markets are a feature of the best areas within downsizing.
- Packaging is a key aspect of downsized products, and good packaging should be watched for in both hardware and software components.
- Inexpensive products can be as good or better than expensive ones - you do not always get what you pay for.

3

The problems with mainframes

For four decades, the mainframe computer has been the dominant type in the industry. Despite recent incursions into its territory, in many ways it still is. Very large organizations still base their computing heavily on mainframe designs. Traditional hardware vendors such as IBM, Unisys and Fujitsu/ICL allegedly derive disproportionate profits from their mainframe sales, whereas smaller machines generally provide only thin margins.

Though the downsizing revolution is increasingly a threat to the mainframe computer, it must be recognised that the large machine still has a reserved role. However attractive downsized solutions might be for many situations, there will still be cases at the larger end of the requirements spectrum where a collection of smaller machines is clearly unfeasible. Also, where companies have already invested heavily in mainframe technology, and where applications are running reasonably well and do not require much change, a conversion effort to smaller systems might impose costs and risks exceeding the value of likely savings.

In arriving at a balanced view of the mainframe, and also in examining its likely future, one has to recognize that much of its role is historical. Until the 1970s, there was no alternative for medium- or large-scale computing, especially where commercial record-handling applications were concerned. The product type was designed when hardware was very expensive and when software was in its infancy. Under these conditions, it was justifiable for users to spend large sums on skilled personnel in order to economize on hardware usage.

On the application side, most work was run in batch mode, as technology had not yet come to grips with the terminal-based on-line environment. Usually, only core applications were implemented on the computer. Such tasks as high-volume order processing were first of all relatively simple in nature. Secondly, there was a high payback

Table 3.1 The widening gap.

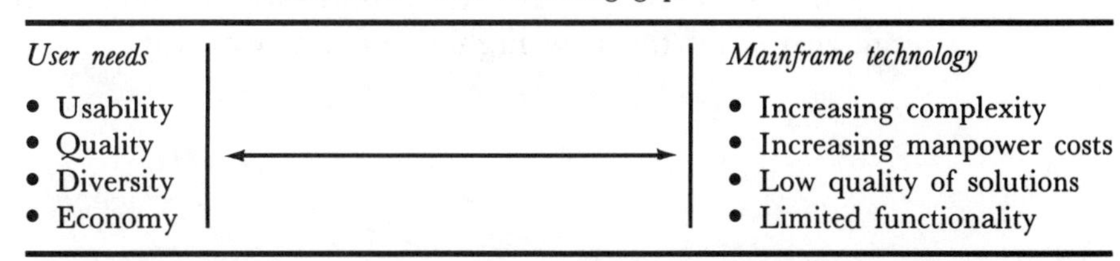

User needs		*Mainframe technology*
• Usability		• Increasing complexity
• Quality	←——→	• Increasing manpower costs
• Diversity		• Low quality of solutions
• Economy		• Limited functionality

The gap between perceived user needs and mainframe technology is actually widening, an unprecedented situation in what is supposed to be modern technology. The size of this gap is one of the main spurs of the downsizing revolution, especially as an increasingly computer-literate user begins to see the vast gulf between what he wants to do and what is possible on the mainframe.

in terms of saved personnel costs, greater throughput of work and greater accuracy.

If one looks at generally assumed business requirements today, some of the above assumptions still hold. However, three major shifts have occurred in comparison with our earlier environment:

- We live in an interactive, on-line world, not a batch one. Except for such housekeeping work as file backups and the tidying up of disk space, batch processing is not appropriate for most applications. Today, the end user must be directly in touch with his computer, not removed from it by layers of data entry procedures and overnight runs.
- The applications spectrum is much more varied than it used to be. Not just core applications, but add-ons to the core work (such as better error-handling and rapid production of unanticipated management information) as well as newer types of task need to be processed. Many of these new areas (office automation, for example) are of low marginal or unknown value, and so are most likely to be implemented where system costs are low.
- End users know much more about computing than they did several years ago, and as a consequence they expect more from their systems.

The mainframe design is ill-equipped to deal with the above points, though with careful selection of software components and with astute design its deficiencies can be minimized. However, many mainframe personnel are wedded to doing things in traditional and very deliberate ways, and they may not be able to react quickly enough to suit the new highly interactive world.

Mainframe design goals

One standard criticism of smaller machines by mainframe enthusiasts is that the former represent 'subset' architectures. The downsized item may not have the full mechanical facilities of the mainframe (typically in batch processing and high-speed numeric calculations). It certainly has nothing like the high-volume input/output capability boasted by the larger mainframes. Such criticisms, so far as they go, are accurate enough, and form the essence of the argument that says one should not tackle the mainframe in its strongest areas.

However, one should note that mechanical capability is not everything. In some respects the mainframe is a lesser design than many newer items. It will not perform graphics or word processing efficiently. Where both mainframe and small machine can perform similar types of work at similar load levels, the mainframe is usually several times as expensive to buy and to operate.

In assessing the mainframe as an overall proposition, it is important to remember that there are specific software concepts underlying it as well as the hardware architecture. It is as much on the software side that high costs and other operating problems arise, the latter including resistance to change and the absorption of human time that might better be spent elsewhere.

If one examines the combined hardware–software mainframe package, the only type of workload it is particularly good at is batch processing. If the need exists for, say, ten large and separate batch streams to be processed within a minimum elapsed time, then the large mainframe is the tool for the job.

When one turns away from batch processing, the mainframe architecture begins to pale. The problems reside mainly in the software, and are threefold:

- Layered software – meaning many different components which are dependent upon one another. Because such items were developed at different times and by different people, incompatibilities are inevitably created, implying performance, functional and quality problems.

- The full functionality illusion. Mainframe software tries to meet a very deep level of function within one product of its type (even though it often fails to do so). In other words, it tries to be everything to everybody (one of the world's most dangerous business propositions). The software items are typically very intricate to configure, tune and amend, so adding high running costs to their initial high purchase or rental prices.
- Fragmentation. Because, despite its theoretical design goals, one product fails to work as expected, others are introduced to fill the gaps (there are many examples among operating systems, transaction or time-sharing monitors, and databases). Such fragmentation in turn creates high machine overheads, extra technical support effort and greater rigidity. Users are inconvenienced and confused, as passwords, error messages, screen formats and operating procedures may differ between the separate software environments, even while one is connected to the same physical machine.

The overgrown mainframe

From the late 1970s onwards, the traditional mainframe has grown at a high rate in terms of hardware power, but without changing most of its design fundamentals. The growth in hardware capacity was fuelled by sharply falling prices of circuitry for central processors and solid-state memory, and by more gradually falling prices of disk assemblies and terminals. This notion of sharply falling prices misleads many into supposing that mainframe power is now cheap. When adjusted for inflation, mainframe units of power are indeed more economical than they used to be. However, one is still paying from roughly $1 million to $20 million for one of the more substantial products of the type, scarcely the mid-point of consumer durable territory which the PC now occupies. Mainframe hardware remains expensive because of the complex designs and the low-volume manufacturing inherent in a declining product. Also, the traditional style of mainframe marketing and pre-sales support is very human intensive, and so requires very high gross margins.

Expensive though the hardware product appears, one should focus equal attention on other areas of mainframe cost to arrive at true comparisons with alternatives. Also, one wants to avoid creating similar problems in the new environment, so there are lessons to be learned in examining the mainframe even though one may not wish to use it. Software fragmentation, for example, is by no means confined to mainframe computers.

The layered cost case, presented in Figure 3.1, shows the financial consequences of mainframe usage in an understandable form for the user. It emphasizes that there are many items other than hardware that detract from cost-effectiveness, especially if one tries to attach costs to timeliness and quality. Very few small-system salespeople understand such issues, so it is generally up to sharper members of the user IT community to put such mainframe problems into an accurate perspective.

Where operating characteristics are concerned, a central feature of the mainframe is resistance to change. If one is coding relatively static applications for a (fairly rich) business, then the mainframe can

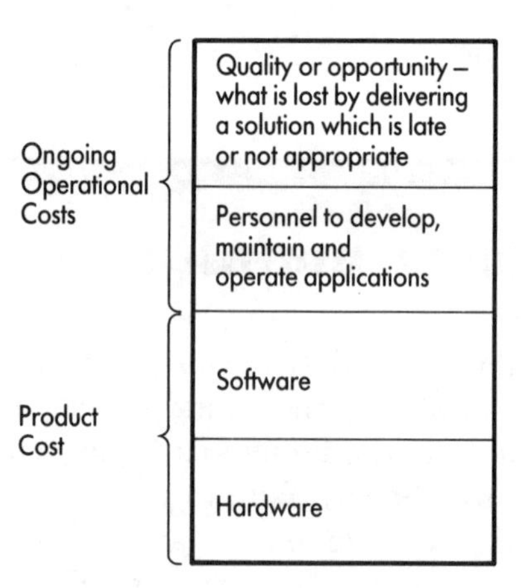

Figure 3.1 The layered cost case against the mainframe.

In comparing downsized costs against those of the mainframe, it is important to include all relevant elements and to do so over long time periods. A point missed by many is the 'quality' or 'opportunity' cost, an area where the mainframe is especially weak against smaller competitors. Adding up the whole list of costs produces some eye-opening figures, all showing that the use of mainframe technology is several times that of the most competitive downsized alternatives on a per transaction, per user or per line of code basis.

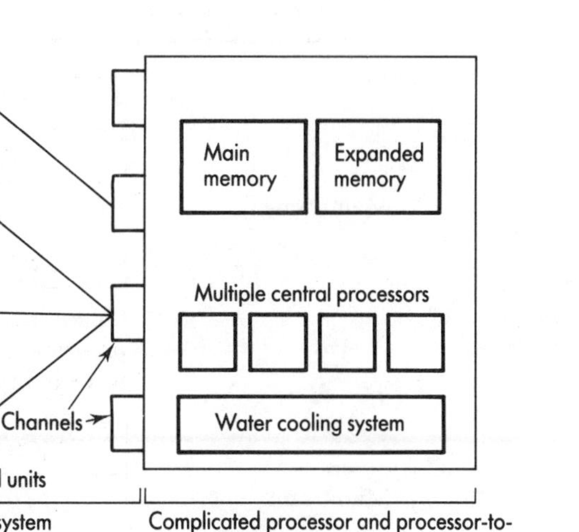

Figure 3.2 The over-engineered mainframe.

As an exercise in hardware engineering integrity, today's mainframe suffers dearly. The overly complicated design is due to a combination of old age and vaulting ambition. Not only are there many components involved, each is expensive for what it is. If you think the above looks bad, wait until you see the mainframe software, Table 3.2.

get by. However, in today's organizational world, there are not that many static organizations lying around. This point should be made forcibly to non-technical managers within a company, as too many end users tend to be impressed by glittering demonstrations and may not realize how rigid the underlying system may be. This rigidity is one of the mainframe's most immutable drawbacks, and in a fast changing situation such rigidity could easily cripple a business.

The mainframe and the corporate database

Both mainframe vendors and a percentage of the mainframe-oriented people within one's own IT establishment are understandably eager to justify the mainframe's continued existence. While there may be reason in some of the arguments put forward, in general it is well

Table 3.2 Mainframe software.

	Transaction or 'Production' Machines	Information-Centre Machines
Large Mainframe	CSP IMS-DB CICS MVS	AS DB2 TSO MVS
Small Mainframe	CICS DL/1 DOS/VS VSE	CMS SQL/DS VM

Operating systems, transaction monitors, databases and program generators are shown. Actual application software is in addition.

The traditional IBM mainframe design still dominates its sector of the market (compatible machines are made by Amdahl, Fujitsu, Hitachi and others, but software is generally the same as on IBM's native boxes). The point we are making here is that, if it is possible for an item to be incompatible with another, it probably is. The different collections of alphabet soup found floating in different sized machines used for different environments imply horrendous problems for any user. Programs, command languages, procedures, passwords, files and libraries are all largely different in the four different environments, creating very high support costs and system rigidities. The software products are generally expensive both to buy and to operate, on top of which one has the costs of incompatibility. The products are antique, and were not designed with today's market needs in mind. As there is little competition in the mainframe sector, IBM has never been forced to rationalise the above *mélange*.

for IT managers to examine such issues with exceptional objectivity. Many mainframe defence arguments are either out of date or do not recognize that there are alternative ways of doing things.

One of the more usual mainframe defences is that of the corporate database. In general, the handling of very large databases is a mainframe strength, especially if the data is structurally complex and has high rates of transaction activity applied. 'Very large' here means in the many tens to hundreds of gigabytes; 'high' transaction rates mean in the many tens to hundreds per second, depending upon the complexity of the transaction.

If such a database needs to be in one place, then clearly the large mainframe is justified. However, an assumption in many minds is that a corporate resource must be centralized within a single machine complex, and it is this assumption that should always be questioned. The central database will inevitably be portrayed as a secure one, under the watchful eye of senior IT supervisors. Such a concept generally goes down well with conservative general management, who distrust profoundly anything beyond their oak-panelled walls. Users in the financial community particular identify with this approach (computer salespeople, like bankers, are skilled at presenting liabilities as if they were assets).

The realities of corporate data are more complicated than many would care to admit, and such issues are discussed in the chapters dealing with applications and database issues. The main point here is that simplistic notions of corporate database should be challenged. Corporate data may be subject to a variety of definitions, from the very broad notion that virtually anything is corporate to a more specific concept that such data is that used by senior managers in their long-range policy deliberations (a favourite myth among IT people is that senior managers actually perform such exercises). Even using this more restricted definition, it may not be appropriate to keep all data in one central location. Much depends upon how specific user groups need to access the data and what role the users wish to play in operating and controlling their systems. Corporate data, centrally stored, may not be of much use if it is unduly expensive to process or too complicated for non-technical users to understand.

The mainframe's bureaucracy

We have spoken of the mainframe's problems in terms of hardware and software designs, both of these being 1960s concepts and not in keeping with many of today's requirements. An equal problem is the organizational one. The combination of human and technical problems adds up to serious cost and productivity issues in most mainframe installations.

There are various ways of measuring the productivity of people involved in computer systems, and it is fair to point out that productivity varies widely in both larger- and small-machine situations. More alert mainframe users, or those with simple application needs, may be able to use tools and techniques to extract much more from their mainframes than would be the average case. However, in many such cases better results would ensue if small systems were used, so the broad comparison holds.

A fairly common measure of productivity is the number of lines of program code implemented, operated and maintained per IT employee. In a mainframe site, this is likely to be around one thousand lines per IT person per year (not, please note, per programmer, which is a much more favourable yardstick). If the average overall cost of an employee is, say, $50,000 per year, then one is talking of some fifty dollars per line of code, or tens of thousands of dollars to create and run even a fairly basic program over a period of time.

There are other ways off measuring productivity. One could separate application development from maintenance and operation, which would be fair for certain types of environment (say, transaction processing) where programs are run many times without change. In such cases, however, the high costs of mainframe hardware and operating software, plus the costs of human machine operators, would to some degree counterbalance the lower cost of development if the latter were calculated on a per transaction-run basis. Purists would doubtlessly be arguing the point forever, but the end result of the various measures is much the same: the human costs of running the mainframe are as high as its other costs. And, despite the high expenditure on what tries to present itself as a 'luxury' product, one is still faced with inflexibility. The human bureaucracy in the large mainframe installation actually *adds* to the rigidity inherent in the underlying system.

There are two reasons why this bureaucracy exists. The first is that much of it really is required to operate the complex software outlined earlier. One does not, as with a PC product, simply pour programs into a machine and expect them to work. In the mainframe world, large numbers of specialists, each with years of experience in a particular product area, are required to make operating systems, database managers, transaction monitors and communications systems work.

The second reason for the bureaucracy has to do with the mind set of many highly technical people. Such people are undoubtedly astute within their defined areas, and most see themselves as conscientious employees. IT managers generally recognize that technical

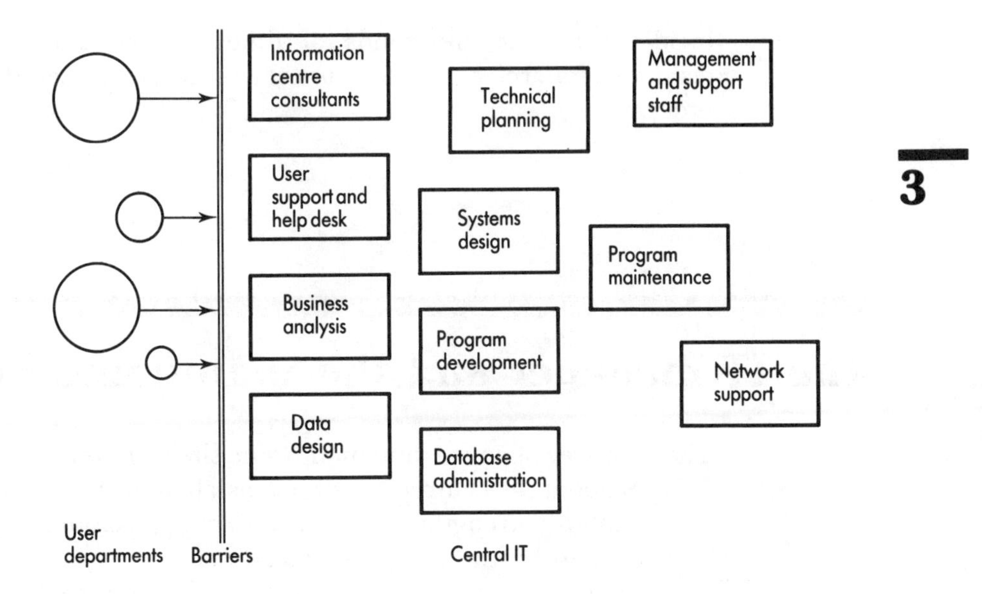

Figure 3.3 The mainframe's bureaucracy.

If the hardware and software do not manage to stop the mainframe in its tracks, then the maze of associated staff groups will do their best. Note that only a minority of people talk to users, and those that do often spend minimal time with them. The large number of units is necessary because of the complicated and monolithic nature of mainframe software. If mainframe software is simplified (which it can be), then the numbers of units and the numbers of people within them can both be reduced. However, in practice this rarely happens.

people need to be narrowly focused in some ways in order to concentrate fully on the very difficult problems they address, but that such mentality can often miss broader issues. Some technicians sincerely believe that being 'professional' involves investigating every last aspect of a problem, and that it is their duty to provide within a system virtually anything a user could think of and much that he might not.

This observer has seen a room full of a dozen or so such technicians arguing for nearly an hour as to whether a data field should be thirty or fifty characters long. The twenty characters of disk space in question, times the number of records involved, cost something like two dollars. The cost of the discussion was several hundred times the cost of the possible disk saving. In addition to this, most of the meeting's participants should have had vastly better things to do with that hour. When yours truly pointed this out to the group, he was thought very unsporting indeed - and the discussion continued. Such incidents happen thousands of times a day among the world's technical fraternity, wasting untold millions of user dollars in the process.

The IT manager and the mainframe ethos

The manager of an existing mainframe site will inevitably have mixed feelings about the centrepiece of his installation. While he may accept the monolith's strengths for some types of application, he may equally be frustrated by the problems encountered.

It is important for managers to exhibit objectivity in their dealings with the split cultures of downsized systems and mainframes, and also to try to pass this objectivity on to others. There is already an abundance of politics between large- and small-machine cultures, and any IT manager's goal must be to minimize this. In many large organizations, mainframes will be running core transaction-based systems for many years to come. The morale of people dealing with such systems must be maintained, and it must be recognized that theirs is a difficult and essential job. To treat mainframe people as last year's fashion will only jeopardize the stability and security of mainframe systems, much to the detriment of the organization as a whole.

In managing a split culture, some consideration should be given to relationships with the existing mainframe or large-mini vendor. It may be that the mainframe supplier also provides downsized equipment, in which case the supplier should feel reasonably wanted even though further sales of his high-margin large products may not be as he would have wished.

In cases where the mainframe vendor is not significantly present in the downsized area, extra care should be taken to illustrate that his territory is as secure as can be reasonably represented. Where the mainframe's duration is obviously going to be short, then artificial attempts to create feelings of security will be seen through, and the

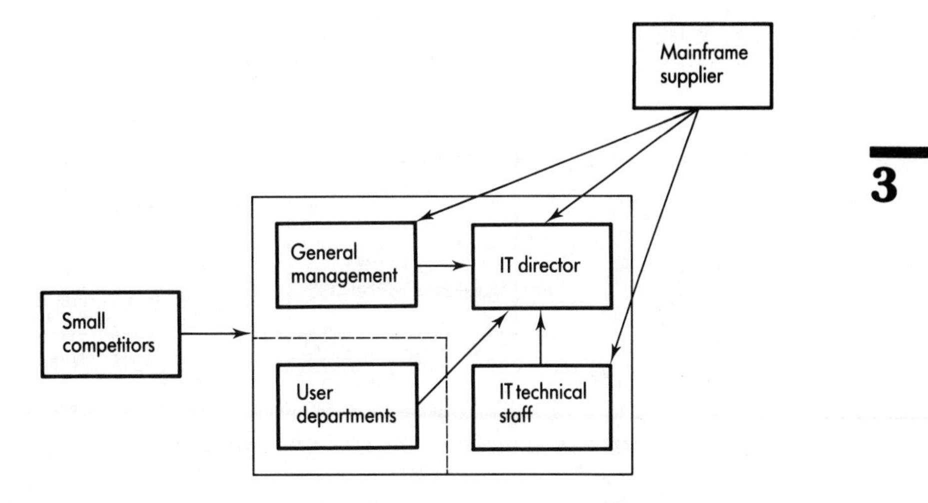

Figure 3.4 The man in the middle.

Mainframe suppliers have well developed techniques for keeping their products installed. A central strategy is to keep as much pressure on the customer organization's IT director as possible. Not only does the mainframe salesperson exert much pressure, he encourages other groups within the customer site to do the same, but from complementary angles. The result is a highly polarized carrot-and-stick scenario for the IT manager himself. In theory, if he sticks to the party line and delivers results using the approved (mainframe) technology, he advances within his own organization until the IT supplier eventually finds him an IT directorship with an even larger concern. If instead the IT director toys with unsafe technology and experiments with unstable suppliers, then he faces perdition and the dole queue. It may sound childish, but it still works with amazing reliability.

best will have to be made of a dubious situation. Whether the installed mainframe has a short life or a long one ahead of it, it is essential to split the two worlds clearly. Except where communications to the host machine or across a wide-area network are involved, mainframe and downsized cultures generally do not have to interact to a high degree. Each group is likely to feel more secure on its own clearly defined territory. This is one reason why, elsewhere in the book, we suggest using different management structures for development and for most ongoing support.

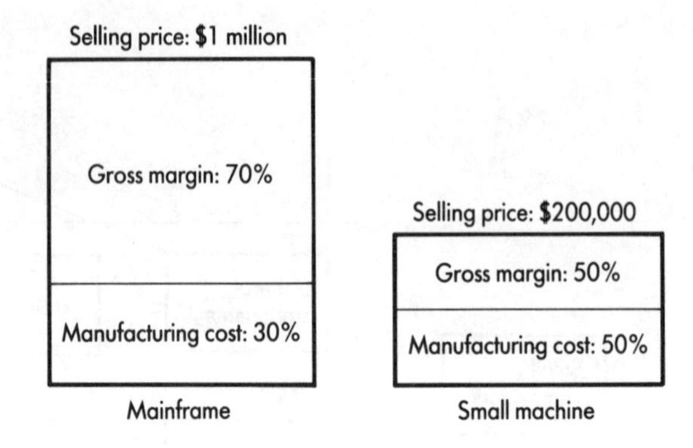

Figure 3.5 Why you don't get what you pay for.

The mainframe's expensive and complicated hardware and software are exaggerated by the high profit margins associated with the product. The high margin is due to lack of competition in the mainframe sector (the IBM design being by far the viable in the industry) and the high marketing and support costs. Smaller machines are simpler in design, and prices are further reduced by competition and lower distribution costs.

The mainframe's future

While mainframes, performing similar roles to the ones of today, will long exist, it is nevertheless likely that the power of downsized systems will change the character of many large machines. The more one transfers certain duties away from the mainframe, the more functions such as application task management, program development and centralized communications will become superfluous.

Given that client/server architectures are very new, and that they will take some time to reach the input/output capabilities now boasted by mainframes, there is a theoretical case for the mainframe to evolve into a very large server or database engine. While some mainframes are already performing such roles, there are problems with the scenario. Much modification of both hardware and software would be required to make the mainframe both efficient and cost-effective in this role. Such development would be expensive even for the likes of IBM ('a bank with a manufacturing subsidiary', as Wall Street *used* to say). Given the increasing capabilities of smaller machines, including such specialist items as data servers and disk arrays, this large-server version of the mainframe would be viable only at the very top end of the market.

An alternative scenario might see the mainframe becoming simpler in both hardware and software designs, so competing more effectively with larger minis such as the Sequent and Pyramid high-volume transaction processors. However, a mainframe vendor might think it easier and cheaper to expand his own UNIX product line to meet such competition, rather than to modify a product type that is visibly past its best.

Beyond a certain point, the 'what is a mainframe?' argument becomes meaningless. As small systems grow in power, so they grow in complexity, though such complexity tends to run along different lines from mainframe intricacy. Until the mainframe can copy the small machine's trick of passing many of its problems from IT over to the end user, it will be perceived as an awkward product, and its position in the computer marketplace will continue to decline.

Key issues

- Though the mainframe retains areas of comparative strength, these will be steadily eroded due to the more rapid progress of downsizing technology.
- Many defences of the mainframe are based upon out-of-date perceptions of downsized alternatives, and so should be questioned rigorously.
- Software, not hardware, is responsible for the high ongoing costs of mainframe ownership.
- Where continued mainframe usage is necessary, separation

of the old and new environments can help to maintain morale in both camps.

- While mainframe productivity can be improved, this is unlikely to to happen if traditional attitudes to development and end-user liaison are maintained.

4

Why small machines work

If one turns away from the mainframe, and in a cavalier fashion lumps most downsizing systems together as small machines, one discovers that there is some commonality within the lump. Lower prices and ease of use are the two items most usually associated with small machines (which, as we noted earlier, can be as big as mainframes for certain types of work).

Both the price and the ergonomic issues can do with much investigation. Small machines are designed differently, use different software and often operate in very dissimilar environments both from each other and as compared to the mainframe. One is rarely comparing like with like, and this makes many common comparisons misleading. If the downsizer misses too many of the key characteristics of the small machine, he is quite capable of winding up with a worse situation than he would have had with a mainframe. The most fundamental point about a small-machine design is that it is not capable of either the high-volume processing or the application complexity of its larger ancestor (high volumes and application complexity may or may not need to go together). The success of the small machine instead relies on a different rule of human organization:

> At any given time, a user wants to perform only one coherent task, and it is usually a relatively simple one.

As we saw earlier, the mainframe concept has very little to do with this rule. One sees this particularly in the design of software products, where the mainframe items must be fragmented into separate and incompatible items because their size and complexity limits them to doing a subset of a job, even if they are capable of doing this job very thoroughly. Simplification of its software helps the small machine to do several things:

- One product can do the job of several mainframe items, because the depth, or detail, of functions offered within an item is fairly basic.
- Economical machine usage results from emphasizing simple functions - there is less central processor and input/output activity.
- The product is coherent, and this plus its obvious functionality make it easy to use. One has a few consistent commands for the things one wants to do most urgently and frequently, and these are relatively easy to remember. A smaller product can more easily incorporate help and training facilities that are understandable.
- Simple software can be developed and distributed quickly. It can change more rapidly to altering market conditions, and is easier to convert to different machine platforms. These factors combine to create a wide market, facilitating economies of scale, so prices drop. Because of the wide market and the development potential, competitors come in quickly. This further lowers prices and speeds up the appearance of attractive features across the market, as such features can be copied either directly or indirectly.

The PC and its software market vividly illustrate the above characteristics, though UNIX, AS/400 and VAX also participate to a degree. The mainframe market has very few of the market characteristics of the small machine, just as the design characteristics are nearly opposite.

The self-directing small machine

One long-established feature of small machinery is its self-limiting nature. By being best suited to doing a wide range of simple things, users and third-party developers are effectively discouraged from being too ambitious. If a software package or a user program tries to do too many things, and so turn the product into a mainframe, one simply hits a brick wall. Most of the following will happen:

- The software will occupy too much machine space (processor, memory or disk input/output subsystem), and performance will suffer. Or the user will have to buy a much larger machine than intended, so raising the effective price of the offering.
- The code will take too long to develop, and it will be very difficult to change or to convert to another type of system.
- The user may not understand the result. The more commands, record types, screens and error procedures an application contains, the more trouble the user will have in learning and remembering it.

The above principles are changing, as small-machine capacity grows, and this presents certain dangers to downsizers. While most small-system software designers learn their lessons early, some do not. Also, many mainframe types are now trying to implement downsized systems, and they typically do not appreciate either machine limits or the desirability of sticking to the tried and true formulae outlined here.

The bigger small machines, first of all, do genuinely present the danger - or opportunity - of developing complex software, whether one needs the complexity or not. The other issue is that the growth in capacity is uneven and often illusory. The central processor speeds now being quoted - up to 400 mips for some very new chips - do not

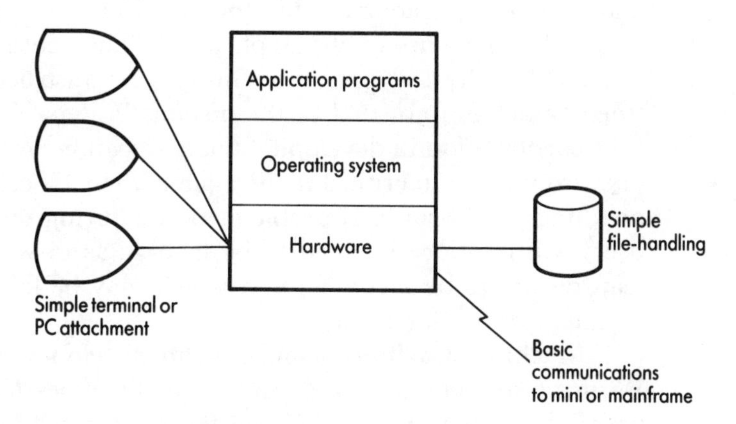

Figure 4.1 The simple machine.

The small machine's simple design confers not one but two benefits, adding ease of use to the more obvious cost-effectiveness. Such designs do not have the mainframe's power (especially in input/output capacity) or its capabilities in batch processing. For basic interactive work, however, such a small machine can outperform a mainframe costing several times as much.

bear any comparison to mainframe mips. One can usually divide by three or four and still overrate the small machine. Also, growth in input/output power has not kept pace with the increase in processor speeds or the size of main memory. Thus, the small system of today is unbalanced by traditional standards, though by its own rules it uses its power effectively (for example, the very fast processors are useful for numeric or graphics work). Most computer salespeople in the small machine area are unaware of the unlike comparisons, and some seriously believe that they are in fact offering mainframe systems at a bargain basement price. Some users, desperate to escape the mainframe, are overly eager to believe them.

User proximity

One reason small machines are successful is because they are physically and logically close to the actual user of the system. This provides some obvious benefits, and others that may not be apparent at first glance. The machine is – or should be – brought in for a clear and urgent requirement. This encourages users to focus on the most important elements of the application. The sense of proprietorship fostered by physical proximity implies a constructive attitude (it is 'their' machine, not that of the distant IT department). This assists user participation in developing the application and renders users less likely to jump into critical mode against their IT colleagues whenever anything goes wrong. If problems occur during the implementation, users will be more inclined to be flexible as to which functions and features are to be included, and which may be left out altogether or perhaps until a later stage.

Machine proximity should mean developer proximity as well. We have already criticized traditional IT types for neglecting their users. The small machine IT professional can afford to spend more time out with his user department, because he has less bureaucracy and technical intricacy behind him.

Once initial implementation has taken place, ongoing operation works better as well. By being in control of day-to-day scheduling, computer tasks can be reorganized at short notice to suit peak business workloads or unexpected conditions. By being able to set its own priorities, the user department may be happy enough to delay other work or to run into the evening, whereas if it were the IT department who suggested such things there would be vigourous complaining.

Physical proximity of a small machine is often welcomed by new users, or by users who have used the central system only slightly. While such people may feel some trepidation, they may also be flattered by the trust placed in them and will typically look forward to their new roles as computer-literate beings. There should be a genuine expectation (as opposed to the more cynical views of many long-standing IT users) that the machine will help them materially in their local business processes.

Fitting the application

When one engages in downsizing, some traditional IT attitudes have to be modified or go out the door entirely. One of the most pertinent of these is the unctuous, patronising 'please state your requirements' approach (in other words, 'please demand everything you can possibly think of'). Such an attitude encourages the user to cover his application needs in great detail, and the average analyst will offer very little guidance in helping the user organize or prioritize the material.

Even in a large IT setting, such attitudes are dangerous. In a small one they are fatal. The motivation of the large-system analyst may be pure enough, and it is often part of a defensive mentality which is trying to show that IT really does care about its users. However, the upshot of long, unguided discussions is a mass of too much detail and a general absence of structure and prioritization. While some current 'methodologies' (they are rarely anything of the sort) do impose some structure, they are meaningless without the application of common business sense. In some ways this mentality of throwing everything in suits the empire building schemes of IT management, as the resulting large applications boost the size of the department and the perceived importance of IT.

In the downsized world, one engages in a blunter (though still polite and constructive) and more frequent dialogue. In the 'close' environment, the user will accept this, as the developer is at least temporarily seen as an ally or even as a virtual department member.

The main idea in application fitting is to encourage users to move part way toward computer technology, just as the developer and his set of product offerings is moving towards them. The idea is to meet somewhere near a conceptual mid-point, not to have the whole IT effort drag itself over into user territory, where they understand little or nothing. The result of this two-way movement will ideally be concise systems which meet most application needs in the short-term. Longer-term needs, or extraneous features, can be left until later or never, depending upon subsequent discussions.

IT theorists invariably rail at the very notion of application fitting (squeezing the problem down until it is manageable), fearing political kickback from the users and even further undermining of the IT position. In reality, if done properly, this does not happen. The sense of proprietorship and the real results achieved quickly and cheaply override any misgivings that may linger. The user sees that he has made an effective decision on a business-like basis, and that the result is a system which he likes and can use with confidence. This is a far better result than that normally achieved by the 'give them everything' school of IT professionals, and no sensible user is going to complain.

The application packaged – or shrunk, if you like – for the small machine should at the same time be thought of as having been fitted to the user as well. When it comes to operating an installed system, the running of the application software should be consistent with the

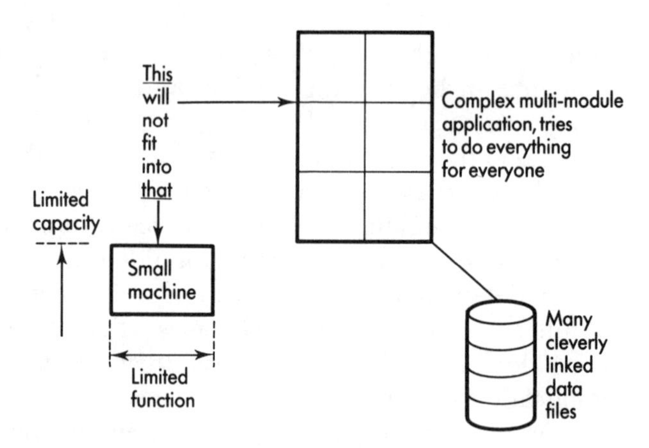

Figure 4.2 How to mismanage the small machine.

In cases where small machines do fail, the most common reason is where the application software and file structures have not been designed with the machine's obvious limits in mind. Mainframe specialists are particularly prone to this misdesign, and often get worse results than would a new user.

relative ease of using the base machine. Most small machines can run relatively unattended, with users themselves (not trained operators) being able to switch machines on and off, start up local networks, change printer stationery and run day-to-day housekeeping jobs. Backing up large disk files to tape (for security reasons) is often done overnight, with no one in attendance.

If an application has too many separate files or programs, operating simplicity is severely compromised. There is more likelihood that programs may be run in the wrong order, perhaps corrupting files, or that file backups and recoveries may be either insecure or overly time consuming. In other words, designing straightforward applications provides follow-on benefits to the operational phase of the system.

The de-skilling of IT personnel

A major objective of downsizing is to reduce IT staff costs in three ways:

- By reducing numbers of IT staff, particularly in certain areas not so relevant to the new environment.
- By using more junior people or those with lower skill levels.
- By transferring some responsibilities to the user department.

The last issue does not at first glance represent an overall cost saving to the organization, though such cost transfer is desirable on the grounds of system quality. By taking on some responsibilities, the user will become more involved in his system and so overall is likely to use it more effectively.

Such staffing issues are of course extremely contentious, especially if one's own job might be eliminated or downgraded. While the goals should be firmly pursued, there will be many situations where politics may delay certain exercises, or force the re-phrasing of terms like 'de-skilling'.

What the downsized environment requires are relatively large numbers of business oriented analyst/programmers and very small numbers of anything else. The small machine and its software have been designed to use such people, and too great a quantity of other skills will either cause trouble or at best will be superfluous. Within a large IT department, it is rare to find many genuine analyst/programmers. In most cases the two functions are split, with analysts, designers and database administrators providing the specifications of an application, and mere coders carrying out the writing and testing of programs.

The programmers and highly technical staff pose a problem for the downsizer, in that most of these cannot be used profitably in the new environment. The analysis, design and database personnel in theory could be used, but many would consider themselves too senior for the new positions, and would not wish to get their hands dirty by writing programs.

An option one should keep open is to use new or very junior people to develop small-machine applications. Experience shows that such people are often more productive and cooperative than experienced, rigid types. In the downsized environment, motivation and attitude are relatively more important than in the more static and compartmentalized traditional IT function. A technician, however knowledgeable, will demoralize users and fail to do proper analysis and programming work if he is unenthusiastic about his new position.

The de-skilling issue, as with many related social issues related to downsizing, is both fundamental and, for many people, difficult to deal with. The simple fact is that many old-world types are no longer required within the user organisation, though they may find rewarding careers in other areas of computer-related work.

Software and productivity

The small machine has long proven itself to be a high-productivity tool, both for the business purposes of the end user and as a platform for the rapid development of application software. Software suppliers use this productivity to provide packages that are both low in cost and easily modifiable.

There are several reasons for this small-machine productivity, and it is well to note them so all can be used to maximum effect:

- The basics of the machine provide simple interfaces to such resources as disk storage and communications lines.
- Different programming languages from those of the mainframe world are used, typically being more interactive and less procedural (meaning with less of a step-by-step orientation).
- Application programs are (or should be) small and simple, and use straightforward file structures.
- Applications are often new, and such systems are generally much simpler than long-established ones or conversions from currently running systems. New systems have few interfaces to other areas, and so complement the basic simplicity of the operating system and the programming languages.

Most measures of small-machine development productivity put it at around twice that of the mainframe. With good practice, the advantage might be increased further, perhaps to as much as three or four to one. With small-machine technology, there is an even greater premium on keeping things simple than with the mainframe. This is partly because most mainframe programs have a high start-up

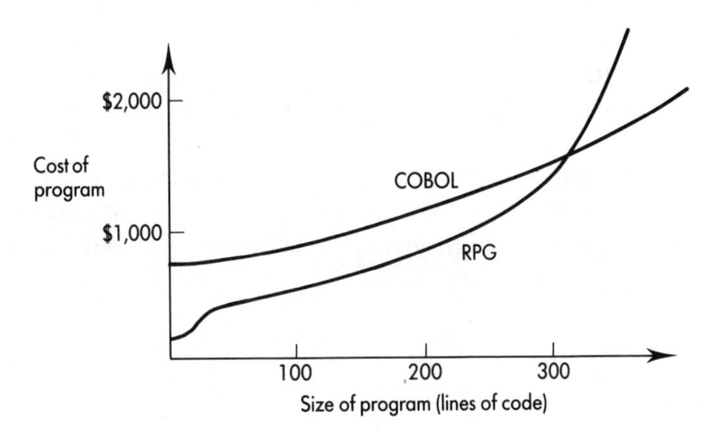

Figure 4.3 The productive small machine.

Simple programming languages have enabled the small machine to show major productivity advantages over the mainframe. Languages such as RPG or BASIC, though now aging, are still suitable for small programs performing simple functions. For extremely simple functions, around the 20 or 30 lines of code point on our graph, a program that works first time can be written in a matter of minutes. Critics of small machines inevitably miss many points regarding the interrelationships between the simple platform, the small program and the basic application function coded in a special-purpose language. The combination was never meant to compete directly with the mainframe, but used in the way intended, the product set is formidable indeed.

cost, with much defining of data and the coding of preliminaries to the actual coding of programs. With the small machine, using such languages as RPG or BASIC, there are few preliminaries - the programmer simply gets on with the job. Thus, very small programs can be coded with extreme efficiency, often to the tune of several per day, whereas the average mainframe item may take a number of weeks.

Aside from programming capability, the small machine benefits from much lower design effort. There are two reasons for this. The most obvious is that the simpler applications involved and the machine's simpler data-handling mechanisms require less design effort. The less apparent reason is that the high-productivity programming tools effectively let the programmer design as he goes to a limited but meaningful extent. Minor design mistakes or alterations can be corrected or incorporated quickly.

IT purists again object to the shortened design effort, as they have been trained to think that faults in the design stage create disasters downstream in the development project. To an extent this remains true in downsized projects, but critics of the minimal-design school miss the point. Small, simple systems are much less likely to contain serious faults, as the user has stated only a few obvious things which he needs. Any serious fault would be obvious at a glance, and minor ones can be sorted out during program creation. Design faults are insidious in complex applications where there are intricate file structures and many links to other complicated processes. These simply do not occur in a good downsized project. What matters is that the size and the shape of the project are right to start with (and arriving at these does take a certain amount of experience). Once these preliminary high-level borders have been put into place, there is little scope for serious error.

Experience and risk with small machines

Because the small machine has been with us for a number of decades, one knows with a high degree of certainty how to handle the basics properly. Where the machine type is best established is with the simple commercial application in a relative standalone situation (meaning with little communication to anything other than its own terminals -

dumb screens, PCs or printers). Running a few programs composed of only a few hundred lines of code each, and with a few dozen busy users running concurrently, the machine is a very safe bet indeed. File structures are those which are clearly essential, easy for both user and IT personnel to understand and maintain. Database sizes are low, perhaps in the thousands to tens of thousands of master records each for customers, products or employees. In this environment, we know not only that the machine is low-risk, we also know what we can get out of it. A small number of analyst/programmers should be able to create and maintain the few hundred programs involved (only a minority of which are key tasks for daily usage). If an application package or a turnkey solution has been purchased, one can probably run without any in-house programmers or technicians at all. A consultancy or the native hardware vendor can be called upon to provide occasional help to reconfigure the system, to provide software updates or to perform trouble-shooting exercises. Day-to-day technical matters are simple enough for a so-called system administrator to look after. This person may be the manager of the installation, or a more senior and technically astute analyst/programmer, as systems administration is far from a full-time occupation.

Where there is necessarily less experience in small-machine usage is in territory more recently occupied. Here, much care is needed, as the user-friendly pet can suddenly grow into a man- and money-eating tiger. Complex applications, high transaction rates, intricate data structures, communications systems of unknown capacity and loading, and new base technology such as windowing can create uncertainties or worse. Many of these issues will be covered in more detail in subsequent pages, but the issue here is to keep aware of where likely

Table 4.1 Classic small machines.

• IBM's System/3x and AS/400	
• DEC's PDP-11	
• The Pick system	Software systems, available on a variety of hardware
• MUMPS	Software systems, available on a variety of hardware
• IBM's and Apple's PCs	

There have been a number of excellent small-machine designs in the market over the past $2\frac{1}{2}$ decades. While all of the above achieved at least some success, not all were marketed well nor developed appropriately.

DEC's PDP-11 lives on in the smaller end of the UNIX product type (in concept if not in fine detail), which is fragmented among a number of different suppliers with different hardware types and different varieties of UNIX-based software.

problems may lie. If one wishes to achieve maximum benefit with the least trouble, then it is apparent that one should keep the downsized machine as close to its historical base as is feasible.

Aside from risks related to broad technological issues and narrow people, a main area of concern is the small-machine market itself. A popular illusion of the early 1990s is that the computer industry is recovering from the recession, and that therefore a period of profitability and stability lies before virtually everybody. While the recovery may help some organizations, there are other factors operating which are expected to polarize suppliers into the very lean and eventually non-existent on the one hand and the fat and prosperous on the other. Rapidly falling prices of small machines, primarily in the PC market, will first of all provide severe competition for more traditional suppliers. Despite a whiff or two of grapeshot in the 1991 recession, most of these are still not geared up for tough conditions. Many are still hoping for a return of the easy 1980s, when high demand and vapid competition meant that high prices could be charged for quite mediocre items. A secondary effect of this competition will be to force prices lower of both UNIX and proprietary items, otherwise the less competitive suppliers would lose sales altogether. The few sales that remain for many of the weak will be unprofitable.

The major impact of the above developments will be felt by the older minicomputer suppliers, as they have limited resources and have no mainframe profits upon which to rely. While any specific instance is a matter of probability, one can say with some confidence that a fair number of hardware vendors will disappear, whether politely (via takeover or merger) or by simple evaporation.

New users should therefore avoid this plagued territory where they can, no matter how cheap or attractive (in the short term) the offering appears. Many frightened vendors will virtually give boxes away in order to gain an installed base which they hope to milk later via upgrades, software charges and services.

For existing customers of suspect suppliers, if instant escape is not justified (perhaps because of the impossibility of converting large applications quickly), then very careful product selection and system design can at least minimize likely future problems. However attractive a small machine may be, to have it accompanied by an ever-shrinking supplier is not a good business proposition.

Key issues

- Small machines gain much of their productivity by being simple and straightforward. Low hardware prices, though important, are secondary in the long-term cost picture.
- Specific types of software development tool are at the heart of small-machine productivity and flexibility.
- Simple and well-packaged applications work best on small machines, whereas an overly complicated one can virtually destroy such a system.
- Relatively junior and less skilled personnel can operate small machines more cost-effectively than can highly specialized technicians, unless exceptionally complex conditions apply.

5

The evolution of client/server systems

One of the main threads of downsizing is the rapid development of client/server architectures. As might be expected, a variety of suppliers have tried to bend the definition to suit their own vested - and high priced - interests.

True client/server should be seen as two complementary systems which have been *designed* to work in conjunction with one another. Among other things, this means they should use as many common components as is feasible, from hardware platforms through operating systems, database systems and development languages. Older systems are commonly described as servers, even though their hardware and operating systems originally had no concept of such an environment. For certain purposes, such client/server marriages might be feasible, but users should keep in mind that they do not represent the mainstream.

True client/server architectures include PC to PC systems, using Intel basic circuitry and similar or related operating systems. Still legitimate, if less ideal, combinations might include UNIX to UNIX or DOS/Windows to UNIX systems. Normally, clients and servers interact with each other via a local-area network, though the concept need not preclude other types of wiring, for example, RS232 connections or wide-area connectivity.

Where client/server fits

True client/server, according to the above definitions, is ideally suited to many types of departmental usage. It is a fair comment that the relative immaturity of the architecture, plus current technological limitations, do restrict the size of the implementation to be considered. However, as development is exceptionally rapid in this area, it is highly likely that very large organizational units will soon be able to take advantage of client/server's economy and responsiveness. Today client/server fits those situations where:

- The department is relatively self-contained.
- Numbers of concurrent users are less than 100 or so, depending obviously on how active each user is at peak times.
- Application types are simple, whether there are a few or many types of application on the given local network.

Because of current limits inherent in client/server, it is doubly important for potential users to evaluate both the types of application to be processed and their volumes. Servers commonly used are based on small-machine architectures, and as such can hit sudden limits in input/output processing, whether for disk access or communicating across the network. One should not be misled by largely theoretical central processor speeds or the variety of equally misleading benchmarks circulating around the industry.

Client/server technology

Client/server technology is progressing rapidly on a number of specific fronts, but unfortunately not on all required ones. Nevertheless, overall the systems are becoming more powerful and lower in risk.

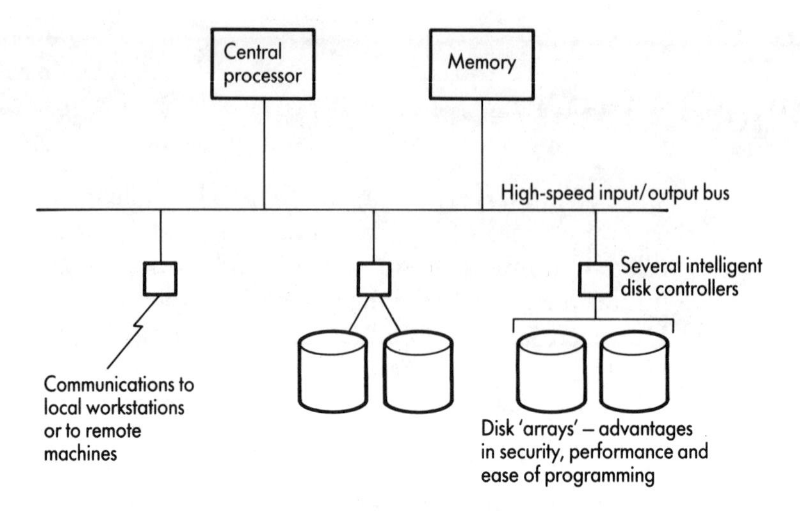

Figure 5.1 Essence of the server.

The server in a client/server system is often an expanded PC design or a standard UNIX platform. Aside from the processor speeds that gain most of the headlines, prospective users should examine the input/output structure of the server, particularly where disk drives are concerned. The better server will allow several accesses in parallel to the disk subsystem, so gaining much better performance than would be available from standard PC architecture.

The more positive threads are:

- More rapid Intel central processor circuitry. The forthcoming Pentium chip (sometimes called the 586), promises 100 MegaHertz and 100 million science fiction instructions per second. Nevertheless, it should be perhaps twice as powerful as the current 50 MegaHertz 486 chip, and should eventually be very cost-effective. Also, 486 chips are increasing in speed (the maximum is 67 MegaHertz at this writing) and are also failing rapidly in price; slower 486 chips are currently going for around $100. This means that central processor prices will become more acceptable to departments with tight budgets. Also, greater speed from a single chip means that expensive multi-processor designs can be avoided in many cases, or that a second processor can be used to give a fail-safe operation rather than more speed, again lowering costs where reliability is a paramount concern.

- Cheaper, faster and safer disk subsystems. Many server suppliers now use disk arrays which can spread input/output loads across several drives. Such data protection features as disk mirroring and data guarding are widely on offer (data guarding means writing disk data, in compressed and recoverable form, onto a separate drive, such that the data from several disks can be compressed onto one drive).
- Larger disk subsystems and larger-capacity backup devices. Servers offering more than ten gigabytes are common, and backup tape systems with capacity in the low gigabytes per cartridge are available.
- For larger UNIX processors, a new generation of very fast chips from Sun, Mips and DEC will provide servers with virtual mainframe levels of processing power (though not with corresponding input/output capacity, at least for the time being). These systems, unfortunately, are likely to remain much more expensive than Intel-based ones, so the price plus their non-standard nature may slow acceptance at this end of the market.
- Better database systems. These have improved substantially over the past few years, and in ways that suit highly distributed situations such as client/server. A number of products (such as SYBASE and INGRES) contained elements of client/server in their designs anyway, which made them especially suitable for this type of operation. New alliances between network suppliers and database providers (Novell-Gupta, Microsoft-Sybase) imply better performance and greater viability for the product combinations involved.
- Better operating systems. NetWare and OS/2 were both designed for the Intel hardware platform, and offer a reasonable blend of performance and ease of use. Better versions of UNIX for the client side of the equation are now entering the market. The recent acceptance of OS/2, and the earlier (and continuing) popularity of NetWare, provide stability for the Intel-based client/server world. If Microsoft's forthcoming Windows (NT) is successful as a server operating system, then this will boost the client/server market even further.
- Rapidly falling PC prices, and to a lesser extent those of UNIX workstations. Currently, PC prices are declining at around 30% a year. A minimal 486 workstation can be bought for around $1000 (not including software) – less than a

dumb terminal cost a few years ago. The fact that most corporations will have PCs in place anyway, plus the related cabling systems, means that the extra cost of the server will appear modest – a matter of a few hundred dollars per user.

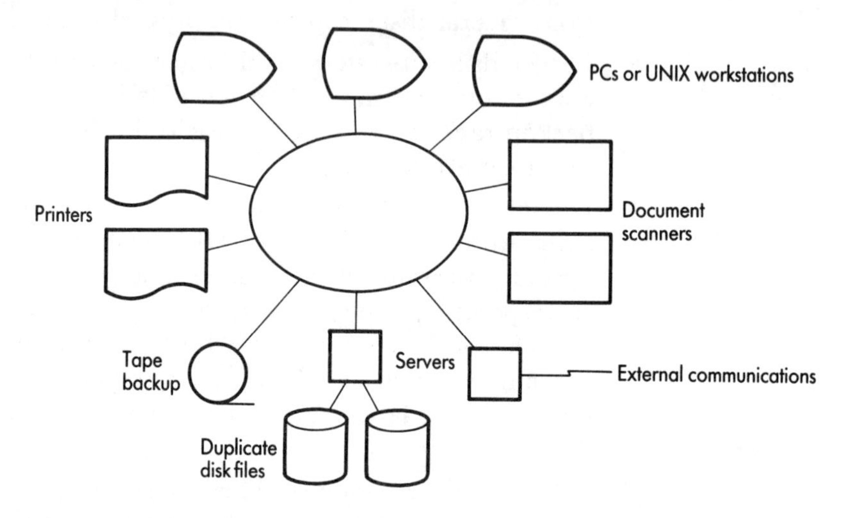

Figure 5.2 Reliability and client/server.

Reliability is important with any system directly under the user's eye. Overall reliability depends upon both hardware and software products performing as planned, and on meaningful alternatives being available to the end user when things do go wrong. Client/server is strong on many aspects of reliability. Because the system is under local control, use of devices can be altered at short notice should a particular item fail. It is relatively inexpensive to duplicate many of the more critical elements, such as power supplies, disk files, scanners, printers and, of course, the workstations themselves. Careful planning can ensure that at least part of the system is functioning on a continuous basis, and one can do this at much lower cost and more easily than would apply with larger machine types.

Limitations of client/server

Despite the many attractions of client/server architecture, prospective users should exercise care in deciding to move to such systems. As with many other types of downsizing, there are plenty of traps for the unwary.

As pointed out already, high central processor speeds are not matched by corresponding input/output power. Depending upon the type of server chosen, disk access rates of several hundreds per second are achievable (a far cry from the 10 000–15 000 I/Os per second which a large mainframe can manage). In terms of actual amounts of useful information transferred from a server to a client, benchmarks (for example, by *Byte* magazine) have shown that 20 000–70 000 characters per second are likely figures. Whether these transfer rates are sufficient for a given site depends as much upon the type of work being done as the number of users on-line. A transfer rate of, say, 200 records of 280 bytes each per second may look adequate for simple order entry. However, if several users decide to do extensive document transfer or to deal with bit-mapped graphics stored on the server, then response times will plummet. Even such standard activities as reading across a section of a small database can strain both the server and the local network.

The role of the local-area network

Where client/server architectures are concerned, the local networking environment is clearly crucial. Unfortunately, many users do not do enough planning in this area, either short- or long-term. As with processor speeds, what looks impressive on paper may not deliver the goods in practice.

In general, communications is the messiest area with which client/server advocates have to cope. Because of the characteristics of local-area networking, it can be worse than communications generally for downsizers. Common local networking problems include:

- Poor and erratic response, particularly for the older and slower local systems such as Ethernet and 4 Mbit Token Ring. The newer 16 Mbit Token Ring and the 100 Mbit fibre-optic networks are much less likely to suffer these problems.
- High failure rates, due to software, erratic connections, faulty

boxes in key positions such as bridges between networks and protocol converters.

- High management costs, due to complex software interfaces, the problems inherent in tracing erratic faults, and in some cases the lack of system management and monitoring software.

The local network, in a client/server situation, is effectively the system bus, carrying all data traffic between all nodes. It is thus essential to engineer it for maximum reliability and performance. One should be aware of the transfer limits and match expected application usage accordingly. If volumes look like approaching the limits for an older network type, then in most cases it is better to install the newer higher-speed option at the start rather than wait until performance problems occur and so be forced into much dislocation and system inactivity as rewiring takes place. In those fortunate situations where a department is moving into new or refurbished accommodation, it is well to try to get the most up-to-date cabling systems installed - and then to try and pass it off as a normal construction cost rather than an IT-related item.

In managing local networks, a number of new PC-based tools are entering the market. While typically not as comprehensive as

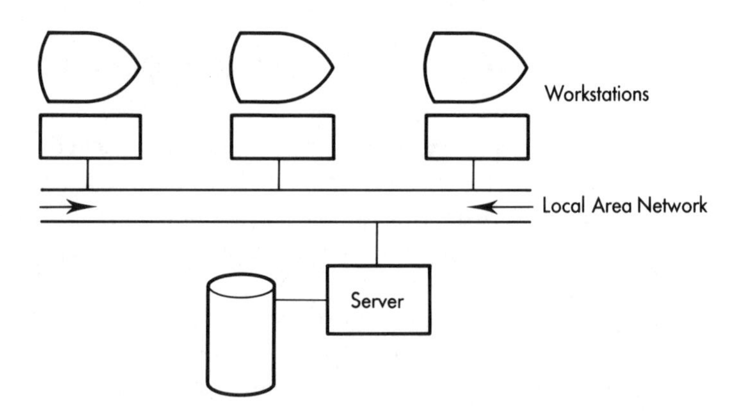

Figure 5.3 The local network.

One should never forget that in a client/server system the local network acts as effective system bus and handles *all* traffic between workstations and servers. The capacity of older network types, while it looks good on paper, is limited in practice, and today there are many instances of performance problems due to inadequate planning or sudden changes in usage. Monitoring network usage and keeping in contact with what users are doing are both essential in order to avoid unpleasant surprises in the form of sudden network congestion.

enterprise-wide items such as IBM's SystemView, they may be adequate for a small to medium local network. Being PC-based, one can store the monitoring software on the server, then download it to whichever PC is idle at the time, so avoiding dedicating a workstation full-time to the monitoring function. Some of these PC items are also very cheap - often thousands of dollars less than mainframe- or mini-based tools.

Software for client/server

While the hardware and communications sides of client/server are well established, software components are more generally volatile. While the operating systems and database levels are becoming reasonably standard, such items as application generators and packages themselves have yet to adapt to client/server needs. Part of this instability is the newness of the windowing environment. Because it changes the elemental nature of the workstation end of client/server, windowing shifts the centre of gravity of the entire system and so has caught suppliers off-balance. Some users may legitimately choose to wait until some of the dust settles before making long-term commitments to application and development tools.

To use client/server to its full effect, application functions need to be processed where the user is and where adequate power is available. Unfortunately, the two locations may still not coincide, though with further technological progress the client and server elements should become more evenly matched.

In the average client/server configuration, the component most likely to be overloaded is the server. In such cases it would clearly be best if the client workstation could perform such offloadable tasks as large data sorts and substantial calculations, even if the workstation took slightly longer to do the work than the server would. In less common situations, a small or very busy client might be better off forwarding work to a much more powerful server, assuming the latter had capacity to spare.

The sum of the two opposing situations is that, in an ideal world, we would like the overall client/server system to decide where spare capacity exists at any given moment, and then dynamically to allocate work from overloaded units. While such technology exists in large clustered systems, it is very expensive to acquire and intricate to operate, so for the time being the client/server world has to subsist on its basic concept of a database box forwarding items to workstations for further processing.

Where splitting applications in a more complex fashion is desired, it can be done using such tools as IBM's CICS transaction monitor in both client and server components. However, this is a complicated solution and should be considered only in extreme situations. In client/server, as well as elsewhere in IT, there are many solutions which exceed the cost of the problem.

Using client/server

Because of the diverse types of client/server component, and also because of the variety of products within each type, it is possible to configure client/server systems that are even more awkward to run than their arch opponent, the traditional mainframe. As with other areas of downsizing, careful planning and forceful leadership are necessary. If these two essentials are missing, systems which are fragmented, rigid and costly to run are virtually guaranteed. Because client/server is basically inexpensive, high personnel costs will be doubly noticeable to users, so configuring for economical ongoing operation is politically as well as economically astute.

Currently, PC architecture is, by a wide measure, the most attractive option for commercial (as opposed to technical/academic) work. This advantage looks like continuing for some years. The main plus points of PC architecture are:

- Very low hardware and software prices.
- A wide array of generic packages such as spreadsheets, word processing, mail and messaging, and database managers. Also, many simple 'semi-generic' packages are available for universal business functions such as invoicing, sales analysis and payroll.
- Relative ease of use compared to alternatives.

- Software which is adapted to the Intel platform, thus adding reasonable performance to already substantial benefits.
- A very wide market base, which ensures stability, openness and viability.
- A highly competitive market, open to imaginative newcomers, which ensures that a continuing supply of new and low-cost products will remain forthcoming.

Unless something totally unexpected happens, PC architecture will advance and gain market share over the relatively slow moving UNIX area. It will also assist UNIX in making proprietary systems such as AS/400 and VAX/VMS appear even more tired and overpriced.

In designing for client/server, one should keep in mind already existing principles for distributed and on-line systems. Applications at both terminal and server ends should be kept as simple as possible. Database locking should come under scrutiny, to avoid delays to other

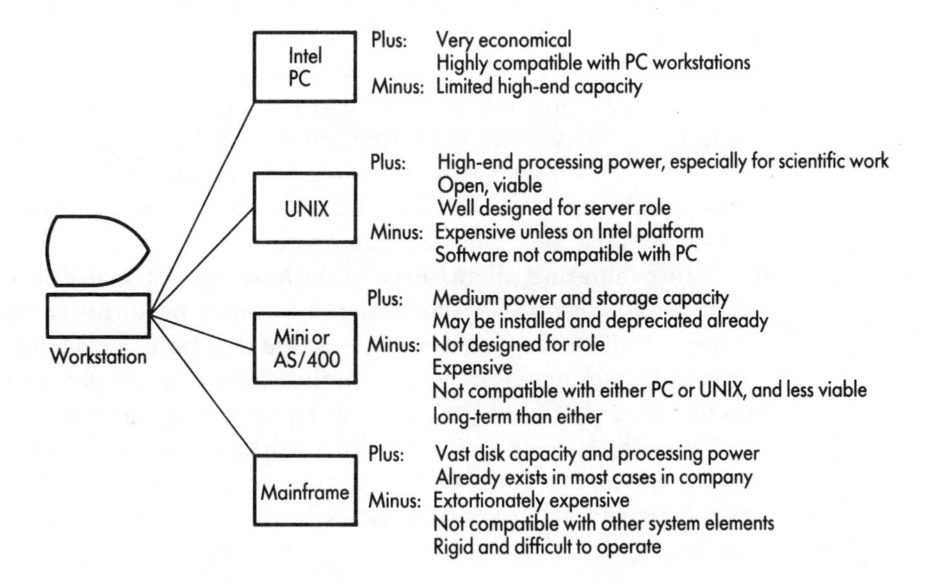

Figure 5.4 Which server?

Because of the fashion factor, all sorts of combinations are calling themselves client/server. Of the main alternatives shown above, systems based on PC and/or UNIX technology are the only ones that really fit the definition. Others might be used in special cases, but such instances should be evaluated carefully as to the long-term implications, which often will be negative.

users in accessing the server. New ways of laying out not only applications but the surrounding business procedures should be examined carefully. For example, if customer-based service points are put into force, then it becomes feasible for a given workstation to contain master data regarding that operator's customer set.

Client/server versus minis and mainframes

The increasing power and acceptance of client/server systems ensures that it will increasingly threaten particularly the established minicomputer sector. Users, when faced with a mini-looking application should always conduct at least a trial fit onto client/server unless it is immediately clear that the latter is unsuitable. In terms of power, existing client/server systems can compete with most minis or similar (for example, AS/400), as only a small percentage of these actually installed today are handling more than, say, 100 busy users. Especially where office functions are involved, client/server normally wins, as most of the activity is carried out on the PC in any case. Products such as VAX and AS/400 are poor propositions for high-volume word processing and local communications, partly because of price and partly because of design characteristics.

In evaluating client/server solutions against mainframe options, one should look particularly at mainframes performing information centre or office work. Unless very large databases or document stores are absolutely necessary, such applications will usually transfer quite readily to smaller systems, often at enormous savings in both machine and personnel costs. As with office work, one should note that much information centre work is processed on PCs anyway. A mainframe acting largely as a passive database engine is an extremely vunerable target.

Key issues

- Client/server is one of the most rapidly developing areas of computing, and it can now be considered seriously for most types of application.
- Client/server is especially a threat to the traditional minicomputer, whether proprietary or 'open'.
- Very low hardware costs are a feature of client/server, plus the fact that the conceptual marginal costs are even lower (in other words in many situations the majority of the system – in the form of workstations and local network – is there already).
- Communications is generally the most difficult part of client/server architecture. It should be analysed carefully for both performance and operability in any given instance.

6

Risks in downsizing

While downsizing to some degree is inevitable for any large organization, the selection of areas to be downsized and their sequence is of great importance. Among the criteria for selecting particular departments or application groups are the risks involved. Risk is one of the most prominent downsizing issues, such that substantial thought must be given to it. Even if an area looks theoretically appropriate for downsizing, an excessive degree of risk should be enough to veto or postpone such an effort.

At first glance, the coupling risk to downsizing looks paradoxical. One has already noted the friendly and otherwise low-risk characteristics of the small machine and its software. There is much less to go wrong with such an item than the complex and unwieldy mainframe. The point we wish to make here is that there are specific types of risk in any effort, downsized or not. Many risks in IT, or in business in general, are related to emotional or political issues. Whatever else downsizing may or may not be, it is definitely both a political and emotional issue. It is of utmost importance to recognize where risks lie, and to have an approximate method for quantifying them.

The main risk issues

There are two points about downsizing that make it a tempting target for those who may react against it:

- It has a very high profile in the user's eyes. The machine is sitting right there in or very near his department, and is running applications crucial to his immediate business duties. If it does not work, he will make sure everyone knows about it.
- It is not the traditional way of doing things, both mechanically and in terms of human organization. Those wedded to the old world will use any failed scheme or dubious success to point out the supposed safety of older technologies and methods.

If these are the reasons why downsizing is risky, one needs to look at the issues that may give rise to an unsuccessful project. At the highest level, we can look at the three key areas of downsizing:

- The user
- The technology
- The application

If any one of these three areas fall below an acceptable risk level, that should disqualify the downsizing project. However, before one goes to that extreme, one should look at ways of minimizing risk and of raising any deficient area above the threshold. A major part of the remainder of this book will cover such topics, especially those sections dealing with the qualification of end users, the selection and designing of applications, and the selection of general technologies, suppliers and specific projects.

It also bears to keep matters in perspective. To the faint hearted traditionalist, using any new technology, or approaching even a mildly unstable end user, or dealing with any new application type, appears to involve a high degree of risk. One must keep in mind the risk of doing nothing, and so dissatisfying everyone in sight (including many of one's own IT colleagues). One must also consider the risks involved in alternatives, as these may be very high. We have already pointed out in the mainframe chapter (Chapter 3) the very high risks inherent in clinging to outdated methods. To provide an accurate evaluation of risks, the assessment needs to consider downsizing versus other alternatives.

Where risks really lie

The genuine risks in downsizing are by now well established, and we will name them. Before we do so, and to edify the super-conceptually minded, one must recognize that, in any relatively new area, a main risk is that an unexpected risk type will occur. In downsizing terms, this is most likely to occur with new communications technology or in the client/server area. Returning to a more down to earth plane, one can start from the highest level and work downwards.

The most senior of these levels is that of the organization itself. Some types of organization are more difficult to downsize than others, though in many cases these are the very organizations that have trouble with IT in any form. Troublesome types include:

- The very unstable organization, whether this instability relates to structure, frequent management changes, an inherently volatile product mix or rapidly changing markets. While this instability causes trouble in any case, if downsized systems are reorganized or relocated frequently, they are apparently more disruptive than if the chaos were to take place behind the steel doors and barbed wire of the old style IT department.
- The organization that does not know what it wants. These are often companies that are not doing particularly well in their chosen markets for the very same reasons. Public-sector

Table 6.1 Models of risk.

- Where does risk reside?
- How much is there?
- What are the consequences if the risk is realized?
- Which risks are near the threshold of acceptability?
- How may risks be avoided or minimized?

Risk management is usually an area of grave deficiency within IT installations, mainframe or otherwise. In downsizing exercises of any scale, good risk management is essential both to avoid highly visible disasters and to force the newcomer's mind onto the most important issues. The objectives of risk management are first of all to avoid risks or reduce them, and secondarily to devise contingency plans for those risks which remain high.

efforts are often in this category, not necessarily because of the faults of the local managers, but because their political masters keep changing their minds and so prevent consistent and constructive action, again perhaps on many fronts aside from IT.

- The highly divisionalized organization. Part of the issue is that it may reorganize into a more centralized company. The fashion for centralization in the business world follows an approximately eight-year cycle. When centralization has had time to fail, the company then decentralizes. When this does not work either, the company throws in the towel and decides instead that it is a 'service' company, whatever that means. The astute IT person can anticipate these moves and plan systems accordingly. A further problem with divisionalized companies is that there is often a great deal of politics between divisions, and this complicates already complicated problems. A plus side of this for the downsizer is that one division may want to downsize simply because the others are moving to mainframes, but this is scarcely the best reason.

Once one gets past the organization itself, common high-risk situations within user and application areas include:

- A vague and uncertain end-user department.
- An unduly hostile end user, possibly because of unpleasant IT experience in the past.
- A very complex record-handling application, even if transaction rates and data volumes are not particularly frightening. Complex non-commercial applications (typically numeric-intensive tasks) are more likely downsizing candidates.
- An application which is not clearly aligned to an organizational department or function, or where distributed data does not have an unambiguous owner. This is particularly likely to happen in head-office environments, where strong managers encroach into the territory of their weaker neighbours and thus muddy the theoretical distinctions between departments. Automating the corporate version of Ivan the Terrible is not within the scope of the user-friendly small machine.

Once one is back within the IT fold, there are numerous risks to note. In theory, they are more easy to control, as they lie within one's own territory. However, as every technician knows, one of the highest-risk factors anywhere is another technician with different ideas. Broadly, one should be aware that the following frequently occur in downsizing projects:

- Inappropriate technology is chosen. It may be too complex, too new, too old (probably because it was lying around unloved) or too unstable.
- Inappropriate people are chosen. These too may be too old, too unstable, and so on.
- Uneven or otherwise uncertain management commitment.

Representing risks

When one is involved in evaluation for downsizing, it helps to draw up simple diagrams to represent common concerns. It also helps to highlight the point that the issue under discussion really is an issue, and so should be thought about. A pictorial representation or graph helps users and technicians to grasp situations where a number of things are proportional, but not precise enough to be represented by, say, a spreadsheet. A number of PC tools are ideally suited to such presentation, and should be used if available.

A suggested way of dealing with risk issues is to specify them, perhaps side by side (as in Figure 6.1). Anticipated benefits should be shown as well, in order to give perspective to the effort. A disqualification line might be shown, to illustrate areas of high risk. While attempts should be made to reduce any risks of significance, those approaching or exceeding the disqualification line should receive extra attention. Depending upon the complexity of the downsized project, separate pages might be used for each topic (user and organizational factors on one page; applications, technology and IT staff risks each on additional ones).

The tactful but accurate method of dealing with IT risks is to discuss them openly with users, managers and one's own colleagues. They are but one element of the project, and should not be overly dwelt upon. By discussing risks and how to minimize or eliminate them, one should gain credibility and add to the perceived security of the project. It is too common a tendency still for IT people to sweep

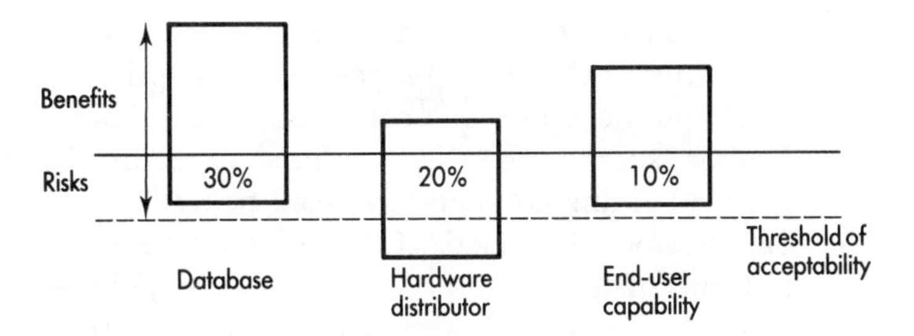

6

Figure 6.1 Identifying and sizing risk.

In order to identify, quantify and present risk issues coherently, simple (and necessarily approximate) representations are useful. Figure 6.1 shows a risk and reward equation for a planned small system. Benefits are compared with risks in three areas where significant risk has been identified: a database package with which the installation is unfamilliar, a small hardware distributor that may not be stable and concerns that the user department may be stretched in managing its new system. The percentages show the likelihood that the risk will be realized at the maximum level anticipated. Note that only one area – that of the hardware distributor – potentially descends below the 'threshold of acceptability', meaning that there is a 20% chance that major disruption to the system will occur. The other two areas are above the threshold, meaning that even if the anticipated worst happened, it would not overly damage the project. A point that should not be missed is that the percentages of likely risk incursion might be summed to get a rough picture of overall risk. If we did this for the above example, we would see that a 60% chance of significant (but not catastrophic) disruption is likely. This is high, and thought ought to be given to reduction of all named risks, not just in the one area that oversteps the threshold.

risks under the carpet, hoping no one will notice. Unfortunately, one's credibility is blown if the risk is realized later in the project. One is open to charges of poor planning at best, or wilfully deceiving managers and users at worst. Discussing risks helps to spread the responsibility to others, which in turn seeks feedback from them to help minimize the risk.

The high-risk project

There will be many instances, downsized or not, where high-risk efforts must nevertheless be implemented. The character of such projects is often evident in the early stages. There are various drivers to such projects, but the general rule is that there is an organizational imperative behind it. There may be legislation, perhaps to do with legal, public safety or ecological issues. There may be a huge cost benefit, such as reducing on-hand inventory by large levels both to reduce holding costs and to avoid being lumbered with unseasonable or unfashionable goods. Or there may be a competitive edge gained in terms of customer service. Early retail point of sale applications are a good example of high-priority downsizing; there were multiple benefits (in both customer service and inventory management), yet the costs and risks were both high.

While red-blooded downsizers should welcome such challenges, one should also devote extra attention to such situations. New technology may be involved, such that its characteristics are not fully known. Point-of-sale machines again provide a good example. Programming for such items turned out to be agonisingly slow, and both time-scales and budgets were overshot by mind-boggling margins. Yet, many organizations still proceeded with the effort and were duly rewarded, despite the overruns.

By far the most important point here is to identify such projects in the first place, in order that contingency planning can take place. Again, many IT personnel choose not to frighten their users, and instead to treat such efforts as if they were programming a sales ledger application. One should understand that a choice has to be made: frighten a small amount now, to concentrate the mind, or a lot later, and possibly suffer more severe consequences.

The high-risk project needs to have extra features added to it in order to allow for contingencies. Extra time, money and manpower have to be allowed for. The awkward issue is the manpower, as skilled resources cannot always be acquired quickly. A contingency plan should always specify the expected source (whether one's own staff, the consultancy market or freelance contractors), and this must be credible. Arrangements might be formally contracted with consultancies to provide staff on a contingency basis.

The importance of risk management

Risk reduction should be a stated objective of every downsizing project, and the issue should be ever uppermost in the minds of project managers as the implementation progresses. One should recognize that pressures to increase risks will come from IT staff themselves in two ways:

- Especially at the beginning of the project, there will be some eager to use this effort as an excuse to plunge into new technology. In some cases the new technology may be justified or inevitable, as suggested in the previous section. In many other cases, it will simply be another case of technocrats trying to use the project for their own ends – perhaps for amusement or career enhancement.
- Where projects encounter problems once they have begun, there are often pressures to change something abruptly. In many cases this change will not cure the ill, but will either have no effect or will even make matters worse. In some cases, the change might be justified, but the issue should always be considered carefully. Sudden reversion either to older technologies – particularly in software – or the acceptance of a new cure-all may be hazardous.

One approach managers may take regarding risk is to perform a trial fit of what are thought to be the lowest risk template of products, techniques and people over the effort in question. In many cases, smaller, older or cheaper versions of products, or more junior

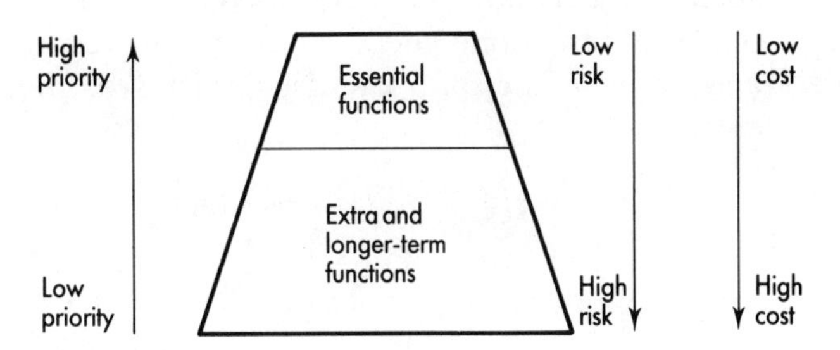

Figure 6.2 Risk and the application pyramid.

Throughout this book we promote the need for application simplicity in the downsized world. Among other issues, the simplicity or otherwise of an application should be seen very much as a risk topic. By following the 'everything now' school of empty headed analysis, the likelihood of project disruption followed by an incomprehensible solution is multiplied dramatically. Where postponable or less essential features of an application are under discussion, Figure 6.2 might be drawn for the user to ponder. Assuming that the user is being properly billed for his system, the point might be made that spending extra money does not necessarily decrease risks.

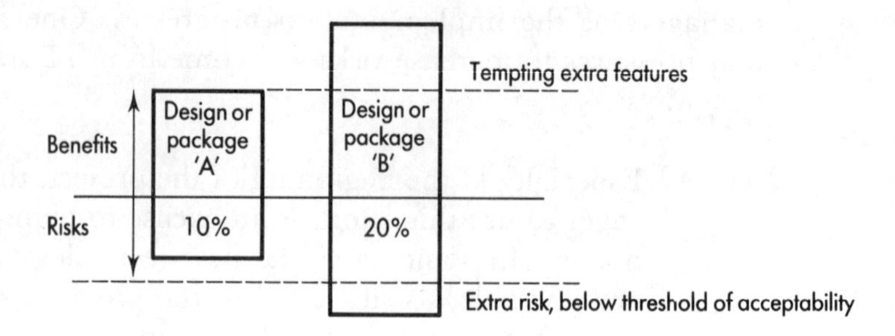

Figure 6.3 The lowest-risk project.

Despite years of experience that should have taught them otherwise, many IT technicians are still feature-crazy, and will choose the product or design with the most of these. While features are fine so far as they go, one should also consider risks involved, especially as new products or untried designs are the ones likely to have the extra features. In Figure 6.3, system 'A' is preferable to 'B', both because of the lower percentage chance of risk being realized and because the downside is smaller even if it is realized. System 'B' has a 20% chance of severe disruption or failure, much too high by normal downsizing standards.

people, can be used without compromising significantly the success of the project. The monetary element is important here, because extra budget will then exist for contingencies or for features the users would value. They may not care that they are on an older release of software or on a 386 PC instead of a more glamorous, faster 486. In downsizing, risk management ties in very closely with other management philosophies. If one gets the basics right regarding application design and end-user liaison, low-risk projects in most cases automatically ensue.

Key issues

- Because of their high visibility in end users' eyes, it is vital to minimize risks in downsized systems.

- Though downsizing technology is essentially simple, the different ways in which it is used pose traps for the unwary traditionalist.
- The character of one's own organization can determine degrees and types of risk. In particular, unstable or uncertain companies may limit downsizing's potential.
- Lucid risk-avoidance exercises are essential in order to minimize risks.

7

Broad downsizing strategies

In approaching downsizing, the average organization will face many choices which need to be resolved early. Selection of application groups or user departments, and selection of technological architectures, should all begin at square one. In parallel with these exercises, the installation should make some attempt to figure out where it actually is at the moment in a number of related areas. Any mature IT department will have a range of hardware and software items, the latter both purchased and developed in-house, plus a range of skills built up over many years.

One of the first major tasks involved in downsizing is to try to split the old from the new. While the two halves will be interrelated to some extent, maximum results on either side are usually best fostered by maximum independence. The mainframe complex, even if it is only to be temporary, must be left to get on with existing systems. The new effort equally must be as independent as is feasible, without continual reference to the more established systems and their supporters.

Depreciation and system values

A key factor in deciding what to do with existing applications and machines will be their assumed value. Depreciation is understandably a sensitive issue, both between proponents of older and new systems, and between financial and IT staff in general. Company policies vary a great deal on depreciation, and formal policies may not exist in many areas (say, the valuing of in-house application programs). Legal and accounting conventions in many countries may bend into artificiality what many consider to be the real world. Most consultants involved in downsizing would probably prefer to see very rapid depreciation of computer products and user-written programs alike. In the real world, especially where technologies and market needs both change rapidly, many items become obsolete very quickly. Resale values on much hardware reflect this. Any computer more than a couple of years old is likely to be worth only a small fraction of its initial list price. One should not be misled in this area by brokers' asking prices for used equipment. In most cases this represents a preliminary bargaining point, and is not overly related to the price they paid for the second-hand machine. One has seen fairly up-to-date kit (perhaps three years old) being offered free to anyone willing to cart it off the premises.

An average company may depreciate a PC over a couple of years and a mini over three or four, either on a straight line or reducing balance basis. Some (perhaps more realistic) people will write off a PC after 12 to 18 months. Probably the most accurate method is the reducing balance one, the problem being that the percentage write-off needs to be up to fifty percent - perhaps too large a lump for many accountants to swallow.

For minicomputers, a less savage percentage might be tolerable. However, if one accepts the scenario that client/server computing will sharply devalue virtually all mid-range machines during the mid-1990s, then brisk write-offs for the mini are justified also.

Mainframe depreciation is less contentious, especially at the upper end of IBM's ES/9000 range or its competitive equivalent. Though the sector is stagnating, there is little competition in it to drive prices down, and such super-economical concepts such as client/server are not yet a direct threat. A depreciation period of five or six years might still be justifiable for a larger mainframe. Non-IBM mainframes can expect much shorter lives, as most non-IBM designs are not going to be around that much longer.

A point about mainframe or large-mini depreciation is that such machines are much more vulnerable to downsizing late in their lives. The newly acquired monolith, partly for political reasons, can rarely be attacked directly. In these cases, downsizing can proceed in other areas, perhaps in the implementation of distributed new applications while the mainframe struggles on with its traditional types of work.

Smaller mainframes, especially old ones, often have a low value because they run obsolete or very limited software. IBM's smaller

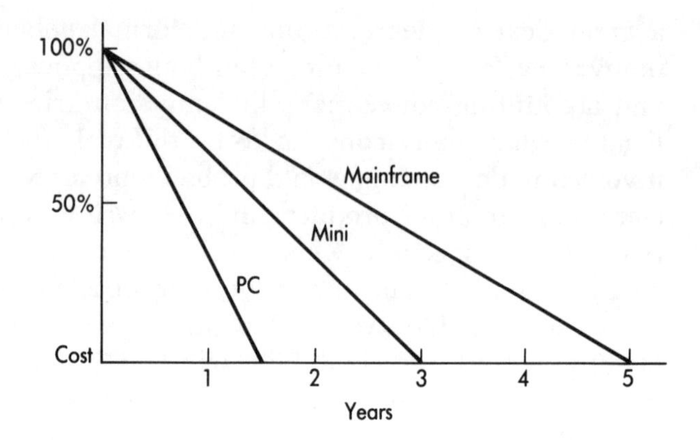

Figure 7.1 Depreciation policies.

In the eyes of a financial director, the high depreciation rates charged to small machines effectively narrows the cost differences between mainframe and downsized projects. Also, if a large mainframe is sitting in the books at a high assumed value, people are tempted to use it simply because it is there. There is some legitimacy in the depreciation policies, as historically large mainframes by IBM, Amdahl and Fujitsu have maintained good resale values in comparison with smaller equipment. However, such resale values may not apply in the future, as competitive technology is growing faster than that of the mainframe. In any case, it is important to talk about *all* comparative costs, not just hardware and its supposed depreciation. Though financial directors may be less receptive to these extra items (many accountants still secretly believe a computer is a piece of hardware and little else), they have to start learning sometime.

areas, perhaps in the implementation of distributed new applications while the mainframe struggles on with its traditional types of work.

Smaller mainframes, especially old ones, often have a low value because they run obsolete or very limited software. IBM's smaller mainframes are in this category, as to perform more work the user must change to a more complicated software set (the MVS-based system). This costs much more both in product acquisition terms and in human running costs, so the user is understandably reluctant to upgrade. If one meets one of these older, smaller mainframe boxes wearing an artificially high notional price tag, one might knock its value down with confidence and so open the way for a better downsized alternative.

Software depreciation

Attacks on assumed application software values are easier to carry out, partly because few accountants know the area and because IT advocates of the old systems generally leave gaping holes in their armour. Two main gaps in software valuation are virtually universal:

- The total cost of development is rarely charged even to an application, let alone to the users who will be running it. Items such as extra technical support and more general overheads (say, for management and operations) are often not included or are minimized.
- Costs of maintenance and hardware running costs are rarely tracked accurately for an application suite.

What the above boil down to is that the real costs of a mainframe application are generally much higher than realized, especially in the ongoing stages. While the upping of development costs might tempt some to place a higher 'value' on the system, one can use these to illustrate what a liability continuing development is, especially as development and the high ongoing maintenance costs have much in common (high hardware usage, poor programmer productivity). Many mainframe applications systems are ten years old or more, and such systems often have very high liabilities in terms of ongoing costs. If someone says a system cost $2 million to develop, this might have very little to do with realities today, especially if the replacement cost of a new alternative is low.

The case for writing off old mainframe software should be argued very forcefully. This consultant once made himself unpopular with a large user by pointing out that for the cost of application and hardware maintenance alone, something like thirty mid-range systems could be acquired and supported each year. These would have been able to do most of the organization's work, and any remaining mainframe requirement could have been so small that usage of a bureau might have been more appropriate than an in-house installation.

The twin-pronged strategy of showing a low present value plus a high running cost of an existing system, plus a low replacement cost where a new type alternative is considered, can be a very effective way of promoting downsizing.

Major machine choices

Once the mainframe position is established in approximate terms, both as to assumed value and justifiable need (the two not often being the same), one can begin to make broad estimates as to what sort of organizational topology and product architectures might be required. Given today's rate of change, it is important to make as large a jump as is safe, otherwise one may be saddled with an obsolete system within a very short number of years.

One of the most important points about offloading existing systems from the mainframe is the speed at which they can be moved. Normally, there will be a spectrum of such items, from the readily movable to the relatively immobile. If both information centre and production centre (the latter basically meaning transaction processing and high-volume batch work) are in existence, one would normally look to the information centre first to find the sorts of small, rapidly changing systems suited to downsizing. Information-handling (reporting and enquiry) programs for either remote or coherent head-office groups should be considered. Any office applications (meaning those dealing with any sort of text, mail or messaging) of moderate volumes should at first glance be considered likely as well.

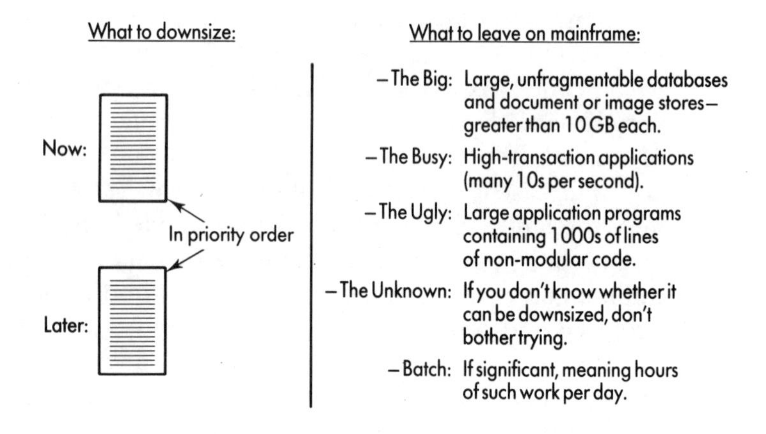

Figure 7.2 Initial downsizing choices.

Rough guidelines on how to arrive at downsizable systems suggest that anything that is not clearly in the mainframe camp ought to be examined. Even where a system initially appears on the mainframe side of the equation, it ought to be examined to see if it can be simplified or modularized to downsizing standards.

On the production centre, while obviously heavy-volume transaction processing is out (meaning transaction rates of many tens per second or more), such systems for smaller departments should be considered likely. Payroll and related personnel systems are an obvious target, and their high reporting content suits the downsized profile.

During this first pass through likely targets, we are trying to get a preliminary idea of all application areas that could theoretically be downsized. For the larger organization, this inventory of possibilities is generally much larger than can be encompassed in the initial year or two of downsizing. One will have to add to the list any new applications that are under discussion, and will also have to consider any need to rationalize or update existing small systems. Essentially, what we are after here is a list of tasks, associated with departments or locations, plus the approximate size of each task (number of concurrent users, data volumes and transaction rates). This will be refined into a more concrete plan later, but this first glance should begin to give us an idea of the types of technology required as well as other insights into specific needs.

The types of likely requirement seen at this stage are subject to substantial modification later, not only to cater for changed or clarified application need but also to accord with specific solution types available such as software packages. In the most general terms, the preliminary pass should suggest technological solutions as follows:

- Small commercial sites of up to a hundred or so users ('commercial' meaning record-handling and messaging applications). Client/server should be looked at for these.
- Sites with hundreds of users, or with mixed commercial and technical work typically for engineers or scientists. Here, a traditional minicomputer, probably running UNIX, would be likely.
- Mixed small and larger sites. In this case, scalability is important (scalability meaning the ability to run small and larger versions of the same system with the same software). If the site is commercial, then a product such as AS/400 is suitable. If requirements include scientific or technical work, then a suitable range of UNIX minicomputers should be considered.

One notes that in all the above scenarios, a homogeneous solution type is the ideal. Like all ideals, it is too readily compromised in real life. However, where downsizing is concerned, the mixing of unlike systems creates so many overheads and other problems that there is a great premium for sticking to compatible hardware and software. Only with the greatest reluctance should one be forced into running unlike systems.

These scenarios have to take into account the existence of earlier mid-range items installed, but at this stage one should not overly weigh in favour of any existing downsized products. Our idea here is to see which items can best handle the forthcoming work, not which actually will. In general, IT managers are overly inclined to use products they have already, and so may unintentionally lock themselves into obsolescent or high-cost options.

In looking at one's existing position regarding installed mid-range products, one can be much more dismissive of single, isolated systems than of a set of comprehensive, linked solutions. One should also downgrade products that come from troubled suppliers, as troubled suppliers inevitably mean troubled users.

Common user types

In dealing with general issues about organizations and technology, one should include some thoughts as to the types of actual user one has within the company. Even within a single industry, and in the same geographic area, there are strong differences in company cultures which inevitably link to characteristics of individual users. Knowing whether users are adventurous or conservative, whether they like quick action or due consideration, and whether they rely on formal procedures or mainly verbal communication, all will help determine the types of system best suited to them.

Perhaps the most commonly observed spilt among user types is that between the technical and the commercial user. In today's world, nearly every user who we think of as 'scientific' has had substantial experience at least with the numeric-intensive side of computing. Such users include scientists, engineers, academics and members of research institutes. In larger organizations, many such people also use simple office automation products which are installed on the same machine that does their equation solving.

A very common mistake in downsizing is to assume that the

technical user understands computing in general. To the layman, computing is technical, so is the user, therefore they are on the same ground. Let the engineer decide not only what machine he wants for himself, but let him determine computing needs for the rest of the organization. This observer has seen a number of cases, and in large theoretically respectable companies, where this has happened. It has been our experience that engineers and technical users are among those who make the worst and least cost-effective decisions about computing, especially in areas which they cannot be expected to understand.

To the downsizer handling an installation with a high content of technical computing, a fine line must be trodden. The people to whom one is speaking do enjoy a high degree of familiarity with the things they want to do on a computer. They are usually thoughtful about their work and have good ideas as to what facilities they most need. In a very scientific or academic setting, they may have enormous political clout, partly because the higher managers in such places are often former scientists or technicians. Such managers identify with both the work being done and the person doing it, and they too may be far removed from so-called commercial considerations and any real knowledge of computing overall. However, being at least partly knowledgeable, they are flexible in some areas. Notably, brand loyalty accounts for little, and they tend to dislike the more slippery type of salesperson.

At this early stage of planning, one should approach such users with a degree of reserve, attempting to find out what is good or bad about the present system and what major improvements they would like, either on their native technical ground or in text handling or messaging. One might test them, without overly implying any commitment, on their reactions to substantial cost savings, in return for converting to new types of system.

With commercial users, one can usually exercise more initiative, partly because they expect it even where they are knowledgeable about many areas of IT. However, there is a spectrum across the commercial user range, and one should anticipate what sorts of reactions to expect. The more approachable users might express more brand loyalty, partly because they may be less secure in computing territory and partly because they are more susceptible to salesmanship on the part of vendor representatives. One should take special care to avoid any suggestion of specific product commitment at these early stages.

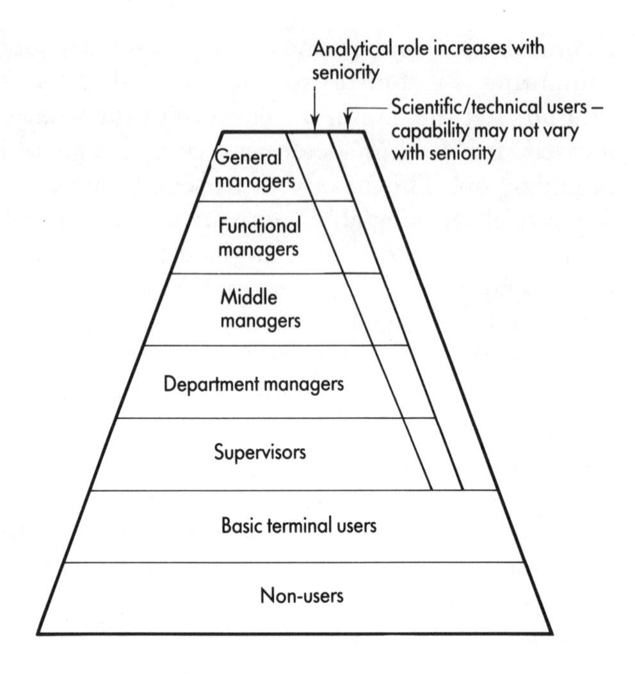

Figure 7.3 Common user types.

Quantifying users within an organization by type and approximate level of seniority is a useful exercise in analysing long-term needs and capabilities. Early in the downsizing investigations we need to begin thinking of the scale of the effort and the types of solution that might be suitable for the various user categories. Once numbers are put into each of the boxes above, they can then be further broken down into more specific topologies described later on.

Organizational quality

A fundamental point that causes problems for IT professionals is the overall quality of the organization that employs them. The company that is having problems in the marketplace (or with its intended function if in the public sector) will almost certainly have IT problems as well.

In such organizations, IT staff, whether traditional or new world in their orientations, may have a substantial portion of whatever intelligence exists within the company. There is a tendency for a strong IT function to push into related areas, and also to try to extend itself into general management. In downsizing, there is a very great temptation to couple machine reorganization with organizational re-ordering. Where one supposes that the mainframe has artificially centralized such inherently distributed functions as customer service, office automation or management information, such returning of power to the people appears justified.

Some initiatives by IT are certainly merited in many instances, but care must be exercised not to overstep one's theoretical boundaries by too wide a margin. Downsizing is a legitimate reason to distribute business as well as computing procedures, should the user department and the organization gain by doing so. Virtually every large organization faces the dilemma of the rigid, overly bureaucratic centre versus the responsive but potentially uncontrollable periphery. While IT contributions should be welcomed in such discussions, overdoing it may cause reaction and retraction. IT people should be sure of their ground where they make suggestions regarding general business administration, as many IT people are not the world's experts in the subject either.

An area of concern in the organization of dubious quality is that both central management and the user departments may be lacking. Distributing computer systems away from a confused central management in favour of an equally baffled user will not solve many problems save for lowering the cost of confusion.

Product politics

IT products have had heavy political connotations since they were invented. In the early days of IT one took great pride in being an IBM or DEC user, and looked askance at products from lesser organizations. As people became disenchanted with offerings from the main suppliers, so-called industry standards became the flavour of the month and acquired political weight of their own.

Today, computer product politics is closely tied to national political–economic issues as well as to earlier ways of thinking. Agencies of national governments are forever trying to tie computing policies to what are supposed to be national economic interests. As such agencies rarely understand either computing or economics, the policies often irritate but seldom produce the intended business results. What occurs is some short-term support of the ailing national computer producer, but at the expense of user budgets and flexibility, and with no long-term benefit to the actual supplier, as subsidizing inefficiency inevitably creates even more of the same. The users most heavily leaned upon are invariably those in the public sector, where competitiveness is difficult to measure and the bill is footed by the tax-payer who has no understanding of what the issues are.

The UNIX world is a main beneficiary of such government pressure. To public-sector users, a UNIX offering may be thrust upon them whether they like it or not. Preliminary downsizing strategy must recognize this and make the best of it. Within the European Community, leaders of large and troubled IT suppliers, many of which are national institutions, are wedded to UNIX because they see it as the only way they can compete with both IBM and the increasingly awkward PC market at the same time. By capturing the UNIX market, they intend to keep prices high, a necessity for such organizations as they have suffered from poor growth and appalling productivity due in part to the very political concepts that sustain them. Until newer systems are able to adapt to the standards set by public bodies (IEEE's POSIX and X/Open), or until the bodies recognize the newer systems (meaning PC-based client/server primarily), one can expect continuing price differentials between UNIX and PC-based systems due to political 'inspiration'.

Non-standard data types

One of the more difficult areas to judge in the early stages of a downsizing strategy is the likely usage of non-standard data – meaning unformatted text, images, graphics and voice (as usual with IT, the terms are back to front, as the non-standard types were in use for thousands of years before the computer came along). Even where such systems are planned for, the activity rates and such issues as peaking can be difficult to predict. One recalls several examples where very heavy unanticipated loads of large documents and images were sent around networks, filling both network and many of the smaller machines attached.

Likely users of such systems are normally apparent: marketing and sales departments, head-office functions that already shift much paper, legal departments, and those areas within customer service that deal with complaints, errors and generally non-standard procedures. Because of its flexibility and low-risk via low-cost character, client/server is likely for such applications, and the majority of packages for such media work are on PC or UNIX machines anyway. A main danger is the overload of either local or wide-area networks, so any likely voluminous usage should compel planners to think of contingencies and the costs of high-speed communications.

Other unusual system types include retail point-of-sale, banking terminals and manufacturing shop-floor items. In the past, such systems were not thought of as part of the downsizing scenario. However, today they should be, as such products can work through and with local servers or minicomputers and so provide local information as well as sending data up the line for more central processing and information production. The inclusion of specialist terminals will of course complicate and extend the time-scales of a downsizing effort, but if one wants integrated local systems with all of the benefits this implies, then the two themes should be combined.

Costs and strategy

With few exceptions, a main downsizing theme is to reduce costs, both directly and indirectly (the latter by providing better business services). This brings up the thorny issue of comparing costs against existing or alternative solution types. There are numerous views on the cost savings involved in downsizing, from IBM's much-publicized 'no savings at all' to a more generally accepted figure of around 25%, once cost transfers to user departments have been accounted for.

As with risk minimization, the downsizing strategy should have a vigourous minimum-cost theme as well. Part of this is because it is worth saving money in any event, but the theme should be there to reinforce other disciplines. Low costs imply simplicity of product solutions and application design, and they imply junior people who are able and enthusiastic enough to get on with basic jobs quickly. Most IT efforts will pay some lip-service to the minimum cost message where hardware is concerned. The issue should apply doubly to software products, especially noting the ongoing maintenance paid to many suppliers for bug fixing, new releases or upgrades and some support (this maintenance cost can be 12% of the purchase price per year). Running costs of all software (including applications developed by in-house staff) should be more carefully estimated than is usual, again partly to cut down the complexity of the initial application.

The average costs savings achieved in downsizing are some way from the potential today. Most historic downsizing has been based on expensive minicomputers which are difficult to use, not the much cheaper client/server architecture now prevalent. By simplifying applications (partly via use of packages) and by using homogeneous architectures, very high savings should be achievable. An ambitious target for today might be a 50% saving in IT costs, *including* cost transfers to users (in other words, the apparent cost to IT should be cut by two thirds). Many will not be able to achieve such reductions, mainly because of politically imposed restrictions regarding products or IT people which are unsuitable. However, it is a target one should

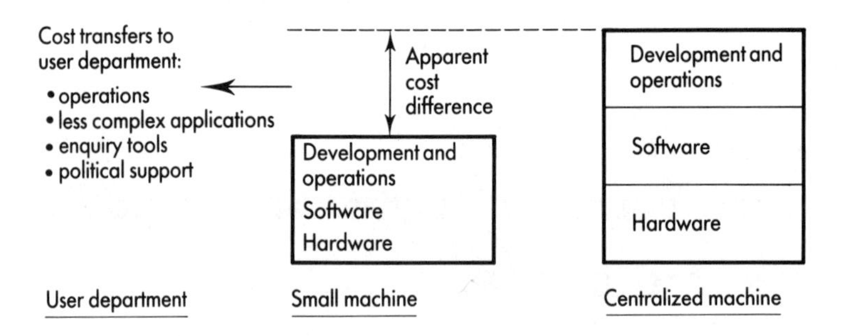

Figure 7.4 Artificial cost comparisons.

Broad strategies should consider cost implications carefully. Comparisons between downsized and centralized systems are rarely on a like-for-like basis, so any fine-tuning of the costing exercise can minimisze the grey areas. In most downsized systems, cost transfers to the user take place, either directly (because the user undertakes some operational duties, for example) or indirectly (because a simpler or packaged solution is implemented than would be the case on the mainframe). The 'political support' item means that IT has to budget for extra support in the centralized case to cater for panic reactions from users, the likes of which more rarely occur when they are in charge of their own systems.

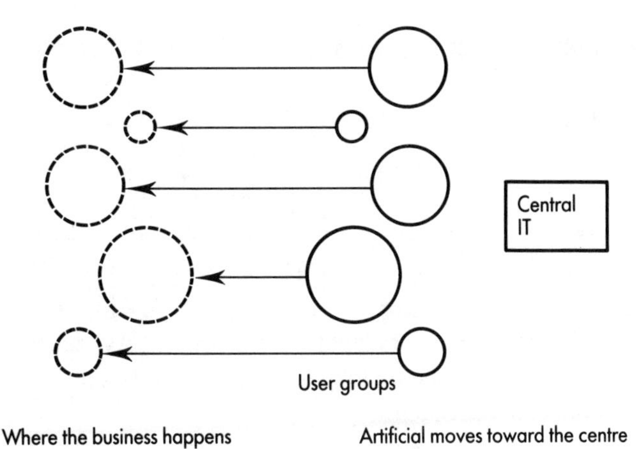

Figure 7.5 Changing the business.

Have user groups been drawn towards the logical centre of the organization, away from the sharp end of the business, partly to suit the needs of centralized IT? If so, downsizing affords an opportunity to put business people back out where they belong, perhaps in smaller groups as well as in different locations. This may be an organization-wide issue, or only a matter of a few departments. If the relocation effort is a large-scale one, then downsizing efforts must clearly wait until the administrative issues are resolved.

keep in mind at least as a benchmark, to see how closely one can approach it.

Cost transfers to users pose obvious difficulties when one is trying to compare like with like, especially as these transfers vary between one user department and another. Once users are established with and confident of their downsized systems, they can undertake several tasks that formerly would have been performed by IT people. These include some machine operation and very simple operation of software packages (for example, enquiry and reporting products). One could argue all day and all night regarding how much of this is a true cost transfer, as often with the new system the user can actually create and run a simple enquiry program much more quickly than he could even specify it in the old world. What we are saying here is that, if IT does less, it is not necessarily true that the user does more.

Key issues

- Policies governing depreciation of existing hardware and software may work unjustifiably against downsized solutions and should therefore be examined in the light of today's realities.
- Existing application software in particular should be evaluated as to its real value. In many cases, even fairly new mainframe or large-minicomputer applications might profitably be replaced.
- In both new and existing applications, attempts should be made to break apparently large and monolithic systems into smaller components appropriate for downsized solutions.

8

Mainframe coexistence

In the very large organization, the downsizing proponent will have to live with mainframes for some time to come. Mainframes still have their legitimate roles, and even where they do not, they cannot be dumped overnight. The very large and monolithic database in the information centre, very high-volume transactions, centralized document or image stores and very heavy communications all need both the architecture and the absolute performance of the large mainframe.

Aside from necessity, there is a large grey area where people perhaps subconsciously assume that the mainframe system is the right one simply because it is there already. The large information database that is better off segmented and distributed, the complex transaction that could (and should) be simplified, and the communications that could just as well be distributed instead of funnelled through one large gateway, all may escape attention unless they are deliberately put under scrutiny. Our preliminary pass at downsizing strategy dictates that we do this, but in a vast installation there are bound to be oversights, unknowns and difficult targets. Hopefully, one notices the major issues the first time around, leaving the relative minnows to be captured later.

Many IT departments assume that new systems will go onto the mainframe unless it can be well established that an alternative system is better. Today, the default policy should be reversed: one should assume a small system unless it is clear that the new application cannot fit, and that mainframe power is genuinely needed. Often a new system will be justified on the mainframe because an application package may be available for it alone. Here, one should look very carefully at the real costs concerned. Mainframe packages for most applications tend to be very complicated. They may require, say, 20 man-years to implement and then have a high cost of maintenance (perhaps several people dedicated to full-time patching and monitoring of the package). The running costs of packages, given that they may not perform efficiently, can be in the several millions of dollars over a life of seven to ten years. In other words, where it is possible, a tailored downsized solution should be compared to a packaged mainframe one - the former is often cheaper as well as better.

A major problem which the downsizing advocate will have, is getting any new system evaluation onto his territory early enough to influence the problem statement. IT investigators of traditional bent will invariably carry out extensive and detailed analyses, generally without sufficient separation of the essential from the vaguely desired, and will not surprisingly come up with a complicated requirement. The longer they take with the investigation, the more complicated the requirement is likely to be. They can do this even in obvious cases. One recalls a four-year payroll study that should have been completed in weeks - it took several people paid a thousand dollars per day to stretch the obvious into the absurd.

If one can get involved in such projects early enough, personal persuasion may be enough to simplify and shorten the investigation to the downsizing standard. At a broader level, one might be able to institute installation-wide standards that suggest short investigations

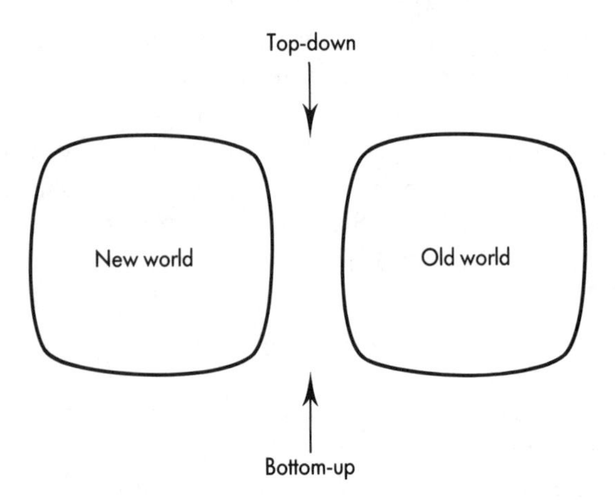

Figure 8.1 Forcing the split.

Initial organization-wide planning need not be as structured as many business school types would like to think. Within a given application area, a combination of top-down and bottom-up techniques can be used quickly to arrive at a decision as to what is likely for downsizing. It helps if a single individual can do this for the application area, as more speed and coherence are likely to result. It is in the interest of both downsized and mainframe systems that the split be defined quickly, then each half of the IT installation can get on with its own work.

to decide upon key elements of an application. If this can be done, more new systems will more or less automatically qualify for downsized solutions.

Offloading the mainframe

In many ways, new systems are much more straightforward propositions than prying existing items off the mainframe. Most IT departments are overworked and suffering under cost ceilings, such that they spend most of their time fighting short-term problems and tend to leave existing applications where they are. Up to a point, this is reasonable. The long-standing IT rule - if there isn't a problem, don't solve it - still applies. However, if one is too lax, then many systems will continue to run on the mainframe simply because they are there already, eating up expensive hardware and overworking the maintenance and operations units as well.

The easiest systems to take off the mainframe have as many of the following characteristics as possible:

- They are old, but they are also necessary, and thus require replacement or major amendments in most cases.
- They are fairly modular, meaning that they are self-contained and share few files or databases with surrounding systems.
- The underlying application is a fairly straightforward one, whether or not the programs have been written to reflect that simplicity.

Not only the information-handling programs suggested earlier, but also small transaction processing systems for minor departments, are likely. Personnel systems or program suites written for special types of business should be considered.

The more difficult systems to offload are those closely linked to other systems, where the latter clearly must stay on the mainframe. It may not be clear which system is which, especially if large numbers of complicated programs are involved. Claims-tracking systems in the commercial or shipping insurance markets might fit such a profile. Often such applications started life simply, then had individual

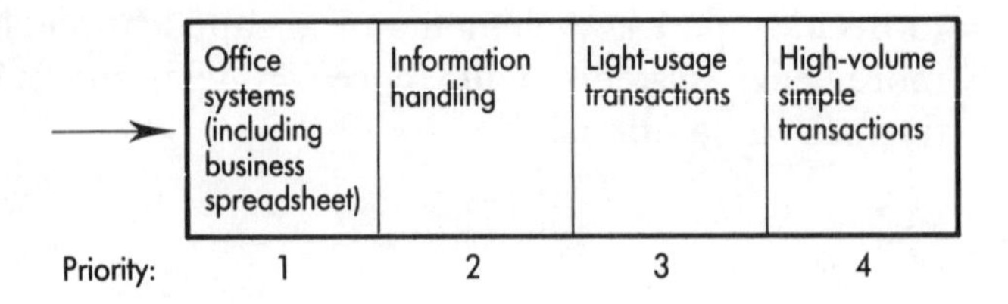

Figure 8.2 The order of attack.

Generally, mainframe systems can be offloaded according to the priorities in Figure 8.2, so long as they obey general guideliness for downsizing. The priorities of likelihood shown above must naturally be adjusted by business priorities. The common element between office systems and information handling is that both are probably using PCs a lot already, which paves the way for further downsizing.

programs grow in size or had many extra programs added on. Both the machine run times and the human resources expended in maintenance may be wholly out of proportion to the actual value of the system to the business, though much of the information may be necessary. Non-IT people invariably confuse value and necessity, as they may not have the knowledge to question costs or evaluate alternatives. 'We have to have it, therefore it is worth what we're paying' is the essence of this mentality, though few would state it as baldly as this. It is up to the downsizer to point out that feasible alternatives might exist for such systems.

Looking for underlying value, then, is a way to get at a downsizable system. If the amount of what is actually produced on the mainframe is on the light side, then one should be suspicious. Many complex systems in the information centre follow this pattern, as they tend to grow haphazardly because of urgent requests and lack of control.

The partial offload of a mainframe system should be handled with extreme care. There is a term for partial offloading, and it is passed around by mainframe vendors desperate to save half their cake rather than losing the lot. The term is 'cooperative processing', meaning let both small and large machines do what they are good at within the same application context, each box closely linked to the other and keeping the other informed as to what it is doing.

There is certainly a role for cooperative processing, and client/server systems among others rely on a degree of it. However, it should be understood that cooperative processing can be very complicated and expensive, in terms of both machines and people.

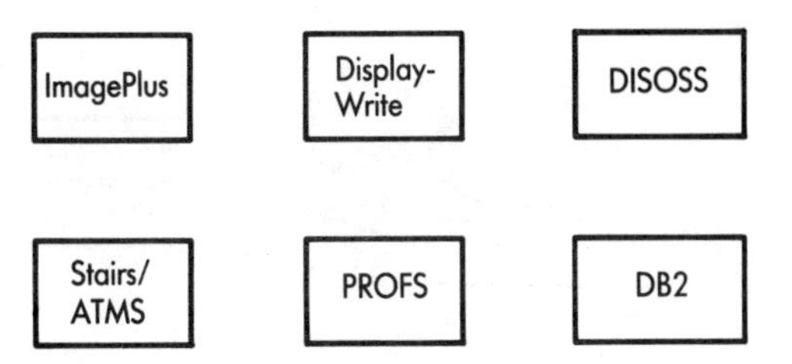

Figure 8.3 The office solution that isn't.

The mainframe's 'deep but fragmented' concept is best illustrated by the plethora of office or part-office systems that run on such machines. Each of the systems in Figure 8.3 is a complicated product, and each is highly incompatible with most of its neighbours. Where such items are installed on a mainframe, it is vital to consider downsizing office functions instead of expanding such functions on the large machine, otherwise very expensive conversions are likely later on.

Programming must be done using intricate tools (perhaps writing in a third-generation language under IBM's CICS transaction monitor), and productivity for both development and maintenance is therefore likely to be very low. Fault diagnosis and recovery can be burdensome. In many cases, the cost of a 'cooperative' system may be much higher than if it was simply put into one place or the other. In time, technology should improve many aspects of cooperative processing, but at the moment it should be considered a limited area.

The mainframe's deadline

The above discussion leads to an obvious point: how long will the mainframe be needed? It should be useful to think of an 'intercept' strategy that says, with downsizing technology developing and the mainframe stagnating, the mainframe will be superfluous by a certain date. One could therefore state the likely date, and aim to have all systems downsized by that date.

The advantage of setting such a deadline is to focus people's minds on the real and most significant issues, and to give clout politically to the downsizing effort. If corporations with annual sales

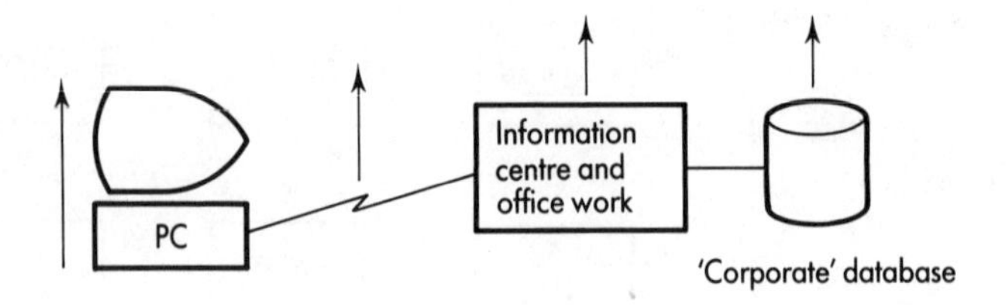

Figure 8.4 Expanding all the options.

A well-known mainframe supplier had the theory that attaching a small machine to a mainframe would actually drive up hardware usage at both ends. Though information centre and office automation tasks were the primary expression of this concept, 'cooperative' transaction processing is also making a strong entry. Such ideas should be questioned on two counts. First, if the PC and its local network are doing most of the work, is the mainframe needed at all? Second, even assuming a mainframe is needed, could a smaller, reduced function version be substituted?

in the low billions of dollars can run totally on client/server systems, with neither a mainframe nor mini in sight, then by the late 1990s organizations many times that size will be able to.

Continuing mainframe development and maintenance

Where the mainframe must be retained, for whatever reason, it is highly advisable to turn it into as passive a system as possible. It might act as a data server to more active outboard systems, or it might run existing applications which have low change requirements. The most important activity to remove from the mainframe's sphere of influence is the development of new systems. Good systems development people (as opposed to passive program coders) are in very short supply, and will be sorely needed in the downsizing environment. If the downsizing projects can pinch the best development people from within the installation, then mainframe development will virtually stop.

Aside from development, program maintenance should be cut to as thin a level as possible. Ideally, the level should be progressively

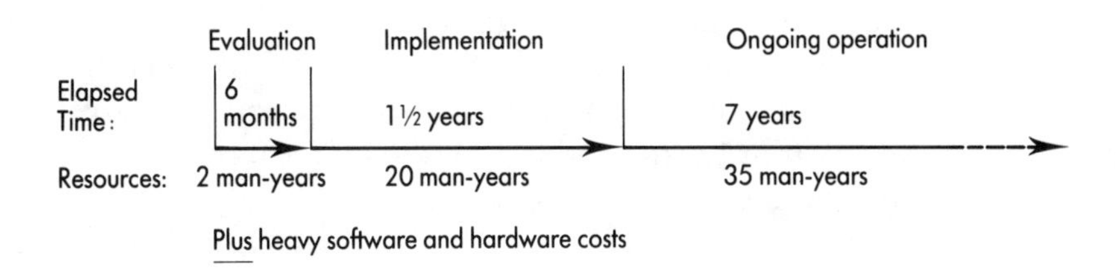

Figure 8.5 The package defence.

Because of the mainframe's increasingly proven awkwardness, many users are considering the use of very complicated software application packages, assuming that these will solve their problems. While the package may be simpler than coding the equivalent oneself, it is still an expensive proposition. The investment of approximately 57 man-years in Figure 8.5 plus the hardware and software costs represent an investment of many millions of dollars. The resulting application may not be all that satisfactory, as it will still suffer from the rigidity and incomprehensibility of typical mainframe offerings. One should carefully examine such propositions in order to see if downsizing either entirely or in part could save money and time on the one hand, and improve system quality on the other.

reduced in order to force the less viable or most troublesome systems off the mainframe, either to be redeveloped on newer platforms or to wither away entirely. Where maintenance is being performed on old systems, the cost should be made visible to users as well as to IT staff and general management. If at all feasible, such costs should come straight off users' budgets. As suggested earlier, this should be the true cost of running the programs, including hardware and operations costs even if these can only be identified approximately. In many cases, the sight of a rising cost for an aging system will be enough to encourage redevelopment or abandonment.

Facilities management and outsourcing

A growing market in current times is what one broadly terms 'outsourcing'. The term often includes facilities management, though strictly speaking the two are different: facilities management might be thought of as a subset of outsourcing. In strict terms, facilities management occurs when the entire in-house IT effort is handed over to an outside company (perhaps the native hardware vendor or a large consultancy specializing in that sort of work). The outside company leaves the computers on the client's premises (many customers like the apparent security of this arrangement), but undertakes to program and operate the machines.

Outsourcing by the narrower definition is where one's own physical computers are abandoned, and programs are run on the outsourcing supplier's machines at a location remote from one's own. This is effectively a bureau operation, though costs and contractual obligations are more defined than the simple bureau case where most charges are related to machine connect time. The reason for the growth of such services is simple enough, and strongly supports many of our arguments for downsizing. Many IT departments are not up to the complexities of running their mainframes. The theory is that a more professional and specialized concern can do the IT job better than can the in-house effort. In many cases, customers expect to save money despite expecting the outsourcing or facilities management company to make a profit. In theory, the specialist expertise applied creates more comparative efficiency, leaving room for the profit while still saving the customer money.

As outsourcing is increasingly seen as an alternative to downsizing, discussion of the very different results achieved is warranted. Despite salespeople's claims, there are rarely any cost savings of significance with outsourcing. Some other benefits are delivered as claimed, most importantly the removing of day-to-day IT worries from the shoulders of general management. In some cases, the outsourcing or facilities management company is indeed more responsive to user needs than was the old in-house IT department. However, this is often because in-house IT was unbelievably bad, rather than because the outsourcing company is especially brilliant.

To balance the above marginal benefits, there are risks associated with outsourcing as well. Contracts have to be drawn up very carefully between supplier and client, as the very close nature of the relationship dictates that there will be many areas of confusion. Where a high rate of interactive development is concerned, or where the customer's machines (say, PCs) need to interface closely with those controlled by the outsourcing organization, then problems are bound to occur. If such issues are not covered specifically by the contract (and they almost never are), then customer management will have just as many hassles with the outsourcing company as they had with their old unloved IT department.

A common occurrence with outsourcing is that contact between user and the IT function is little better than it used to be. The fact that outsourcing personnel are working for a different organization, and that many such staff will not be on the customer's premises, can mean slow response to needs for new systems or changes. Again, the rapidly developing or changing company is most likely to suffer.

Overall, the most likely mainframe systems to be oursourced are those which have been running for some years and are known to be stable. In such cases, outsourcing might be seen as complementary to downsizing. By allowing another company to operate the stagnating mainframe systems, the organization's own development and technical staff are freed to work on the newer systems in the downsized area.

Another valid use of oursourcing is to hand over a defined and complicated technical area so that one can turn one's attention to more business-related needs. In today's world, communications subsystems often fit this concept. Where one is trying to operate a number of different systems across different sites, perhaps in different countries, then this type of outsourcing might be considered for the downsized world as well as for the mainframe.

In general, though, outsourcing should never be thought of as an alternative to downsizing. The actual objectives of the two concepts are very different, and the distinctions should be made clear to management at the very beginning of strategy-setting processes. Outsourcing remains expensive, rigid and remote from the end user. Development times, response to urgent requests and the ability to alter systems quickly are all much as they were in the old world. The outsourcing and facilities management efforts which this writer has seen in practice fall far short of the glossy solutions proposed by salespeople. As with much consultancy effort, the user's work is soon passed over to those lesser beings who inevitably trail in the sales team's wake. People within outsourcing companies often change jobs frequently, either within the organization or by leaving it, adding to communications and continuity problems.

A danger that one should appreciate with outsourcing is that one can be locked into one supplier, perhaps in different ways but just as effectively as if one had an in-house proprietary system. The outsourcing company often runs proprietary systems itself (usually large IBM mainframes), so the programs written by the outsourcing company are restricted to that environment. The customer is usually locked in also by having an inadequate escape route. The ending of an outsourcing arrangement is frequently not covered properly in the contracts, and the fine points of who gets what and how the system may be moved to another supplier or back in-house are often left untouched. If the contractual details here are not clear, then the outsourcing

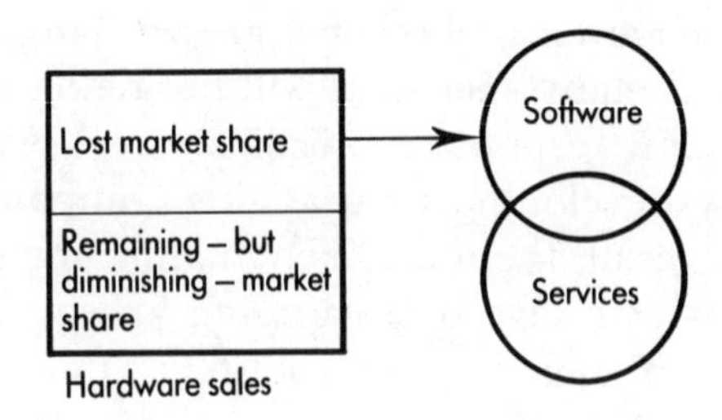

Figure 8.6 The services myth.

Traditional hardware suppliers have lost market share because of 'faulty management policies' (the politically correct term for blatant stupidity). Many such suppliers try to prolong the profile of their ailing organizations by pointing to services and software offerings. Prospective users should have none of this, reminding themselves that the hardware and software/services business are poles apart in terms of people, marketing, management style and actual products. One should also reflect that a loser in the business which he knows best is unlikely to be a winner in an area where he has infinitely less experience and expertise.

company is left free to quote an exorbitant charge to release the materials.

Facilities management and outsourcing are a far cry from true downsizing, and in most cases deserve to be packed away along with the rest of the old world.

Key issues

- IT policies should explicitly recognize that mainframe computing is a declining area, and should direct new developments toward smaller and distributed machines unless there is a clear case for doing otherwise.
- A strategy should be put in place to identify those systems that would most benefit from offloading from the mainframe onto downsized solutions.

- Consider using conversion tools or services to speed up those mainframe applications best suited to downsizing.
- Once offloaded, keeping the mainframe as stable and passive as possible is a good general strategy. Outsourcing mainframe management in such cases can help direct more energies to downsizing.

9

Planning organizational needs

Aside from appreciating the general need for downsizing, the actual process of planning merits much consideration. Downsizing represents a long-term commitment both in direction and in the large amounts of resources to be assigned to the concept. Good planning not only makes clear who is doing what and why, it also adds stability to what might otherwise be a highly erratic exercise, with people tempted to stray from the agreed path for short-term gains or for frivolous reasons.

Though of utmost importance, planning for downsizing should be as short and concise as possible. The twin purposes of this conciseness are to save time and to make the basics clear. Downsizing processes should be much like the systems that one would like to result: brief, responsive and well targeted on particular needs.

One thing a downsizing plan should not be is the industry-standard 'strategic study' promoted alike by hardware suppliers and the more expensive consultancy. Such studies cost tens to hundreds of thousands of dollars, take months to prepare, result in several heavy volumes of nicely printed paper, and sit unread as they migrate from someone's desk to a corner cupboard and eventually to an out-of-town warehouse.

This excessively general strategy, aside from being a waste of time and money, provides insufficient practical guidance for follow-on stages. This leaves too much room for more junior business functions (including IT) to interpret the strategy however they like, which leads to too much diversity in both business and systems terms.

A downsizing plan (or 'strategy', if one must) should first of all state the corporate goals that the plan is to meet. If a corporate goal is to provide better customer service through decentralisation and single point of contact with each customer, then that is enough to say about that particular goal. The next item that should be stated is how, in business terms, the goal will be met. This effectively is the high-level business plan. In our example, it might involve setting up ten regional service centres across the country, but have each region serving its named customers nation-wide. This 'how' part of the business statement naturally relates more to IT than does the more general goal, and IT potential may substantially influence this part of the business statement. If there is not much to choose between, say, regional and branch service for certain types of customer, then technology and economies of scale may dictate that a regional solution in a particular case is better than a branch-based one.

A downsizing plan involves progressing a number of threads in parallel, with each thread exerting some influence over the others. This parallelism is necessary in order for the plan to be formed quickly. To a certain extent, the technique is self-limiting, as are other downsizing concepts. Time is allowed only for the most important issues to be discussed, and for limited communication between the threads. It is not necessarily true that the separate threads, probably operating under our three major headings (application need, user characteristics and technology), should be progressed by different

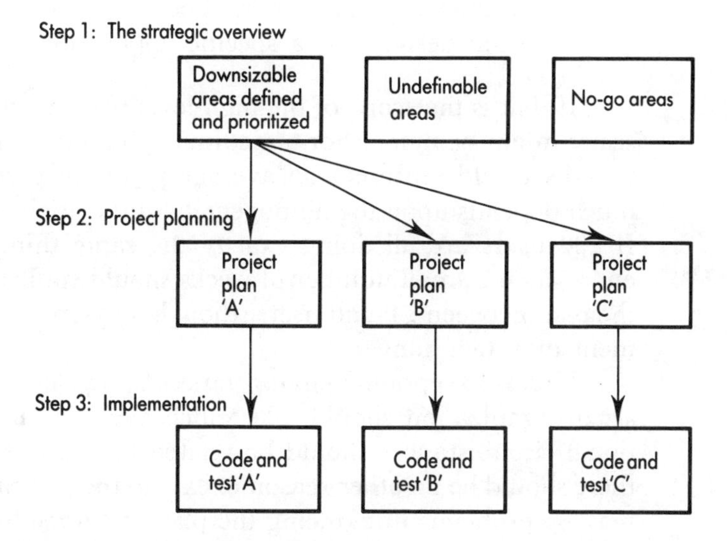

Figure 9.1 The three steps to downsizing.

Planning and project stages should be kept as simple as possible for downsizing, both to save time and money and to make it clear to all what is happening. In a large organization, the 'Undefinable areas' denoted within Step 1 in Figure 9.1 can be quite large. Unless some of these are thought to be of urgent priority, the large number of undetermined futures should not be allowed to impede the progression of the straightforward areas.

individuals. In a small downsizing scenario (perhaps for 30 to 50 users), one person should be able to do the lot, though perhaps with some reference to specialized technicians and to his own management.

There is a tendency with such planning techniques to allow one area to dominate, and so to freeze out equally important areas. The dominant area will inevitably be the pet subject of the person formulating the plan. It must therefore be impressed upon the individual or the team very early on that reasonable attention must be paid to each area (unless that area is either obvious or a solution has been pre-determined). Aside from the initial impression made on the planner(s), two other techniques might be used to reinforce the point:

- During the frequent (but brief), progress meetings that will take place to monitor the planning process, each significant topic will be discussed, and each will be equally prominent on the agenda. This encourages planners to do their homework prior to the meeting.
- The output from the plan should cover each significant topic in sufficient detail for the implementation project to begin. This means that, at the end of the planning process, analysts or analyst/programmers should be able to begin file and program designs for a specific application.

If that is the scope of the high-level plan, mention of likely timescales might be made. For a medium system (say, for 100 users), two months would represent an average planning period. Obviously, as much depends upon the homogeneity of the applications as their size. If 200 users are all doing exactly the same thing, say simple cash entry, then a small number of weeks should suffice to form and agree the plan between IT and users (though agreement by higher management may take longer).

Unless exceptional circumstances apply, no plan for a medium-sized organization should take much over two months. The exceptional circumstances should be related to application complexity, as there should be no other reason to extend the planning period. If there may be problems in agreeing the plan at 'immediate' level (between IT and end-user departments), then these should be sorted out before the plan begins to take shape. There is no point starting to plan something if too many issues remain in the air afterwards to enable a solution to proceed. Obvious though this inaction after planning sounds, it is nevertheless a very common IT error. It is a usual consequence of the vast and misconceived 'corporate strategic study' outlined above as well as of more modest efforts.

High-level benefits and costs

Statements of estimated benefits and costs should accompany any planning process. As with the other steps, they will be refined in stages. During the early organization-wide discussions on downsizing, information will arise as to how many people might be saved in particular areas, what the costs of implementation and ongoing running might be, and what other organizational benefits will ensue.

If such statements cannot be made, there may be little point in going ahead with the planning process. Such types of people as IT and accountancy personnel often shy away from approximations, preferring instead to believe that things do not exist unless they can be specified to the penny or to the IT technological equivalent. Broad benefits and cost estimation is the very essence of business, as otherwise significant efforts would never get started. Exactness will be approached progressively as one goes down through more specific levels.

To frame the planning process, one should present formally both at the beginning of the planning exercise and then again at the end. Intermediate discussions (for example, on draft topologies) should also be held. Presentations should be verbal, as opposed to the circulating of written reports, and senior managers should attend if they can be convinced to do so.

In general in IT planning, there is insufficient formal verbal presentation between IT and users, and this is another reason for the failure of many plans. A formal presentation, using reasonably professional overhead foils (perhaps PC produced) in a brightly lit room, will establish the right blend of authority on the speaker's part, yet will not be too formal to prevent participation from the audience. Documentary handouts, including copies of any foils shown, should be given out before the presentation starts. Aside from the overhead foil copies, documents should be rich in diagrams and thin on text and overly detailed numeric tables. IT departments should consider carefully the means of communicating to users. Too many tend to copy the marketing techniques of computer suppliers, which are generally appalling. The mumbling technician in a dark room with visual aids which alternate between pure waffle and total inscrutability is to be avoided at all costs.

Presentations on a less formal plane should be conducted within IT. These can be brief, and should follow more of a meeting format,

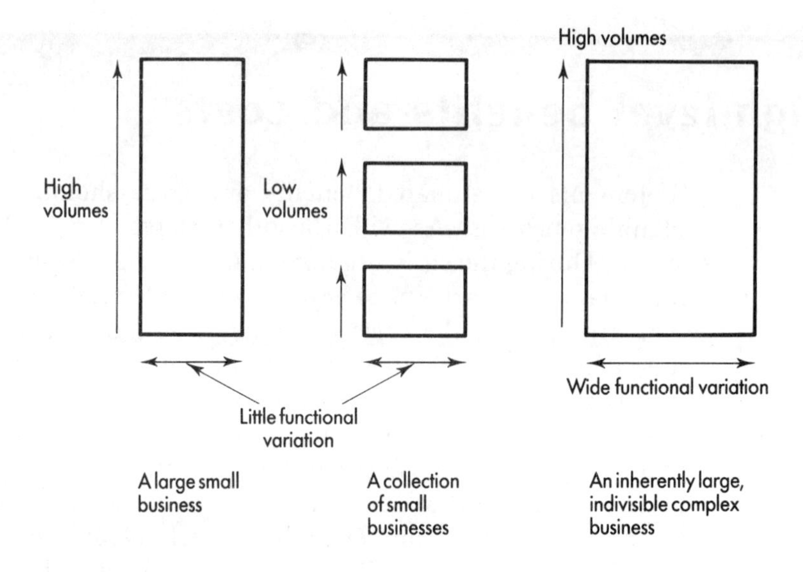

Figure 9.2 Which large organization?

A large company should be examined carefully in order to see if functional modularization is likely. If either volumes or functional diversity can be reduced within defined modules, then that subset of the business probably has downsizing potential.

though the lead speaker should still be on his feet. Some presentation materials or drawings should be used, possibly including some from user presentations. Gamesmanship applies as much within IT as with users. Downsizing staff should be urged consciously to aim for the right blend of authority and approachability, otherwise too much detailed and irrelevant discussion may take place, or else feelings will be too stiff for meaningful feedback to occur. Attitudes suggesting initiative and control should always be displayed when communicating with any IT person outside the specific downsizing project, almost as if such a person were a user. There is no more fatal mistake than to assume that one's IT colleagues are allies. Even if they mean to be, many will still be more loyal to their own pet ideas than to the actual business purpose of the project. By overly inviting them to contribute, they are likely to introduce needless complexities.

To control discussions within IT, reasonably strict rules should be applied. Technicians should only be invited to contribute within their areas of expertise, and then according to a definite sequence of questions:

- Will the item work in the present project context?
- Are there *significantly* better alternatives, given that risk, cost and delay are material factors?
- What is the best way of using the item in this project?

The above can be applied to most technical areas such as communications, database, system platforms (hardware plus operating system). In many cases the finer technical points will have no bearing on the results of the project. While one hopes to minimize such extraneous discussions within IT, one should make doubly certain that they never reach users' ears, as confusion and loss of credibility are likely to result.

9

Recognizing existing positions

Whereas early discussions may speak of ideal machine types or communications networks, where an existing commitment exists to products one must rapidly become more concrete. In many organizations, the use of existing components is a requirement, whether or not they are theoretically the best ones for the downsized project. Some items may be immovable because of politics (for example, the IT director has just bought a hundred small, slow PCs during a very good lunch). Other elements of rigidity may be due to physical factors (for example, Ethernet wiring already exists within the building and to replace it would be both time consuming and expensive).

In downsized systems, being forced to use inadequate components can bend other elements of a system out of shape. The inadequate PC or the sluggish local communications system may tempt one to use less than ideal products elsewhere. One might, for example, choose a minicomputer over a client/server architecture just to get better response, even though the costs, compatibility and long-term viability of the mini create obvious problems.

When faced with such situations, it is generally better to adapt to existing components rather than to be forced off the path into unwanted solutions. A key question is whether the right *type* of technology is present, but at the wrong performance level or with obsolete features. If this is so, then adaptation may be possible, and pressure might force upgrades to larger machines or more recent models. If, however, one allows the wrong *type* of solution through the door, then this will create ongoing deficiencies, including the likelihood of a costly conversion exercise later on to get rid of the dubious item.

Beyond a certain point, it is better to abandon a downsizing project than to be forced into too gruesome a product just because it is there. Though this may look like a short-term setback (which it undoubtedly is), in the long term he who chose the inappropriate item should get the blame. Had one used such a product, the downsizing effort would look weak for taking the course of least resistance.

If one has to make moderate adaptations to partly suitable components, it is important that the dangers are recognized. Ways of lowering the risks include using the dubious item for only a defined period (say, until a faster network or PC becomes available). Adaptations to compensate for inadequacies should be kept as crude and simple as possible. One could buy larger components in one part of a system to offset shortcomings in a related one. Perhaps a larger server could compensate in part for slower line times, or simply adding memory to the small PCs could buy some breathing space. Splitting an Ethernet network in half, and then using bridges to span the two halves, may not be the ideal way to gain performance but it will still work.

Where bending away from the best solution is inevitable, one should above all else make it clear that it was forced upon the project against its better judgement. This will put the blame where it belongs, and will help to focus on the genuine longer-term need, hopefully speeding up its implementation.

Short-term technological expectations

At the beginning of the high-level plan, one looks at the organization as it is and envisages the best currently available solution for its various components. One then modifies the strategy in the light of existing positions. This, so far, is a fairly standard way of proceeding. However, where the rate of change in products is rapid, it may be wise to anticipate some developments in order to gain meaningful benefits in system quality.

In any situation which requires very low risk, one should never buy the announced but yet to be delivered product. Nor should one rely on specific features in a new or recent software release, or deal with unviable vendors or distributors. However, there are certain cases where it may be advisable to wait for a development, while still recognizing that it may not appear as one has anticipated. In such cases, credible contingency plans must exist before one decides to wait for the forthcoming product. It is justifiable to wait for an item when both of the following apply:

- The technology in question represents 'more of the same' rather than something fundamentally new. This is most usual with hardware upgrades, where the basic technology (say, a central processor or input/output bus design) is already established, the new item simply being a faster version. This rule *never* applies to software. The obvious problem is that there may be a relationship between the two. If the hardware item relies significantly on software features to realize the increase in underlying performance, the gain may not be realizable until software can adapt. However, this is a confined risk, so long as we know that the software will work at least at current speeds.
- The feature is sorely needed, such as to make a significant contribution to the business benefits of the project. In other words, do not wait for technology just because it would be nice to have some extra speed. However, a side effect of the newer technology might be to drive down significantly the price of existing items, and if this is a large amount of money (say, tens of thousands of dollars), then such a benefit might be worth waiting for.

Our ideal long-term downsizing policy might then incorporate developments that are expected to have taken place when the implementation phase of a particular project arrives.

Organizational stability and disruptive change

In our discussion of organizational characteristics, we looked at broad issues of stability and how they impact downsizing. Organizational volatility and unstable end users effectively provide a base of quicksand for an IT project of any description. If this instability can be anticipated, then one may not deal with the area in question. In the worst cases, one might let the whole company remain with the mainframe.

If disruption occurs once an effort has begun, for political and genuine business reasons it is best to try to proceed on some basis if this is at all possible. There are a number of ways in which this might be done. If disruption occurs because of an unexpected change in structure, the major question to ask is: how long will the new structure last? A typical case might be where a highly divisionalized company suddenly rationalizes in order to gain economies of scale not possible with a fragmented effort. Such major shifts so commit senior management that they are not likely to be reversed for a number of years. Otherwise, continuing disruption would virtually paralyse the company, and the managers who reversed the earlier decision would be committing near-suicide.

The above is a fundamental and long-term example. In other cases, where departments shift ground continually within an artificial environment (with no externally imposed business disciplines), then there is no particular reason to suppose this will stop. We mentioned the organization's head-office as being the most likely area for this to happen.

One tactic that may be valid in the last of the above situations is to downsize more or less completely. In other words, try to put as much computing power on the individual's desktop as is possible, so minimizing the role (and the all too visible expense) of the other components. Client/server is appropriate for this, as servers can be moved around or have their roles changed. In the worst case, a server can be abandoned without too much exposure if it eventually turns out not to be needed due to a reorganization. The use of packaged software will cut down development budgets correspondingly, and many generic packages can be used in the new structure. However, only certain environments can follow these 'completely downsized' principles. Applications which demand complex, tailored software on

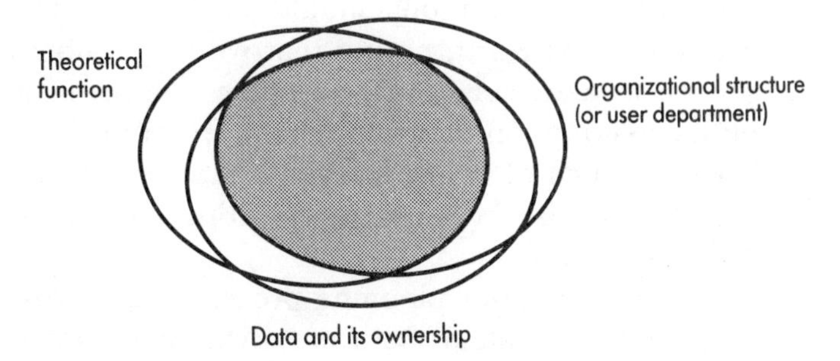

Figure 9.3 Defining topologies.

Properly arriving at topologies or application groups is one of the keys to downsizing success. The point made here is that only where business function, company structure and data usage meet (the shaded area) is it safe to proceed with downsizing. What we are after is a coherent picture of who is doing what, and with what data. If too many departments share *different* parts of a business function (as opposed to many departments, say retail branches, doing the same thing), then downsizing might not be right at that low level. However, sharing a system at a higher level still short of centralization might be feasible, and if this is thought likely then topologies should be drawn at this higher level.

minicomputers would be highly exposed in such rapidly changing structures.

Where only moderate instability exists, it might be worth trying to reduce it simply by having constructive discussions with parties concerned. Some businesses are so inherently intricate that it may not be clear from externally driven market needs how the organization should be structured, hence the continual experimentation and change. In such cases, downsizing can act as a catalyst, as it necessarily focuses the mind on organizational issues. Such activities as drawing application topologies and data layouts can help users as well as IT people think about such matters. A good systems topology might actually encourage stability, as people will then happy with the successes being achieved.

Setting priorities

Once the broad strategic view of downsizing has been completed, the setting of priorities for the next two stages (project planning and project implementation) should begin. In terms of traditional IT activities, it is worth noting that we are combining what used to be several separate stages into a smaller number of steps. We can do this on the assumption that we know much of the business already (partly because much of it has been mechanized by the present IT department), and also because the resulting application groups should be clear and simple.

Step one of our planning process, the downsizing strategic overview, has elements of both organizational strategy and feasibility in it (the two of course interact - there is no point in having a strategy if an effort is initially thought to be unfeasible).

Step two, the project planning stage, also incorporates some elements of feasibility, as the initial view from the top is necessarily approximate. Though Step two should not be begun unless there is thought to be a high chance of success, it should be made clear to all concerned that either IT or the user has the right to veto the effort before Step three (actual implementation - meaning the coding and testing of programs) begins. This cancellation potential should not be thought of as rebounding on anyone concerned. It is an acceptable and recognized risk in return for the great savings in both elapsed time and actual manpower as compared with traditional efforts. One should think of the risk of cancellation as a device to lower real risks - those involved in installing a poor solution.

The Step two (project planning) stage, which will be covered in more detail later, includes detailed feasibility and general system design, as in smaller projects it has been repeatedly shown that this approach works.

Because we know something about the costs, benefits and methods to be employed, at the end of the high-level view it is reasonable to set priorities. The decision to proceed with the remainder of the project should depend upon reasonably structured estimates such as:

- Overall monetary benefits, initially and once the system is fully efficient, for the business as a whole.
- Qualitative business benefits, such as service and morale.
- Savings and costs in the user department's personnel budget.
- Savings and costs within the IT department.
- Systems costs.
- Net monetary benefits to the user department, if these are different from the overall benefits for the business as a whole.

Most of the above can be presented by a spreadsheet package. It is important to state all benefits together – on the same screen or page if possible – as one will then have a coherent picture of both financial and qualitative gains. As with other downsizing documentation, clear, straightforward diagrammatic presentation is more effective than mass text or instantly unmemorable speech.

The remaining variables related to the setting of priorities are mainly based on IT issues, technology and people being the most important. If these quantities are known for but a few of the possible downsized projects, then the system with the highest overall organizational benefit should be chosen. If organizational benefits overall are the main criterion, this does not mean that departmental benefits should not be substantial as well. Otherwise the actual users of the system will not be motivated properly to complete the implementation.

In considering priorities, the question of running a number of projects in parallel should be examined. While new downsizing efforts inherently incorporate more risks than will later ones, one should not be overly timid. If a number of projects have clear benefits, and if they are reasonably straightforward, then there is nothing against implementing them in parallel. To do otherwise would stretch out time-scales of the downsizing effort excessively.

One term that frequently crops up when projects are being organized is the 'pilot project'. It is a concept of which any competent manager should be wary. 'Pilot project', in its broadest sense, means

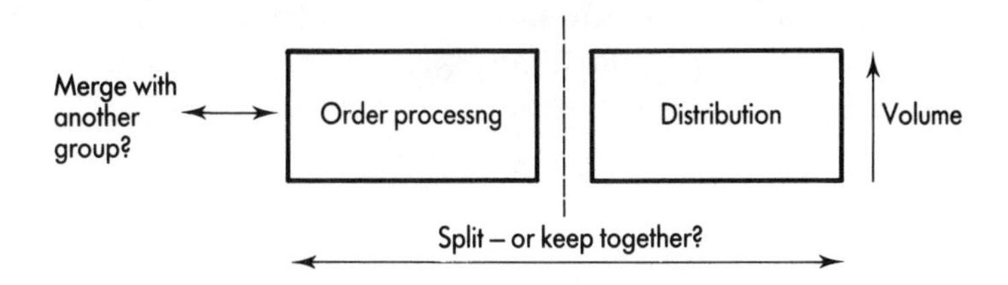

Figure 9.4 Splitting and merging application groups.

Preliminary application groups or topologies may need to be drawn in several ways before a clear picture emerges as to which is the best way to continue. Such issues as breadth of function, volumes and which departments actually do the different pieces of work are all relevant. In the example in Figure 9.4, choices might exist between merging order processing with shipping on the one hand and with order entry and customer service on the other.

any venture into a new area. However, it can also mean a largely artificial exercise, implementing a system in a small and insignificant area of the business. The rationale is to experiment with new products and techniques, and so determine whether they can be applied later on to 'real' systems.

The idea appeals to non-technical types in certain kinds of business. To the car stylist, it might seem analagous to building a mock-up of a new body design so that one can see what it actually looks like. To the marketeer of fast-moving consumer goods, it appears somewhat like a test marketing campaign, getting useful feedback without committing oneself to the full costs and risks of a proper product launch.

However, as a downsizing exercise, pilot projects (in the experimental sense) are generally worse than a waste of time. They can sidetrack or delay meaningful efforts. Because such projects are usually overmanned and overly observed, they can cost much more than the same system would in the real world. It is therefore difficult to obtain cost-effectiveness measures that could be applied to other projects. If the result is bad, the pilot project may scupper legitimate downsizing implementations. Yet, if the result is good, the go-ahead might not be given for further downsizing for some time. Because technology is changing, any experimentation here might be superseded by new announcements.

If experimentation with technology needs to take place (often it does not, but it is fun for the technicians whose vast salaries you are paying), then one could do this in more economical ways than wrapping a whole make-believe project around it. However, we have stressed that, if technology really needs experimenting with, then it is probably too immature and too risky to participate in our low-risk downsizing scenario anyway. Downsizing is about getting on with it, using known values.

Key issues

- Planning procedures for downsized installations should reflect the economy and simplicity of the anticipated solution.

- Because it sets expectations for further activity, the planning process itself should be thought out carefully where it involves end users.
- With basic downsized systems, a number of planning activities can be carried out in parallel, further shortening time-scales.
- Frequent but brief meetings with both users and IT colleagues help to ensure that the planning process remains on track.
- Use of existing machinery and communications lines should be considered, but only where these will not compromise the quality of the downsized application excessively.

10

Arranging organizational topologies

For an organization of more than a couple of thousand employees or $100 million turnover (these being very rough numbers indeed), the laying out of an organizational topology is part and parcel of good downsizing practice. Some organizations smaller than this, perhaps in the few hundreds of employees, will also benefit, assuming that they are diverse geographically or in terms of business functionality. For the smaller, more homogeneous company, the laying out of a topology should be so straightforward that it should not take much time or effort.

By 'topology', we mean an organized way of laying out what goes where within the organization. While this should bear some relationship to the more generally presented structural diagram of the company, it is not the same thing. The topology we are talking about here is for direct input into a high-level IT plan, and therefore is drawn out in terms useful to an IT person. The topology, much of which is in diagrammatic form, should make clear:

- What major groups exist within the company.
- What business functions they perform.
- What information they deal with.
- What links exist between the groups, in terms of passing responsibilities back and forth, and in terms of accessing information.

Approximate quantitative information should be included in all four items above, such as numbers of people in each area, broken down into three or four levels, rates of activity (noting any significant peaks either seasonally or at ends of accounting periods) and volumes of information that need to be available. In the ideal case, the topology

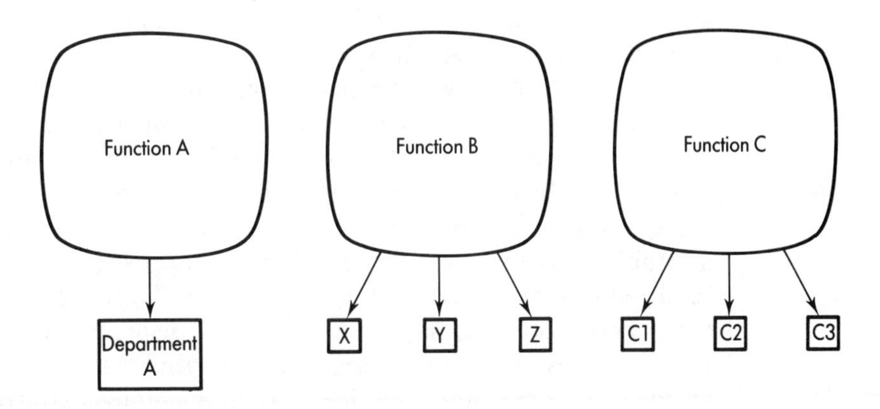

Figure 10.1 Examples of topologies.

Applications map quite differently across departments, and this needs to be sorted out early in downsizing planning. In Figure 10.1, Department A is a management information unit and is the only user of the system denoted as Function A. Function B, a desktop publishing system, is used by several completely different departments (personnel, marketing and investor relations). Function C is an order processing suite that is used by three more or less identical departments performing order entry at regional sites. For the three different cases, aside from the applications themselves, such issues as machines, communications, operating procedures and support are all going to be quite different.

will suggest reasonably self-sufficient application groups, with clearly defined and quantified communications links between them. In some companies, or in certain types of industry where functions may be piecemeal and decentralized (for example, manufacturing, merchant banking, insurance broking), matters may not be so orderly. What one has to do in these cases is to infer or assume a likely logical topology and then derive physical topologies, perhaps several alternative ones, from these.

Deriving topologies in imprecise situations

If matters are too unclear and disorderly to draw logical pictures of the organization, or to state approximate quantities of people, transactions and data volumes, this of course is a factor mitigating against downsizing in the first place. However, as it is just these organizations that may benefit from downsizing, one should be persistent in trying to find suitable downsized solutions and not give up too easily.

Though for political reasons one has to tread gingerly in such cases, one obvious solution is to advise a degree of administrative reorganization before mechanizing the disorderly situation. If this is desirable anyway, then downsizing can be used as a catalyst for a required organizational change and so may be welcomed by many in the organization. If, say, order entry is dispersed across too many product lines, perhaps in separate geographical areas, then better productivity, customer service and management control might be gained by doing it in fewer places or departments.

If such reorganization for whatever reason is not thought suitable, then one might consider a more complicated topology than the one originally envisaged. In the example cited, an order entry machine might be placed in one department, but with a responsibility for servicing others. The computer service so provided might at least be better than the existing mainframe one.

The highly divisionalized organization

In some very large organizations, fragmentation and duplication of functions may be a deliberate management policy, rather than just being the result of haphazard growth. The highly divisionalized organization may have become that way because the very separate divisions can either produce or market more effectively. Such divisions may be geographical or product based or, in the worst cases, both. This poses a problem in deriving a functional topology, as the separate empires may resent having all their accounting or inventory control systems thrown in together.

The best IT solution in these cases clearly is to use common systems across the separate divisions. These separate divisions often have authority to make some of their own IT decisions in practice, whatever the 'corporate guidelines' may state. As in the case with smaller and more casually disorganized companies, one might have to draw the topology more tactfully (see Figure 10.2). As a general rule, the 'common elements' shown across the divisions should be as

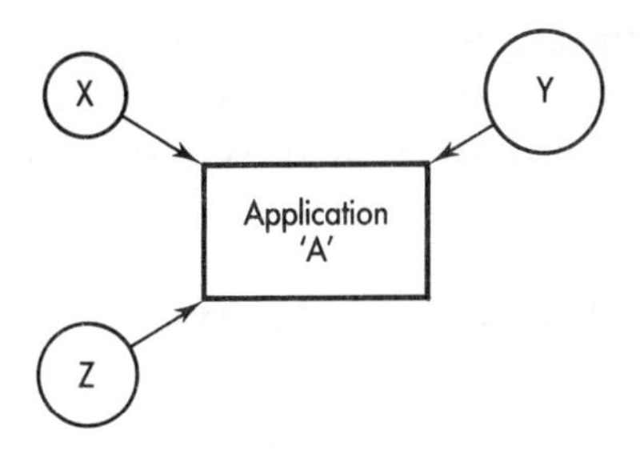

Figure 10.2 Politics and topologies.

Where several (possibly competing) departments use common application facilities, it may be tactful to suggest no ownership of the application and its data, at least initially. The above is one method of doing so. There is no inference from the above that any of the user groups (X, Y and Z) are more in control of the application than any of the others – they are merely represented as equal users, even if of different size.

large a percentage of the functionality as one can justify, as this will be the base for arguing for common systems across the division. To identify only a small percentage of common function would give too much leeway for continuing fragmentation, such that both the economies and control inherent in good downsizing would be lost.

The application blueprint

Once the right political overtones have shaded the topological picture of the organization, one has a *preliminary* downsizing blueprint to place before the organization's senior managers. It should be made clear to them that it is not a final document but that in many ways it represents a map for further exploration. It is effectively the initial suggestion as to how downsizing might be done, and is to stimulate discussions and further refinement before formal approval is sought.

Once the high-level logical diagram of the organization has been laid out, those in IT should confer among themselves as to how best to agree the next stage of the plan. There are several areas that need careful evaluation before any firm implementation plan, however high-level, can be put before a management committee. Because the planning process we are suggesting here is a compression of more usual ones, and because several elements are running in parallel, there are certain exposures that must be covered. These relate to the feasibility of each of our three traditional areas of downsizing concern:

- The end-user department
- Technology
- The application itself

As a very negative assessment of any one of the above for any defined topological area can veto downsizing, one must have a reasonable degree of confidence in advance that the majority of functional areas will pass. In other words, even before presenting the initial topological layout to anyone outside IT, one should have a reasonable idea as to downsizing's feasibility in more than one area. One does not want to present a diagram covering five application groups that are apparently suitable for downsizing, only to have to veto four of them later because either the end user or the technology is not up to scratch. Where technology is concerned, it bears mentioning that all areas must be up to the job (hardware, software and communications). Too often, superficial assumptions are made about the less obvious aspects of products (particularly software ones), and such a skating over the issues can cause problems later or even stall a project.

The uses of imaginary machines

In the scenarios outlined above, we have assumed that the business functions are well known, and that the end users and their departments are equally familiar. In a mature IT department, obtaining a broad knowledge of such subjects should not be difficult even from sources within the IT department. There should be some people who are aware of all but the most obscure backwaters of the company.

Surprising as it may seem, at the relatively high level about which we are talking, a very common weakness in IT departments is inadequate broad technical knowledge. Traditional mainframe or even minicomputer technicians may be well behind in their appreciation of downsizing technology. They may also make assumptions that the new solutions are much like the ones with which they have been working over the past *n* years. They may not realize the limitations of small machines and their software, and in particular they often do not question the possible loadings of local communications facilities. The applications they may be considering for the downsized system may be very different from those on the mainframe (for example, document processing and messaging), and these applications may imply very different technical problems.

This is why, within the IT department, it is well to envisage an imaginary machine which one can test against the approximate volumes occurring in the topology. It is partly an exercise to focus technicians' minds on what technical requirements matter most. This estimate of mechanical capacity should go to the level of physical input/output operations per second (input/output capability being a better measurement of small-machine loading than central processor instructions per second). Communications links in terms of characters per second should also be estimated.

In the most general terms, if the loadings required by the logical business functions look like requiring more than 15 or 20 physical disk accesses per second, or if more than a few hundred thousand characters need to be transferred between one local machine of any sort and another within the space of a few seconds, then one should investigate further.

This imaginary machine exercise serves two purposes in our downsizing planning. First, it tests the technical feasibility of the solution in terms of hardware, software and communications, and it also provides high-level parameters which will be useful in configuring specific systems at a later stage.

The most common problem with the imaginary machine scenario is that it is difficult to use it for application packages. At this early stage, one might have a reasonably clear idea of hardware, systems software and communications items to be used, and therefore be able to make reasonable guesses as to their capacities. However, if an application package is to be selected later, then the product may have unexpected performance traps. Regrettably, one cannot assume that packages are well-designed from the performance standpoint, their main aim generally being to provide functionality for the user.

Therefore, if an application package is to be chosen later on in the project, it helps to have a short-list of such items in mind partly so that if one does not measure up in performance terms then alternatives can be considered. If there are only a few packages in a given

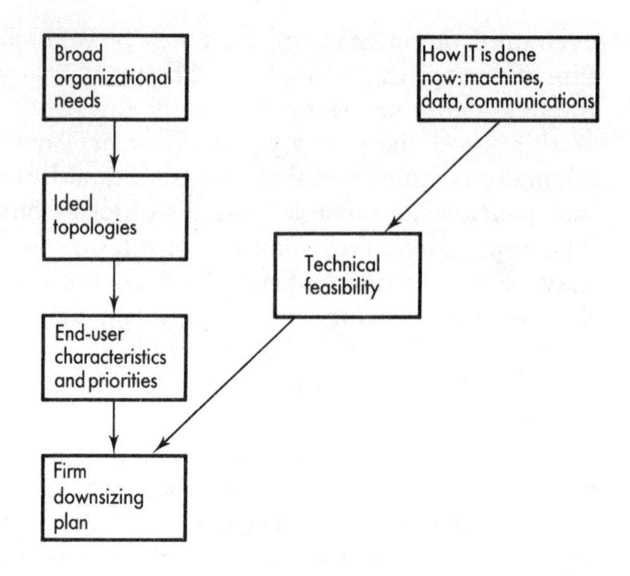

Figure 10.3 Steps within high-level planning.

For a larger organization, Figure 10.3 might represent the main steps in planning for downsizing. The result (the firm plan) dictates which projects will be implemented in which order. Where the IT department knows the users, applications and technology likely to be used, the above steps can be executed quickly.

area, then it is prudent to have a quick look at a few offerings strictly from a performance viewpoint, before the packages are placed in front of users for a more functional evaluation.

Refining topologies: the nearly standalone system

One feature that made the earlier versions of small machines so easy to install was their isolated nature. Not only were communications links (nearly always a major source of trouble) absent, there were also few links of any other sort to applications on other machines. In many cases it sufficed to send a tape or diskette periodically to another location so that summary management information could be processed.

One of the major goals of our topological exercises is to create as nearly a standalone system as possible. This at first glance may seem contradictory, given the frequently extolled benefits of the distributed environment, but in fact the longstanding dictum that 'the best distributed machine is a standalone machine' still holds true.

Topologies can cover many different dimensions of an organization. Early in the downsizing process it is worth drawing all of those that look obvious:

- Theoretical functions, irrespective of who performs them.
- Actual departmental functions.
- Geographical topologies, if these are relevant. Communications topologies might be part of this exercise.
- Data topologies.

The obvious hazard in rationalizing a number of topologies based upon different considerations is that a mix of the lot will result. Such a mix is highly unlikely to represent the best mechanizable system. The normal IT reaction 'when in doubt, compromise, especially if you don't understand the issues' definitely works against project coherence here.

The purpose of drawing several types of topology is primarily to see which one works best. The differing diagrams should be thought of as looking at business needs from different perspectives. A *mix* of different perspectives, however edifying to the twentieth-century artist, is a nonsense in terms of systems design.

During high-level planning, it should be made clear that the physical location of machines other than workstations is being left open at this stage. A departmental machine may or may not be located actually on the physical premises occupied by the end users. Such considerations as space, physical conditions (heat, humidity, pollution), quality of electrical power and local data lines, security and the responsiveness of local support services may all influence physical siting.

Also important in this discussion is whether the user actually wants the main machine in his department. New or insecure users may like the application itself, but may not feel able to operate the system, especially in some of the more challenging aspects such as fault diagnosis or recovering from corrupted data. Physical siting may change well after implementation, perhaps because the user will then feel more confident in using the machine.

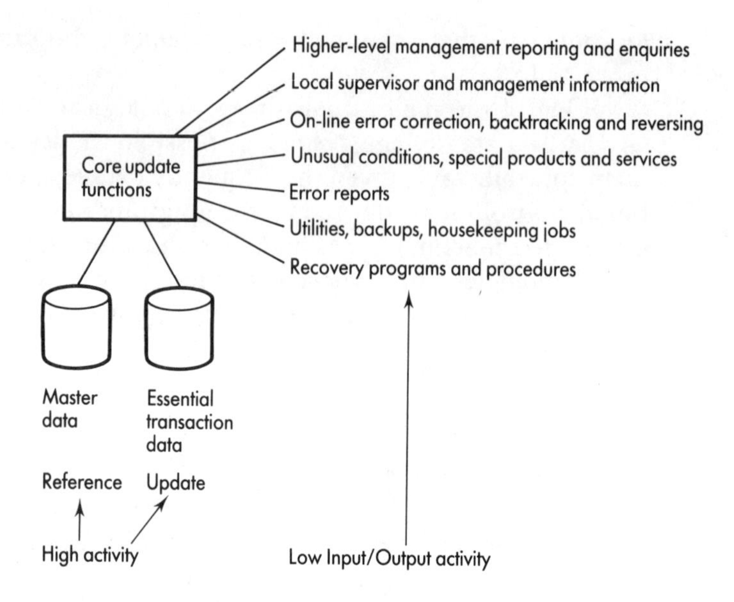

Figure 10.4 Mapping application complexity.

Getting to grips with application characteristics should begin with topological studies. The functions plus their volumes under the topics named above will help designers to begin to estimate the size of the problem. A point not appreciated by many IT people is that a very large amount of useful design and configuration can be gleaned from very early and high-level investigations.

Criteria for arriving at what is a semi-standalone system can be outlined broadly. As minimal communications is the most immediately measurable goal, a small system that only sends or receives high-volume data at the beginning or end of the day would meet the test. 'High-volume' here means more than a few thousand records (or a few hundred thousand characters) on low-speed remote communications lines, or perhaps ten times that on local links (say, between servers or minicomputers on the same logical local network). Where high-speed remote lines are in place (using digital technology), one might approach the local-area rate. However, aside from long transmission times, other problems can follow from high rates of data transfer. High error rates or excessive processing time at either sending or receiving machine can cause problems.

Should data transmissions be required between nodes (meaning anything but a workstation) during the business day, then these are ideally as low and simple as possible. The requirement to read occasional remote master records (rather than processing large sets of transaction history) should not cause problems. Most small machines could handle a few of these per second without trouble. What should be avoided is high-volume updating of records across nodes, or transferring large sets of either traditional or non-traditional data.

Our limits here depend in part upon how many users are likely to be performing heavy tasks concurrently. Broadly, if several users on a given node undertake transmissions that require several seconds each to complete, and if they do this many times per day, then a fair amount of disruption would appear on most wide-area systems. Local-area networks are more tolerant, partly because of the higher speeds and partly because there may be fewer individuals attempting such hostile workloads at any one time. However, all assumptions regarding heavy workloads especially should be checked. Those conducting these topological exercises should understand the basics of queuing theory (if not the detailed mathematics), particularly that aspect that says that long service times impact response more than does a series of short transactions.

Problems with topologies

One of the most challenging activities the downsizer will face is getting his chosen topology accepted. People with other interests (database, communications) may argue for a design that suits their area in particular. Users will fear that they have too large a system or too small a one, depending upon their imperial ambitions or their timorousness. In one way or another, attempts will be made to complicate the system by compromising its boundaries. A measure of tact ('perhaps we'll look at that in Phase two'), management backing and simply sticking to one's guns, explaining the benefits of a short, sharp, targeted implementation, should do the job in most cases. Any examples within the particular company or within one's industry at large where the preferred approach worked and particular alternatives did not will be especially welcome.

To stress the importance of getting topologies right, and to illustrate a few points, a case study might be in order. The head office of a large bank decided to downsize, assuming that each major department (money market, corporate lending, treasury, foreign exchange)

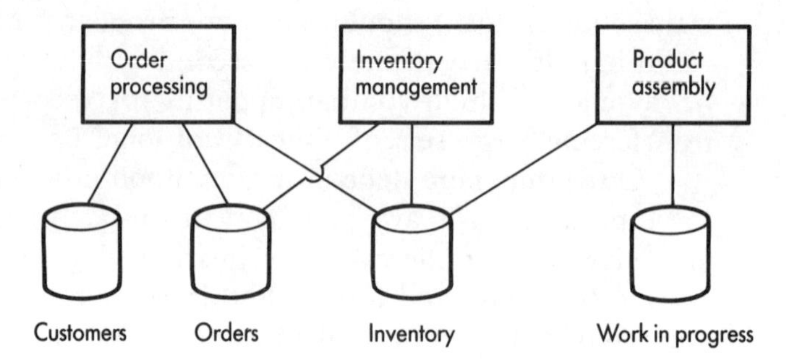

Figure 10.5 Closely and loosely coupled applications.

The notion of how closely separate application groups are coupled is useful in planning machine locations, communications facilities and shared databases with the attendant issue of data ownership. Figure 10.5 shows closely coupled groups (order processing and inventory management), with substantial usage of common files. Product assembly, loosely coupled to the others, does not communicate or share file usage substantially with the other groups, requiring only occasional reference to the inventory database.

ought to have its own small machine, and that mainframe computing would eventually be abandoned. Initial estimates of cost savings were large, as the ten or so small machines involved were each one-twentieth the price of the mainframe upgrade that would be needed.

The effort proceeded rapidly, and was equally rapidly unsuccessful, as the bank had made one of the classic errors of downsizing. It had not realized that user departments and application groups might not be overly related to one another, and so had not attempted to rationalize the two into a coherent topology before considering whether downsizing would really work. Other problems contributed to the confusion, and reflected the overall lack of management and planning. No one was willing to decide whether customer information should be considered a central resource or whether such data should be stored in each department where a given customer had an account. Management also could not decide whether to separate corporate customers from the wealthy individuals who used many of the same services.

The upshot was that too many copies of the same information were stored on different machines, with great efforts needed to transfer and check data. Rather than rationalize the distributed system, which could have been done albeit at some cost and delay, management got cold feet and put the lot back onto the mainframe (which, incidentally, has not been very successful either). Several elapsed years were wasted, which otherwise could have been used to advance applications systems substantially. A few million dollars went down the drain, and the morale of IT and many user staff went down even lower faster.

Just giving a user department its own machine is no way to downsize. Functional clarity and coherence of tasks and data is as necessary an ingredient as integrity of organizational structure. A second message from the above study is that, even if bad mistakes in planning have been made, it might be better to continue with the commitment rather than to back out and set the organization still more years behind its competition.

Key issues

- The arranging of coherent application-related topologies is crucial to downsizing success. To violate such logical groupings is a clear invitation to disaster.
- In cases where sensible topologies cannot be drawn at a highly distributed level, then proceeding to the next-most-centralized solution should be considered.
- Arriving at the 'as standalone as possible' situation is the objective of any topological experimentation. Such a system not only minimizes troublesome communications technology, it also simplifies application design and overall system management.
- Volatile departmental structures and varying responsibilities represent a major problem in arriving at stable, coherent topologies. In such situations powerful desktop machines communicating directly to a large minicomputer or a mainframe might be considered.

11

End users and their departments

We have stressed already that the role and character of the end user are of crucial importance in gaining success for our downsized system. We specified the end user as one of the three critical success areas, along with technology and the application itself, for a downsized project, and that substantial IT effort needs to be spent in dealing with the user.

No end user adapts instantly to computing, and those who do are converted by degrees, generally over a period of years. The results, even between individuals of the same theoretical ability, vary widely. At the end of the years of training and exposure, the end user is still rarely equivalent to an IT professional, and it would be an error to expect him to be. He should, in business terms at least, have better things to do.

In the two stages of our planning sequence, one should both analyse the user on one hand and educate and motivate him on the other. While difficult end users will always exist, the majority will respond to some degree to the right IT approach. Unhappily, IT's approach in the past has not always been ideal. A user who has been treated badly by IT, whether intentionally or not, is going to be a much tougher proposition than one whose opinion is neutral or better.

The new role of the end user

In user departments, the downsizing effort is usually anticipated with mixed feelings. Potential for an improved computer service is tempered by fear of failure of two types: collapse of the system itself;

Table 11.1 Why standalone is better.

- Less communications cost and complexity
- Greater sense of end–user proprietorship
- Easier operation by user department
- Lower management overheads and lower skill levels employable, both in user and IT areas
- Clearer database ownership and simpler data maintenance procedures
- Programs quicker to develop, easier to change quickly

The superiority of the (nearly) standalone system is one of the fundamentals of downsizing success. The more it is compromised, the more one is likely to wind up with the costs and complexities of the mainframe. A major purpose of our discussions on application groups and topologies is to arrive at the almost-standalone system.

and the inability of the users to cope with the system. This polarized mentality may, among the weaker or less experienced users, cause them to shrink from the sense of responsibility or ownership so essential to success. The insecurities can be exacerbated by insensitive handling. If the users simply have their lists of responsibilities dumped upon them, and particularly if they do not understand what is expected of them, then they are naturally likely to react. They may do so subtly, perhaps gradually attempting to disown the system or perhaps by expecting the IT department to shoulder an increasing percentage of both work and responsibility.

In dealing with end users, it is essential for downsizers to use a two-pronged approach. Users must first of all be evaluated carefully, both as to their general ability in IT matters and also where particular talents may lie within a given department. While keeping an objective eye on user potential, both initially and as the project develops, the IT representative must also try to educate and motivate as much as possible. Objections or misgivings are often expressed in indirect ways, perhaps showing as hesitancy or in asking rather too many questions about things which we as IT people think are obvious. Such feelings need to be fished out of users very diplomatically, but also firmly so that any problems can be clarified and resolved.

It is important right from the beginning to make the point that, though some duties may be unfamiliar to the department, they are straightforward enough, and are probably no more complicated than much of the administrative work already carried out. One might stress, albeit tactfully, that many very simple organizations have successfully managed to shoulder their responsibilities in operating basic computer systems, and that there is nothing to worry about unduly. In return for learning a few computer-related duties, the work of the department should be made simpler and easier, to the net profit of all concerned with that particular area.

Equally, the IT person should make it clear that training the users in the operation of their system will be a step-by-step process, and only a small amount of new material need be absorbed within any particular week. IT professionals will be on hand during the training and handover to cover any problems. If more training is needed on a particular subject, then it can be provided. By having such discussions early, one can both ease users' fears and also spot any areas or people likely to prove troublesome later.

End-user responsibilities

Though much depends upon the nature of the system being installed at the specific site, in general a number of things are expected of end users that would not apply to the same degree in a centralized situation. These include:

- System operating responsibilities, such as starting the local machinery in the morning, closing it down in an orderly fashion at night, and ensuring that end of day work, including security backups, is properly completed.
- System security.
- Data integrity.
- Cooperating with other departments directly where shared information is required.
- Broad knowledge of how the application software works, rather than just what it does.
- Limited operation of *ad hoc* enquiry and reporting packages.
- Taking initiatives in suggesting changes or enhancements to the system.
- Trouble-shooting - performing preliminary diagnoses when local hardware, software or communications fail to work properly.

In a very small and simple system, the user might be encouraged to play a major role in all of the above areas, though obviously where problems were more than superficial he would have to call upon IT support. Where large, complicated local systems are in operation (say, those involving more than 100 users) then the user's capacity for trouble-shooting and understanding complicated application software is going to be limited.

Charging users

The issue of passing computing costs onto users is a central one in the downsizing debate, and it has many ramifications. As usual, there is a traditional school of IT thought that is diametrically opposed to the realities of today.

The 'everything for free' types argue that IT should be treated as an organization-wide overhead, and that the services should be provided to users on an 'as-needed' basis. This need is determined by a steering committee in which the IT department plays a central role. The fact that the steering committee itself is remote from the ground-floor user means that the apportionment of resources may depend unduly on IT's opinion and not on real business needs.

The broad thrust of downsizing says that, in return for better and cheaper computer services, users have to assume responsibilities in order to play a meaningful role in their systems. There is no more fundamental responsibility than paying directly for what one uses. Therefore, the issue should be thought about. Broadly, two situations arise.

The first, and most favourable, case is where the various users are already being charged for most, if not all, of their services. The second is where no departments are charged at all, even in 'funny money' (inter-departmental cost transfers) and without any published breakdown of costs according to departmental usage. In between these two extremes lie various types of charging, either partial or imaginary, the latter meaning that some costs are nominally attributed to users but no actual figures come off the departmental budget.

In the downsized world, a user department should bear directly all costs that can be attributed to its computer usage. We feel strongly that these costs should be on an as-incurred basis, rather than trying to uplift them (often by factors of two or three) to show an imaginary 'profit'. The profit centre approach does have its advocates, as some imagine that this makes an IT department more efficient and also enables users to make comparisons on a like-for-like basis when considering whether to buy a service or product in-house or from an external supplier.

One has seen many cases where the profit centre approach has been counter-productive. The assumption behind it is, in most cases, false (the assumption being that the user can evaluate IT matters on a comparative-cost basis – most can do no such thing). Users may go outside the company for frivolous reasons such as dislike of IT personalities, or for corrupt ones such as bribes from suppliers. The process of presenting astronomic charges to users may offend them (IT's costs are astronomic enough, even with downsizing, not to benefit from any uplift). The process of artificial tendering and marketing adds costs and delays to projects, especially to downsized ones where a few days effort can cost as much as several useful products. On a purely aesthetic plane (downsizing is not simply about crass risk-and-reward matters), the last thing any company needs is still another computer salesman with his industry standard smile one meter wide and a micron deep. The profit centre approach, in short, embodies many aspects of bad IT practice which downsizing is trying to eliminate. To accept it is to encourage expense, ill-will, fragmentation and delay.

Where expenses are charged to users, they should be shown in a simple breakdown on a monthly basis. Such a statement should include:

- Purchased hardware and software.
- Rental of hardware, communications lines and software.
- In-house IT personnel costs.
- External personnel charges (consultants, for example).

Such a cost statement should be kept simple, and show the cash liability incurred. Let the user worry about such subtleties as depreciation, as if too many parties get involved only confusion results.

Though users should bear costs and have a planned budget to accommodate them, IT should initiate and approve all purchases and process all invoices. Without this degree of control, users will wander off and purchase all manner of odd and incompatible items, the longer-term (or even shorter-term) implications of which they may not understand. This happened with a vengeance when the PC revolution first took hold, such that many organizations took five years or more eventually to rationalize their PC acquisitions.

Once the principles of cost allocation have been agreed, thought should be applied as to how to convert to such a distributed charging system. If user departments have no budget for IT when downsizing begins, this fact should not be allowed to delay projects. Temporary measures, such as the distribution of some of the large central IT budget, may be used to oil the financial machinery until a longer-term and orderly system can be put into force.

The charging of users complements our other downsizing goals. If a user is paying for products and people, he will simplify his needs, get on with the job, be willing to do some things himself, and will generally appreciate the low effort and low costs involved in having a soundly engineered system underneath his applications.

11

Levels of understanding

Most end users today actually understand very few IT fundamentals, even if they have been using computers for some time. In downsizing, it is important to gauge end-user capabilities in order to tailor applications and operating procedures to a given department's needs.

One way of estimating user abilities is to look at the work they are doing already (both on and off the computer), and at how long they have been doing it. One will therefore have a good idea as to what users do understand. It is vital not to make any assumptions beyond this unless one sees positive evidence (as opposed to mere enthusiasm) that users actually do comprehend such concepts as, say, abstract data in general or a database structure in particular.

Seniority of users in relation to their understanding of computer matters is a delicate topic. The frankness of some managers can be at once refreshing and frightening. This writer recalls a senior banker who, after several discussions, said simply 'I don't understand anything you've said so far'. Suppressing an urge to downsize the manager then and there, one instead engaged in some tactful research that established that the man understood nothing about banking either. It pays to ascertain these things in advance if one can, as

Table 11.2 End-user computer knowledge.

0	No experience
1	Dumb terminals for existing transaction programs
2	Dumb terminals for simple, formatted enquiries or office work
3	Basic PC usage (spreadsheet or word processing), or free-format enquiries on mini or mainframe database
4	Uses PC database (say, dBase or PARADOX), or substantially manipulates larger database using FOCUS or SQL
5	Designs own databases on PC or information centre machine

Table 11.2 is a rough guide for estimating a user's familiarity with computer topics: the higher the number the better. Areas that cause the most trouble are the understanding of abstract data (hence the emphasis on database experience) and the way complicated interlinked programs work. One emphasizes that this estimates familiarity only, not 'maturity' in general, where attitudes are as important as experience. For example, a new user may be more 'mature' in many respects than an experienced user, but much training will still have to be given.

personnel departments often assign to computer projects those users found gathering dust on the particular afternoon when the request for application users was made. In general, a user who understands his applications well is more likely to adapt to computing, both because he is innately superior and because he knows the application already.

The PC expert

One phenomenon which is common enough in larger companies with numerous analytical departments is the user PC enthusiast who thinks he knows all about computing. While his facility with dBase, spreadsheet or even traditional programming languages may be undoubted, his understanding of the real world of multi-user medium sized systems will usually be lacking. Comprehension of database, metadata, communications and recovery problems will be limited or non-existent. He is unlikely to have any appreciation of the vast differences in scale between the single-user personal box and the server or minicomputer (many well known writers on computing topics also suffer this gap in understanding).

Such people have to be handled carefully. The PC expert's opinion of IT people may be contemptuous, partly because of their actual shortcomings, but also because they do not realize that the computing world can be conquered simply through the fiendishly clever use of DOS and C.

There have been numerous cases where such enthusiasts have been turned into innovators and catalysts of change within their own departments and neighbouring ones. If one can keep the person's energies confined to constructive paths, which are almost always within his area of interest, then he can be an effective ally. Often such people are among the first to see the business benefits of a new approach, and will propagate the message within their areas. Numerate, rather than administrative, users are usually the ones to display such attitudes, though one should look for them everywhere.

11

The system proprietor

However one may term it, the 'system proprietor' or 'system supervisor' concept is a useful one in downsizing. In a broad sense, the system proprietor is the user department as a whole, though somebody at relatively senior level should be chosen to wear the actual title. In a small or specialist department, this might be the actual departmental manager, though in most cases it will be another person close to the manager in seniority or specialist knowledge.

The function of the system proprietor is to look after the day to day running of the system from the user's point of view. He is not the system administrator, who is an IT person (probably an analyst/programmer) maintaining the more technical side of things. A system proprietor and administrator would normally communicate on more or less a day to day basis.

System proprietorship should be a growing concept, with tasks being added to keep pace with the user's learning and the increasing size or complexity of the system. Simple operational tasks should be assigned at the beginning, and these should be coherent and related to the more obvious business activities such as opening up and closing down at the beginning and end of the day. Early activities should be closely monitored by the IT person watching the department and, in the early stages of a system's going live, weekly meetings of a semi-formal nature may not be too frequent.

The system proprietor should be named if possible during the project planning stage (Step two according to the method outlined here) and should be closely involved in the implementation. Not only the user department, but the actual individual named should be positively agreeable to the tasks assigned him, not merely acquiescent. If doubt or insecurity is expressed on any topic, then extra training and confidence building are worthwhile investments so long as the person himself is thought to be capable. If it turns out otherwise, then changing the system proprietor is not a particularly pleasant task, but it is better to change early rather than to wreck the system later.

The system proprietor should be the primary contact between user department and IT for all computer-related functions, meaning specifically application development and maintenance, operations and training. To cater for his absence, an alternative or two should be named, and these should be trained up to a basic level in operations and fault diagnosis. In general, the system proprietor should see training and motivation within his department as primary responsibilities, and should spend a percentage of his time on an ongoing basis in carrying out such activities.

Cooperation between end users

One thing an IT professional learns early in life is that people who appear to be working for the same organization in practice rarely are. While being politically correct about organizational purpose in public, in private many users are hostile to other units and protective about their territory. Often these feelings are related to personal rivalries and animosities between unit managers. Many such people see the sudden emergence of computer facilities as an ideal means to carry on long-standing civil wars.

In a downsized environment, it is essential to secure cooperation with everyone in sight: IT, one's own users, users in other departments, general managers, plus any customers or suppliers who might be involved in the system. Efforts should begin at square one, and should be progressed from then onwards. Inter-unit liaison might be

Table 11.3 Questions *not* to ask the end user.

- What is an invoice?
- What does a payslip contain?
- Why do you need to issue a delivery advice?
- Why do you need a separate customer number from account number?

The questions in Table 11.3 were all asked by experienced IT consultants or analysts in the course of early systems investigations. The loss of credibility was instant, and in most cases not regained. Such incidents must *never* be allowed to happen in the downsized world. No analyst or analyst/programmer should be placed before an end user until it is established that he has a reasonable understanding of what the user's business is. Such basic levels of understanding should not take more than a few days at the most to acquire, and in many cases a few hours of to-the-point discussions can furnish adequate background.

an agenda item at progress meetings. End users who bottle themselves up in their own departments will substantially slow down the downsizing effort and in the long term they will slow down themselves, as they will not benefit from the discoveries of others. They are also more likely to cause incompatibilities between neighbouring systems. Users must be convinced early on that insular behaviour is not in anyone's interest.

Ways of encouraging end-user cooperation include inviting representatives from different units to one's own meetings on occasion. This may be particularly justified in the project's initial stages, when broad commonalities of applications, techniques for exchanging or sharing data, and staffing matters might be examined. If the right tone is set here, ongoing meetings can be organized separately to cover inter-departmental issues, and people should be encouraged to trade ideas at such events. Establishing liaisons early will help to set a tone of corporate responsibility as well as increasing the likelihood of success for a department's own system.

Key issues

- Downsized systems are characterized by a high role for the end user, but one that can vary substantially in type and degree from one department to another.

- End users should be graded in terms of experience, abilities and attitudes in order to fit systems to them properly.
- End users should be treated like neighbours or long-established customers, and not as members of the IT family on the one hand or as complete aliens on the other.
- Charging users as fully and as accurately as possible for *all* IT facilities and services is essential in order to manage downsized systems in a disciplined fashion.

12

The project plan

Ideally, construction of the project plan for a downsized system should begin shortly after the initial strategic overview ('Step one'). However, in some cases this might not be possible because of other priorities or because of delays in decision making. If more than a few months elapse between completion of the overview and the beginning of the specific project plan, a quick review is in order to establish whether anything significant has changed. In most cases, such changes will be minor, and the project can then proceed.

Before beginning this second and more project-specific phase of the planning exercise, it is assumed that:

- A topology defines the application group with reasonable accuracy, meaning that functionality, user departments, databases, communications items and any geographical issues are covered to a reasonable standard of accuracy (say, within a conceptual 20%).
- The end user is eager to proceed (note use of the word 'eager').
- The right amounts and types of IT and user personnel will be available.
- There are no likely contingencies that would disrupt the project, particularly on the user's side of things.
- Any products required can be obtained within the time-scales foreseen.
- Training as well as implementation duties can be undertaken.

The project plan should be a concise document, using similar (perhaps PC-based) media employed in the initial planning step. It should state:

- The scope of the plan – the departments and applications covered.
- Expected benefits and costs (refined from the higher-level model). These will have been meaningfully revised during this stage of planning.
- People required and their levels of involvement, for training and for actual work. They should be named if at all possible. Levels of involvement should also be stated for live running, after the implementation has been completed.
- Managerial structure of the project, and how monitoring is to take place, both during and after development.
- A level of application definition should be included sufficient to begin designing the most important programs. If application packages are to be considered, a short-list of these should be provided. (This phase of the project should not be entered if it is unlikely that a suitable package will exist, assuming that the presence of a package is crucial to the effort.)
- The application definition should include or have attached a database scenario, and responsibilities for maintaining this data should be stated either here or in the 'people required' section.
- Specific types of technology should be named, and approximate sizes and costs of machines, software, communications facilities and any other essential products or services. Specific products may or may not be named, depending upon how much is known at this stage.
- Time-scales and agreement procedures for the plan itself.

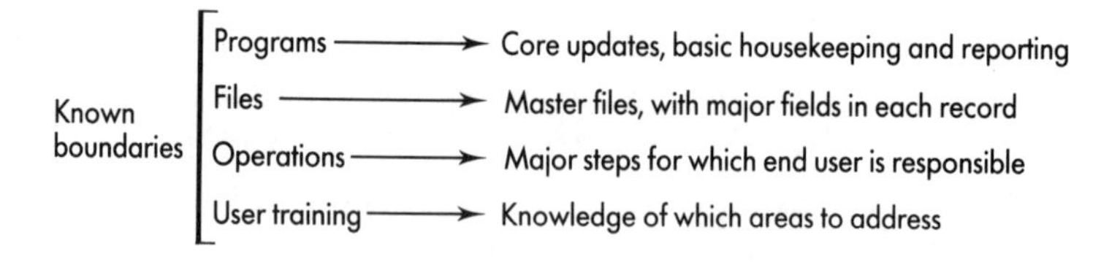

Figure 12.1 Planning and defining.

The setting of firm boundaries in the earlier stages of planning makes subsequent project planning more secure and accurate. By the *beginning* of the project planning stage, the points in Figure 12.1 should be obvious, leaving staff free for detailed definition of files and programs. As a number of subjects will be progressed in parallel by an individual or a small team, it is important for management to ensure that no one subject gets squeezed out.

Time-scales

This second stage of the planning/design process, being a concise effort and having meaningful and time-critical activities on either side of it, should not itself be overly time-consuming. The previously suggested figure of two months is probably right for a medium-sized project. If one supposes that project planning might take longer than this, the reasons should be carefully reviewed, as the possibility will exist that something is awry with the initial assumptions. Where a small to medium organization is performing the exercise, it may be decided to combine Steps one and two. If matters are straightforward (where fairly standard commercial applications are required, for example), then there is nothing wrong with this.

If several people are involved in planning, it is important to apportion their time across the three main areas (end user, application, technology) in order to give appropriate attention to each. However, the areas do not necessarily require equal time to be spent on each. Because one is talking to the end user in relation to other topics, opinions regarding his capabilities can be formed, and motivation and training given, in the course of these discussions. Nevertheless, in order to make sure the ground is covered, a conceptual breakdown of effort should exist in the minds of IT personnel concerned, and it might look like this:

- End-user characteristics, including producing a training plan and considering operational duties - 10%, meaning about 3 man/days.
- Application - 70%, or 20 to 25 man/days.
- Technology - 20%, or approximately 7 man/days.

Such might be the involvement of the IT personnel on the project, adjusted according to the complexity of the exercise and the contributions from users themselves.

One point that stands out from the above, and which is worth making to one's IT colleagues and users alike, is the overriding importance of the application itself. Keep in mind that this is still a planning stage in part (combining feasibility plus general design), and the percentage looks much higher than considered polite by IT traditionalists. Also, the amounts of time devoted to technology appear small. One makes an assumption that the technology is reasonably known (if it is not, then one has no business beginning this stage of the plan). Most of the technological attention should lie in configuring the products and in providing familiarization to those IT staff who need it (mainly the analyst/programmers who will be developing the applications). Any very detailed technical matters might be passed to technical specialists within central IT.

Staffing the plan

For a basic effort, a business analyst from IT is normally the only person required on any continuing basis. One or two representatives from the user department complete the picture (one of these should be the 'system proprietor' or 'system supervisor' defined earlier). Any analyst/programmers to be brought fully on board later might be undergoing some familiarization at this time.

Management and sponsorship of the project plan deserve some consideration. The project sponsor should be a senior manager from the user side, either the actual department manager or, if he is unavailable, then his immediate senior. Anyone higher up than this is unlikely to know much about the area covered.

On the IT side, the business analyst will be supervized by the IT manager in a medium sized installation or by a systems development manager in a larger one. Progress meetings should take place no less frequently than fortnightly. At these meetings, the project sponsor, the business analyst and any other IT analysts involved should be present. The business analyst's superior should be present at occasional meetings, depending upon conditions, and any needed user representatives should also attend (particularly those guiding the specific applications covered). Other people, such as technicians from IT and more senior user managers, can be drafted in as required. It is a necessity to retain a practical and flexible attitude to project membership and meetings, and to adapt as conditions change. The system proprietor/supervisor should be at every formal progress meeting, and should also be kept closely advised of off-line meetings between the business analyst and such people as technicians or supplier representatives.

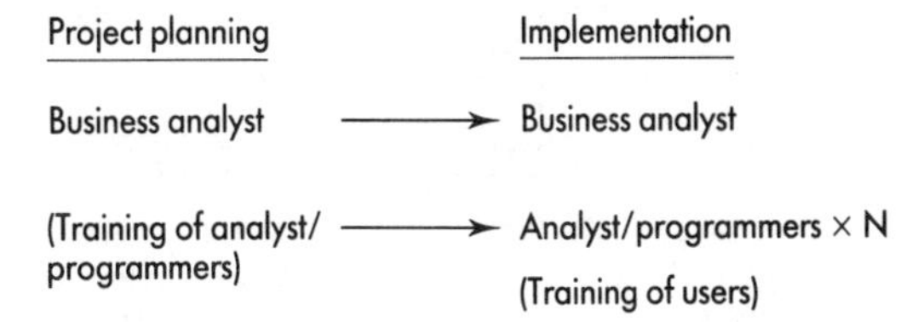

Figure 12.2 Naming the people.

Throughout downsizing, it is important to maintain momentum, but especially during the two specific project phases (planning and implementation). To this end, during project planning the team to work on the implementation should be named. In many cases these analyst/programmers will require some training, either with technology or with some phases of the application, before the implementation stage actually starts. If application packages are to be used instead of tailored programs, then such evaluation should start as early as possible in the project planning phase.

The unfeasible application

We stated a couple of times that this stage of the planning process contains an element of the feasibility study in it, as would any planning process. The likelihood of project cancellation should be very small, assuming the strategic overview performed earlier had any validity. A more common case is that, during the detailed planning process, it becomes clear that the project cannot be completed as easily as thought earlier.

The most common reason for this is that the user needs time to make decisions about actual business procedures that accompany the application. While such areas of indecision should have been spotted earlier, in real life the odd little surprise often crops up later than it should. Typically, the user will suddenly decide that he wants to change or rationalize some process, as the effort of investigating applications has caused him to see new possibilities. He may need the approval of a higher-up to effect the change. If it were up to the user department alone, most would make a decision then and there, with some help from their IT colleagues.

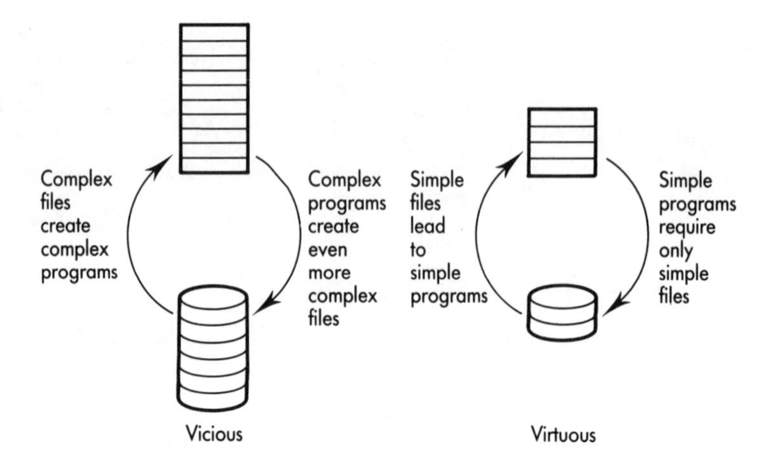

Figure 12.3 The alternative circles.

In striving for application simplicity, one tried and true technique is to limit the number and complexity of data files available to the programs. This in turn encourages simple and small programs, easy to code, test and maintain. A complex file system, on the other hand, not only requires more complexity in the application code, it also needs many more housekeeping and utility programs to keep data clean and relationships intact. The relationship between data and programs is much easier to keep under control when both are designed by a single person or a single small team.

Where such decisions take more than a few days, it is obvious that the planning effort itself will miss its deadline. If the decision is a fundamental one, impacting many programs and large areas of the database, then too much will remain in the air to make any firm commitments. The more fundamental the decision, the longer it may take to resolve. If an indeterminate but probably long delay is on the cards, then project postponement should be considered. Politically astute handling of such situations is obviously required, as the user must not in the future feel inhibited about approaching IT.

In those cases where IT has to postpone the effort, the reasons should first of all be made clear to the user, and presented honestly if not in an overly grovelling fashion. Such IT-induced failures should be extremely rare, given the preliminary work and the simplicity of the exercise. The most common reason would be the unexpected departure of the business analyst performing the planning, and such an eventuality would normally be viewed sympathetically by the user. If the abrupt departure of such a key person is even remotely thought likely, then prudent IT management should devise a contingency plan or else should not begin the planning effort.

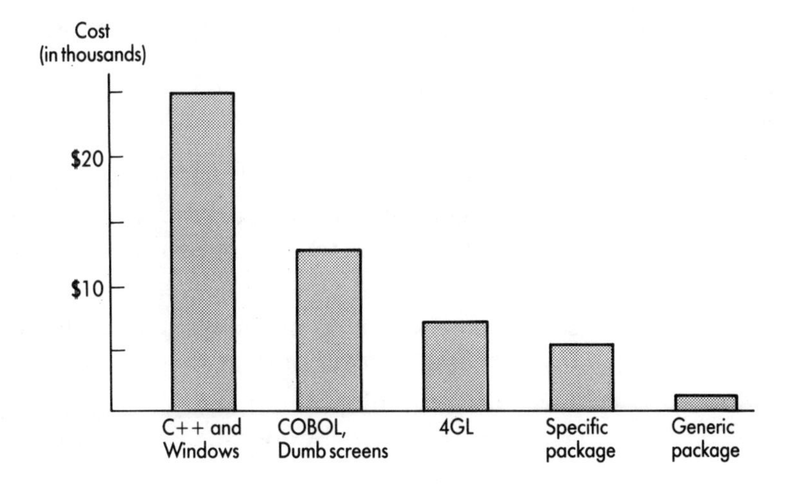

Figure 12.4 The cost of application functions.

The cost of an application can vary enormously, perhaps by a factor of ten to one or more, even on a small, supposedly easy to use machine. By far the cheapest solution is to adapt a generic package or packages to do some or all of an application. Users should be well acquainted with the trade-offs between the high-cost tailored system and the more general packaged approaches. Especially where they themselves are paying the bill, they can then make an informed decision.

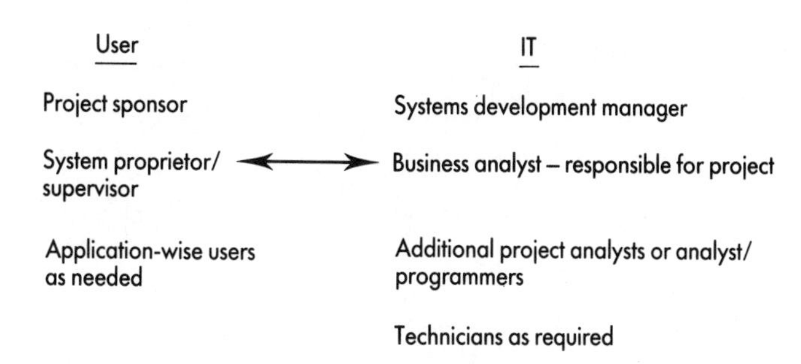

Figure 12.5 Progress meetings during project planning and implementation.

The key link during all project work for a user area is that between the project-responsible business analyst and the so-called system proprietor or supervisor. As with other meetings and user-IT contacts during downsizing, progress meetings should be frequent, brief and very much to the point. A progress meeting is *not* a forum for the discussion of application or technical details – such points should be sorted out offline.

Key issues:

- Project planning, as the effective start of a specific project, should begin as soon as possible after the general company overview in order to maintain momentum and credibility.
- Staff continuity is especially important in downsizing projects, so such key people as business analysts should maintain their involvement over all project stages wherever this is feasible.
- From the beginning, build in diplomatic escape routes should a project suddenly be found to be unfeasible.

13

Data and database policies

To the large existing installation, the whole issue of database causes much puzzlement. By now, most such installations have long-established policies governing data design, standards, methodologies and documentation, and they have large specialist departments to deal with various data-related issues. One might see several sections containing several people each involved in:

- Logical data design (data seen from the business's point of view).
- Physical data design (data designed for the machine's benefit - meaning for performance or ease of recovery).
- Operational matters, such as tuning the database and guaranteeing security and integrity.
- Data dictionary maintenance and use of CASE (Computer Aided Systems Engineering) tools.
- The management and coordination of all of the above.

Managing data can involve very high overheads. In theory, the overheads are recovered via savings in program coding and in making information clear. But theory and practice, as in much else regarding IT, can be well apart.

While practices and results both vary widely, in the average case the database administration function acts as a constraint on development, whatever benefits it may provide elsewhere. It is well outside the scope of this volume to go into all of the fine points about database in the large-machine environment. Our purpose here is to cover what is or is not needed in the downsized world.

Downsized data requirements

Insofar as an individual downsized project goes, database needs usually appear to be quite basic. The standard data-handling tool will be a relational database, either PC-oriented (dBase, FoxPro, PARADOX, and so on) or a server- or mini-based larger product, geared to multi-user processing of data. These larger products can usually handle some degree of distributed data as well.

The point about the relational product type here is that it is first of all an industry standard item. In terms of how data looks to the user or to an application program, the products are much the same. The retrieval language used with relational products (SQL, for Structured Query Language) is more or less a standard (as usual with standards, there are variations, though there is a reasonably common core). This language is relatively easy to use for *very* simple enquiries on simple data structures. Beyond this, it is as complicated to use as most other programming languages. In any case, for data handling in the downsized world, there is no alternative to SQL and its underlying relational database.

The problem with large IT installations is that they associate a vast array of methods and departmental structures with database in general and with relational database in particular. Part of this is because of the 'guru factor' which plagues much of the computer world. A number of prominent database theorists, with most of their experience based on 1970s research, formulated sets of principles and specific rules that bear little relevance to the world of today. Among their most significant shortcomings was not to foresee the downsized world of today which emerged predictably and on schedule from the long-term popularization of technology. IT professionals in the database area often find it very difficult to give up their theories and to adapt instead to a much more practical world. Some of these types can be the downsizer's greatest enemies, as if they cannot prevent downsizing they will try to cripple it with obtuse yet intricate design exercises.

The downsized project itself needs almost none of the 'professional' methodologies. If the application and data topologies have been drawn up correctly, the structure will above all be simple, even for large sets of data. There is simply no requirement for the involved methodologies, and if used they would only add expense, delay and rigidity to the system.

Downsized data should be straightforward, and related to fundamental items with which the business deals. Orders, customers, parts, products and services should be most of what databases are about. Such items as documents, spreadsheets, images and other less traditional forms of data are not encompassed in either database packages or the methodologies designed to handle them. Much of the whole database concept is irrelevant to the wide spectrum of need visible today.

Corporate data

Yet, in the downsized world the individual system is not on its own, much though it would like to be. It too must be a good corporate citizen and enhance the quality of the business as a whole. We made the point that an application group should cooperate with its neighbours, that management control is still required, and that this control is inherently a centralized function.

The corporate data concept was mentioned earlier as an expression of the 'all data in one place' mainframe defence. There are widely varying definitions of corporate data, and that is one extreme (and one which most database administrators would love). In today's world, the concept of corporate data should encompass only a small subset of its earlier scope. There are two ways of defining it:

- Data which is needed outside the application group.
- Data which is needed for the management of the organization as a whole.

Both concepts are valid enough, and one does not want to waste time bandying definitions. The real issue behind the phraseology is how the above two requirements should be handled, and by whom? The most indefinite definition is that of data needed outside the particular downsized system, as central control is not necessarily implied in all such cases.

Where data needs to be exchanged between nearby or coupled systems, and where only a few such systems are involved, it is reasonable that the neighbouring parties should agree common

Table 13.1 Key questions on data ownership.

- Will the user take responsibility for local data?
- Does the user understand basic definitions, meaning record layouts in master and essential transaction files?
- Is the database management product simple enough for the user to operate at least in part?
- Does the user understand the major aspects of integrity and recovery?
- Does the operation of data-related procedures unduly complicate the user's overall role in operating the system?

For a downsized system to be effective, the sense of system proprietorship must extend to the data involved. The abstract aspects of data are beyond most users' comprehension, and IT professionals should not use or try to explain database jargon or the more abstruse areas to users. Data ownership should be thought of as a growing concept, with initial support by IT giving way to more user control on a carefully monitored progressive basis.

definitions. That is one purpose of the working parties operating between departments which were suggested earlier.

For data that needs to be exchanged between a large number of widely separated groups, a corporate policy clearly needs to apply. A reasonable definition of corporate data, meaning that controlled by a central agency, might read:

- Data which is common to more than a few application groups, such that it would be cumbersome to agree and enforce common definitions. This still leaves room for negotiation. In some cases three groups might be too many; in others six may be able to cooperate successfully. 'Cumbersome' might be taken to imply that more than two meetings are needed to agree a definition.
- Data which is essential for management reporting. It is management itself, or a related management information function (see Chapter 17, on management information) that should determine what this data is and how it is ideally defined.

We thus see that in a highly distributed environment the role of the database coordinator changes drastically. Instead of worrying about the definition of virtually everything, he can turn his attentions to much smaller bodies of data, and enforce definitions agreed with actual management. A problem with current database administration is that it is far removed from business processes themselves, and from any notion of what management actually needs, instead being seen as a narrow specialist area within IT.

Coordination of non-traditional data

Whether data coordination of non-traditional types of data by the database administration department is necessary is very much open to doubt. Database administration is not equipped to handle text, image and similar, and in many cases it is not interested in doing so. Certainly, some items can be standardized (perhaps defining a common style for documents, brochures, reports, overhead foils and slides), but existing data specialists are rarely the ones to cope with such tasks. Other - non-IT - management can often handle these functions, or matters can be left to local groups to agree their own standards. It is not a key business or IT issue.

Local control of data

Certain data-related functions still need to be carried out, aside from definition. Definition itself, if relatively local, can be agreed by business analysts or analyst/programmers involved in the actual systems. Security, recovery and performance tuning may need some technical backup from the central IT function. Whether or not this technical expertise is in a department called database administration, systems programming or operational support is irrelevant. The important point is that some central technical resources are needed to provide expertise and to do so economically. If a technician is supporting, say, ten different server databases, he soon builds up expertise quickly, as differing systems will encounter different problems.

Data design at local level should deliberately be done simply. One should watch for the over-designing described above, in which

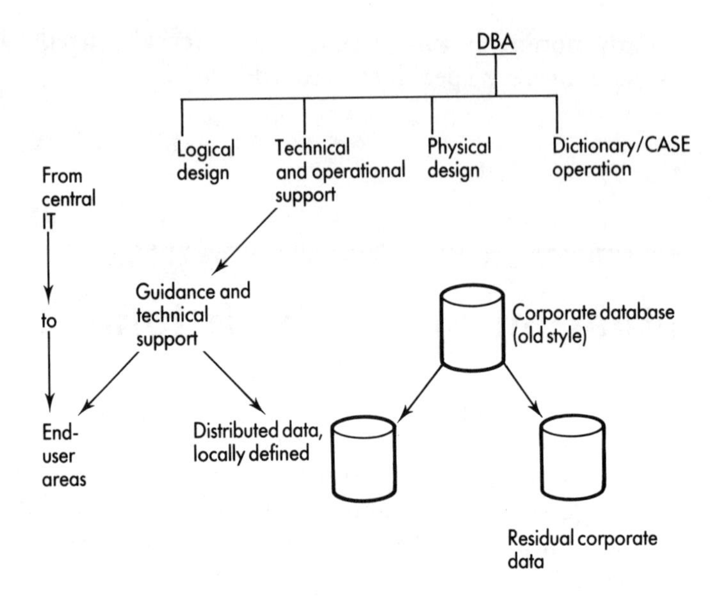

Figure 13.1 Dismembering database administration (DBA).

Most large IT installations have a large database administration function which is not suited to the downsized world. To fit the new environment, DBA must be adapted and reduced in size, and this will inevitably entail a lot of politics within IT. Data skills will be needed in three areas (guidance in design, especially where product related; technical support for performance and recovery situations; and maintaining the now smaller but still essential 'corporate' database).

people try to use all of a product's bells and whistles simply because they are there or to illustrate the brilliance of the technical designer. Databases for local usage should have as few tables as possible (partly because this can act as a brake on application complexity in general), and there should be few linkages between different tables (variously called 'link boxes' or 'junction boxes' in the trade). Few secondary indices should be used, mainly for ease of administration and to aid performance (most database products insulate the end user from the presence or absence of index fields). Many-to-many relationships should be avoided where possible, and limited numbers of meaningless (to the user) codes should be present. Much of this advice runs counter to established database practice, but one must keep in mind two things: established database practice does not work all that well, even in its intended environment; and in the small world there are trade-offs. Needless complexity and obscurity impose penalities particularly in the database area, and particularly later on, when systems need to be changed or performance problems crop up.

Key issues

- Traditional database administration applies only partly to the downsized world. New data management policies should be introduced which are more practical than theoretical and which are adapted to the specific natures of the projects under consideration.
- New and accurate definitions of corporate data should be agreed between downsizing projects and central IT control functions.
- It should be recognized that traditional data administration does not address much of interest to downsized projects. New controls and ownership guidelines should be established for text, voice, images and any combination of these.

14

Communications and networking

Of all the technical areas with which downsizing is concerned, communications is undoubtedly the most troublesome. If downsizing were merely a matter of running separate small machines, life would be very simple indeed. The problems inherent in communications are several, and are largely related:

- The basic technology is complex, especially as transmission speeds rise.
- Actual transmission rates available today are too slow for many types of application.
- The area abounds with conflicting standards.
- Many wide-area (long-distance) systems, especially in Europe, are operated or controlled by national telecommunications agencies, with the inevitable political issues further clouding already murky waters.
- Remote transmission is still very expensive.
- Hardware and software items needed for communications are often expensive, intricate or both.
- Management and control tools for communications networks are generally underdeveloped, which makes fault diagnosis and the monitoring of what is actually going on within a network difficult. Where control tools exist, they can be more complicated than the problem they are meant to solve.
- Networks are inherently rigid, which makes change slow and often expensive. Wiring systems within buildings, and the setting up of wide-area networks, both take time and manpower. The natural tendency in such situations is to buy more

capacity than is thought necessary at first, which adds further to costs.

- Physical aspects of networks, such as connectors, cables and interface boxes, are all prone to trouble. This is especially so when items are moved, or plugged and unplugged frequently.

Because of the integrated nature of networking, it is not possible to isolate completely communications requirements when planning a downsized application. Such issues as distribution of databases and how the application is actually to be coded in turn impact communications needs, just as communications potential may in turn influence system designers in other areas. This need for interactive planning, plus the technical complexities, are what make the planning of communications something of a challange, to say the least.

Communications is closely linked in most peoples' minds with such concepts as open systems and interoperability. As with other notions regarding open or standard systems, the reality is regrettably short of the ideal, though progress is indeed being made.

Over the past few years, surveys (by IBM and X/Open, among others) have established that communications, or issues closely linked such as interoperability between systems and office automation functions, have been among the chief concerns among IT managers. High costs, technical uncertainties and the known high manpower costs associated with managing the area all cause worry.

As might be expected in such an area, it is common for problems to loom large, late and unexpected. Such problems typically occur because of poor capacity planning, or because fundamentally bad choices have been made in related system areas (mixing too many unlike systems being a common fault). Thoughtless application design can compound the problem.

While communications are undoubtedly at the heart of downsizing and system distribution, it is well to be aware that many downsizing failures are due largely or in part to communications problems. Therefore, recognizing in advance where problems might occur, and noting the bad practice of others, can help enormously to skirt the more troublesome areas. The point must always be made that communication at modest volumes between like systems is troublesome enough; to expand traffic unduly, or to make a career of connecting unlike systems, is to ask for more trouble when one least needs it.

Influence of business policy

We have repeatedly stressed one of the primary principles of downsizing: that the simplest and most isolated system possible under the circumstances is the best one. In arriving at this almost standalone affair, one has presumably drawn application modules to fit closely organizational layout, so minimizing communications between both systems and departments.

A factor which can override sensible system design practice is high-level business policy. This observer has seen several instances of this as it relates to long-distance communications. Financial businesses, such as banks and insurers, have an understandable wish to know what is going on at a fair level of detail in remote subsidiaries, and they also like their information to be up-to-date. In other areas, certain types of highly centralized management feel an emotional need to know exactly what is going on at every instant. Such companies often insist on direct communications links between subsidiaries or branches and the head office as a matter of policy. While the need for centralized control exists in any organization, there may be a tendency to overdo it, and also to assume that frequent data communications equates to accurate or meaningful information (clearly, in many cases, they do not).

Such over-controlling via communications media results in high costs and extra complexity for the IT staff at both central and remote locations. When planning communications aspects of any distributed system, it is worth making a strong case for minimal communications, both in volume and frequency. In many cases, a small amount of data at the end of the week is just as meaningful as transaction summaries shipped down daily.

Planning communications needs

Once business policies have been dealt with either successfully or not, those planning networks should pay great attention to both traffic levels and system compatabilities. While traffic levels are notoriously difficult to deal with in many distributed environments, some attempts should be made, on the principle that a broad estimate is better than none at all.

Where system incompatabilities are concerned, IT staff should have much more control. Like systems should be used throughout the organization wherever possible, but particularly on high-volume local networks. Unlike systems are more tolerable at remote sites, where transfer volumes are moderate, and where traditional formatted records are transferred. Unfortunately, many IT staff will have inherited a mix of incompatible systems about which they can do nothing in the short term.

When confronted with such situations, separating long-term and short-term goals is essential. The long-term objective should be not to repeat the mistake, and to aim for compatible systems. The short-term goal has to be to make the best of it, and one does so by using the most established communications method between such systems (which is often primitive) and keeping the amounts of traffic as low as possible. The fallacy of 'each type of box for its most suitable purpose' (a nuisance in general) is particularly troublesome where communications are concerned, and should be flattened without mercy wherever it crops up in discussion.

When it comes to estimating traffic between systems, the easy part is the basic traditional application. Transaction processing systems deal with manageable record sizes, and the summaries of these that *need* to be sent upwards and onwards are normally concise enough. More difficult areas to estimate are management information and what is sometimes called non-traditional or non-formatted data (documents, colour 3-D graphics, voice, multimedia, animation and other technological nightmares). Particularly, management information and non-traditional data can be problems on wide-area links, as the speeds here are much slower than those available on local-area systems – and by factors of as much as fifty.

Other areas that need to be considered – and which are often overlooked – are end of period data transmissions and recovery situations. Particularly where small remote sites or portable systems are used, it is common to try to transfer relatively large amounts of data at the end of the day in one or both directions so that the remote site and the central one both have up-to-date information, say, on a customer's order position or on local stock levels.

With small units or with portable PCs, it is usual to use basic line speeds either because nothing else is available or to save costs. Therefore, if at close of business one chooses to send several thousand records to or from a remote site, one might be talking of many minutes of transmission time - or worse. Though line quality is improving in much of the world, poor quality can still force a high rate of re-transmission, such that a theoretically half-hour transmission could extend to a couple of hours.

The message about end of the day (or whatever) transmissions is to estimate carefully, and then to try to adjust the figures if transmissions take too long. During very long transmissions, there is a finite risk of a system fault at either end or on the line, which means that the entire transmission might have to be repeated once the problem has been overcome. Common ways of adjusting transmission volumes include sending the data less frequently, or sending only changes to master information, not the full set. The problem with sending only changes is of course that the two sets of data - central and local - may become inconsistent, so periodic checking procedures need to be instituted to correct any mismatch.

Communications systems capacities

In our discussion of client/server systems, we mention some likely transmission speeds on local-area networks. In summary, we may note here that capacities vary from around 256 000 characters per second of actual user data (ignoring control information which the system sends around with the data) to 1.5 million characters per second on established network types. The new fibre-optic network type (FDDI) just coming onto the market (but not officially standardized at this writing) is capable of approximately 9 million characters per second, a substantial improvement on all earlier 'local' networks.

One emphasises that, as with virtually all other computer-related performance information, these maximum capacity levels are partly theoretical. In practice one does not load a network evenly except in specific situations. Also, though the capacities of the newer types of local network may look high, they can still be sabotaged by large amounts of non-traditional data (or even by traditional data if one tries hard). If an ambitious financial analyst tries to transfer several Mbytes of data from a server to his PC while a secretary decides to transfer a digitized photograph or a telephone conversation across the network, then there are many seconds of saturation, during which other users trying to use the network may be inconvenienced as well.

Saturation is particularly a problem with the Ethernet system, as it is less orderly about handling traffic than the Token Ring or FDDI (fibre-optic) system. Token Ring and FDDI would make the offending user wait relatively longer to complete his transfer, while others would be able to use their alloted time-slices at least at a reasonable rate.

When one turns to wide-area networks, potential rates of transfer drop alarmingly. PC modem and line combinations usually transmit at around 400 to 800 characters per second, assuming good line quality. For higher-speed leased lines for larger computers, rates of up to 200 000 characters per second are available (this with the fastest available digital technology). However, these high-speed lines are very expensive, with costs of tens of thousands of dollars per year being common across even moderate distances.

There are a number of developments in wide-area communications that should eventually mean faster, cheaper and more reliable services. New standards on ordinary analogue lines are emerging with speeds of up to 5000 characters per second (this is assuming efficient data compression). New techniques (Asynchronous Transfer Mode and Frame Relay) should mean more options in relatively higher-speed media. Better satellite data transmission and metropolitan-area networks will mean better solutions for portable computers or for those within a large city's catchment area. Unfortunately, these developments have been slow in coming, and often conflict with existing standards.

Table 14.1 Communications' danger areas.

- The SQL data retrieval language
- Multi-page text
- Image, voice, video/animation
- Untested procedures
- Volatile user needs
- Uncontrollable users
- Mixed platforms (hardware plus operating and communications software) and mixed communications systems or protocols
- Low-speed network

The above checklist covers some of the more likely troublesome areas where communications are concerned. In many disaster scenarios one sees a combination of the factors causing not only networks themselves but also the attached systems to grind to a halt. As elsewhere, planning and control are the watchwords. In unusually volatile situations, however, life will remain difficult until better management and monitoring tools become available.

Local-area networking packages

At a level above the basic systems about which we have been speaking (Ethernet, Token Ring, and so on), a number of networking packages are available. These normally require an adapter card in the PC or mini, plus operating software.

Catering primarily for PCs, the product called LAN MANAGER or LAN SERVER was originally a joint IBM-Microsoft development, though the products may be drifting apart (LAN SERVER is the IBM version). Other companies (notably DEC) sell the Microsoft version (renamed PathWorks) under licence. Hewlett-Packard has developed a version of the product for UNIX networks based upon Ethernet. These packages essentially offer a higher-level interface for application programs, plus network management facilities. These include granting passwords and access rights to users, defining sub-areas, usually called domains, enabling software to be loaded between nodes, controlling access to files and sometimes support for data security features such as 'mirroring' (duplicating disk data).

The outstanding success among PC-based local networks has been and continues to be Novell's NetWare, which still boasts around 60% of such units sold. As pointed out elsewhere, NetWare is a prime example of what a downsized product should be: it is well packaged, easy to use (relative to the fiendish level common with communications packages), does not try to do everything perfectly but hits a defined target well. In a market crying out for good communications packages, this is the *only* one that has managed to hit its target at all convincingly, though other offerings are now closing the gap. It did so early on in the PC revolution, while the monoliths were bumbling around with low-level Ethernet or were doing nothing at all.

NetWare today comes in a variety of packages, from the 'Lite' version aimed at simple peer-to-peer PC networks, to more substantial items (NetWare 386), targeted at client/server configurations. NetWare is in fact an operating system, complementary to DOS on the simple PC but dominating server machines so that the likes of OS/2 or Windows (NT) are not necessary. Because of its concept of the Network Loadable Module (or NLM), one can load complementary software such as database managers into the server, and so can have a close interface to such products. The benchmarks provided by the Gupta organization with its SQLBase database manager are run this way with a Novell system, and provide very good performance figures indeed (over 100 simple transactions per second). Many users are still unaware of what a good Novell system on a fast server and with a good database product can do. Basically, it can outrun most mini systems (UNIX or proprietary) costing several times the price. It underlines the basic downsizing point: the fewer components the better, as NetWare with a database loaded as an NLM is effectively one lump of software, providing performance and ease of use by the same token. It also confirms that a good communications system is at the heart of a properly organized downsized environment.

Aside from NetWare's intrinsic features, it is also a very open system. It offers interfaces to virtually every other communications system, and so can fit into an existing environment where older products may still be used, or where other items may need to be supported for application reasons.

When one moves above the PC-level networking systems, life necessarily becomes more expensive and complicated, which is a good reason to avoid doing so if you can. Minicomputers and similar, such as most UNIX systems, DEC's VAX and the IBM AS/400, generally use such networks as Ethernet or Token Ring. DEC's overall network management product, DECnet, is mature and easy

Table 14.2 Emerging communications systems.

Local:
- High-speed Token Ring - 1.4 MB/s
- FDDI/CDDI - 9 MB/s

Local and remote:
- ATM (Asynchronous Transfer Mode - over 10 MB/s eventually)

Remote:
- ISDN Frame Relay - 200 KB/s virtual circuits with guaranteed minimum rate
- Analogue transmission (V.32, V.42, V.FAST) - to 5 KB/s assuming compression
- Portable PC communications - standard modem plug, digital satellite (via GSM standard), modem sockets on public telephones

After many years of very sluggish development, communications are picking up speed. The setting of standards still poses problems, and it may be a few years before a convincing one emerges regarding mobile data. The cost of high-speed links is still very high, and unless it drops sharply many users will be inhibited from sending too much data over such facilities.

enough to use for the product type it is. It is consistent over both local- and wide-area networks, simplifying learning effort and on-going management.

UNIX systems generally use the TCP/IP protocol atop basic Ethernet wiring and message control. Depending upon the supplier, a variety of native management systems are available. A reason UNIX networks are not seen as particularly easy to run lies in the targeting of UNIX systems wholly or in part at very technical situations. In a manufacturing environment, for example, there may be many types of machine connected to one network, some UNIX, some proprietary. The environment may be demanding, with electrical noise, dust, humidity, high temperatures and anything else undesirable that one can throw at computers and their cabling systems. Software may be non-standard, partly to handle unusual machine control devices. Moreover, the very technical people usually – and often necessarily – associated with the UNIX world may devise more intricate solutions than are strictly needed. All of which make for a monumentally unsound operating environment, however theoretically necessary only some of it may be.

A fundamental point about local networks is that they vary enormously in their success. If one chooses a limited set of simple products and keeps data traffic moderate, they can be quite easy to use. If one does the reverse, then understandably the results are opposite. In other words, tight control is mandatory, more so here than in many other areas of downsizing.

Wide-area networks

Aside from being slower, wide-area networking relies upon a wider range of technologies, and one is at the mercy of those outside the organization which serve as public carriers in a particular country. So gruesome is the wide-area scene in some areas and for some applications that one might consider remarkable 'low-tech' alternatives. One organization comes to mind where sending a tape in a van about 50 kilometers down the road was actually cheaper and faster than sending a few Mbytes of data down a line using the primitive X.25 protocol. Other possibilities might include sending a few diskettes with the end of the day's data by post.

However, if data in the tens of Mbytes per day from one site needs to be transferred reliably, or if quick and unexpected access to data at other sites is needed, then one is usually forced into the leasing of lines in some guise or other. In most advanced countries, there are many network companies operating, and these in turn buy line capacity from the basic-level telecommunications provider or providers for that region.

One can thus buy a wide variety of packages, from the basic line service through to total facilities management for the communications side of the business. Prices obviously vary accordingly, though it is true that here, as elsewhere in computing, you do not necessarily get what you pay for. Many organizations add substantial overheads to the more basic services which they sub-contract, and value added by the prime contractor may or may not be proportional to these extra overheads. A good rule is to talk to the lowest-level supplier first, and only if it is clear that they cannot provide the service one expects then go up one level to talk to a more expensive service provider.

If one is undertaking wide-area communications directly, and not through a services provider, there are only a few options that are meaningful today. IBM's Systems Network Architecture (SNA) is the dominant product in the corporate market. However, for many years, IBM assumed that a large mainframe would be the centre of the networking universe, and only recently has the system been adapted to networks of smaller, simpler products. This simplified version is conceptually very much like Digital's DECnet, and like DECnet uses a peer-to-peer rather than a master–slave relationship (its initials, APPN, stand for Advanced Peer-to-Peer Networking). The AS/400 is the main product using this newer version of SNA, and experience to date has established that it is as easy to use and as trouble free as any of its type. However, such networks in general are suited only to light to medium traffic, and it should not be confused with its larger sibling. IBM's protocols on its local- and wide-area networks are similar (SDLC, meaning Synchronous Data Link Control) simplifying much of the software involved.

DEC'S DECnet, the first easy-to-use general networking product to appear on a wide scale in the market, is also a light to medium usage item. It is now well established, and has reasonable interfaces to other systems such as IBM's SNA and public standards such as X.25. Its main problem is that it is Digital's proprietary product (though it is closer to some open standards than are some other such

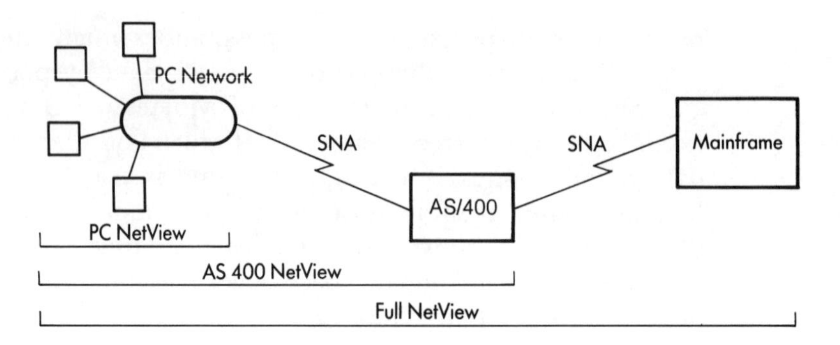

Figure 14.1 Network management.

Network management is a highly involved area, especially where many types of machine, operating system and communications protocol are involved. The more homogeneous the network, including all its attachments, the easier it is to manage, and users should keep this in mind at the beginning when they are configuring product policies. The theoretical 'interoperability' so touted with open systems is today far from a reality. Because of its experience with large, complicated communications systems, IBM has the best-developed set of network management tools, variously called NetView or SystemView depending upon how it is packaged. One can acquire subsets of the product should one be interested only in PC network management, or in AS/400 networks (the latter including any networked PCs attached). The IBM product works best with IBM's own platforms and protocols, though some management functions (for example, spotting alerts) are usable from DECnet and TCP/IP networks. For PC networks on their own, there are a number of products from small software suppliers which can perform a number of local network management functions.

offerings), and so is tied both to DEC's uneven fortunes and to the increasingly obsolescent VAX range.

The supposed international open standard for communications across remote sites is the OSI protocol (for Open Systems Interconnect). This is now available from most major vendors, but because of its newness most organizations are using earlier, lower-level protocols (such as the TCP/IP already mentioned) or sticking with proprietary options. As time progresses, more OSI will obviously be used, though it may be a slow effort.

The user's choice of wide-area products will thus depend upon whether he wants to outsource the lot and what proprietary product he may already be using. The basic proposition is that one should be as open, simple and cheap as possible in view of application needs. As with other areas of downsizing and computing in general, this involves conflicts which must be traded off against one another. The basic overall downsizing message remains: the best communications is the least communications. Design accordingly if you can.

Key issues

- In any distributed scenario, recognize in advance that communications might represent a conceptual third or more of the problems encountered. Pay attention accordingly.
- In considering network sizes, try to avoid an excessive number of very small local networks, in order to minimize administrative overheads.
- Pay close attention to capacity planning as it impacts both local and remote networks.
- Maintain strong pressure for a single in-house standard for both local- and wide-area communications.
- Consider outsourcing the company's communications effort, especially where much complexity and diversity exist.

15

Designing distributed data

If we are to combine the themes of the last two chapters (database and communications), distributed data results is a separate enough topic to merit some consideration on its own. Full downsizing invariably involves at least some distribution of data to locations which need it. Because of the combined complexities of communications, database and applications themselves, data is often distributed incorrectly. In many downsizing disasters, inappropriate distribution of data has played a major part.

The first point to be realized about distributed data is that distribution itself should be minimized in the sense that an item of data should be in a single place if at all possible. Here, as nowhere else, does our point regarding the 'almost standalone' system hold valid. It is worth forgoing a fair amount of theoretical functionality to gain the simplicity of the environment with one record in one machine.

However, in many cases this cannot apply. In the complex organization of today, many parties in different locations may need the same data items. Where they do so with urgency, or where many need to change data, a degree of distribution (or replication) may be necessary. Many of those dealing with distributed data, as with the basic database products, tend to overdesign, and to use facilities that are not strictly needed. With distributed data, the penalities for overdoing things are much more severe than in standalone environments, and in areas that range from machine and communications overload through to complicated system operation. Database products are moving rapidly to handle distributed data more efficiently than they used to, but this is not a reason to plunge in over one's head.

There are several distinct degrees of distributed data (see Figure 15.1) and it is important to use only the minimum required

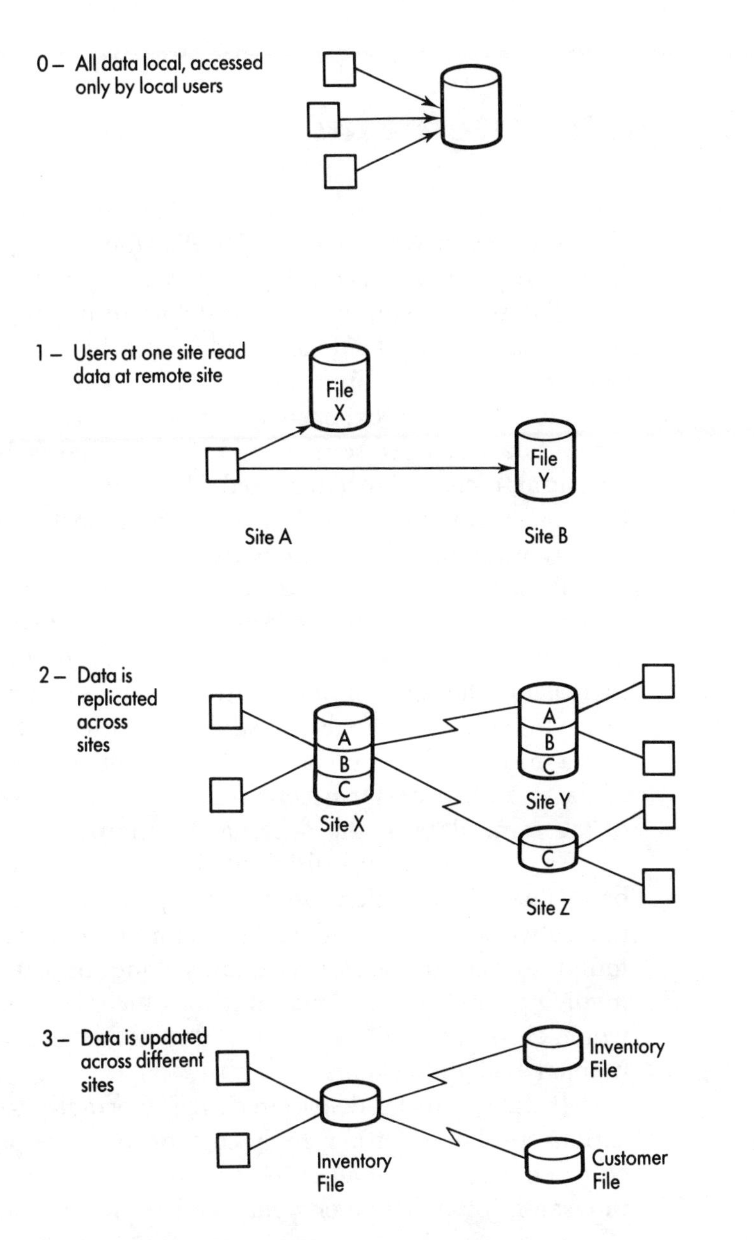

Figure 15.1 Degrees of distributing data.

for the given application. As distributed technology improves and the underlying machine and communications resources become cheaper, then it will become more feasible to distribute for more marginal benefits.

Why distribute data?

Before considering the details of distributed technology, designers should consider why they need to distribute data, rather than leaving it in one place and accessing it down a remote line.

The relationship between the communications system and database should always be deliberated upon whenever the distributed data question arises. In some cases, a faster communication line, though undoubtedly more expensive, will avoid the need for spreading the same data out over several nodes, thus saving both machine space and human costs. Once installed, the faster line will normally involve little more complexity or human effort than the previous slower one did, so most of the cost increase will be in line rental.

If data is likely to be distributed in terms of duplicating or replicating data, then the full cost of the distribution effort must be considered. The extra human cost might involve setting up or increasing the size of the central database administration unit in order to look after the technical complexities of the new data system. Extra procedures may be needed to ensure security and integrity of data, and to perform consistency checks between different copies of the same data at the different locations.

In particular with distributed data, a 'disaster' scenario should be evaluated, in which lost or corrupted data at several sites within the network would need to be restored. This restoration might be found to require an unacceptably long time (one has seen cases involving a number of days), during which the business units involved would either be off the air or forced to devise and operate cumbersome manual backup systems.

If data is to be distributed, it is normally to solve a communications problem (either high cost or poor response times). If the cost penalty on a small system is going to be in the several tens of thousands of dollars per year, and if the distributed alternative is one of the simple ones (say, replicating read-only data), then distribution is usually worth considering without too many qualms.

Though many eminent theoreticians will disagree (understandably on theoretical grounds), we have found it very difficult to find many situations out in the real world where the benefits of complex distribution of data were greater than the risks and costs involved (by 'complex' we mean the replication of several copies of modifiable data). Undoubtedly, the costs and risks of multiple-update distribution will

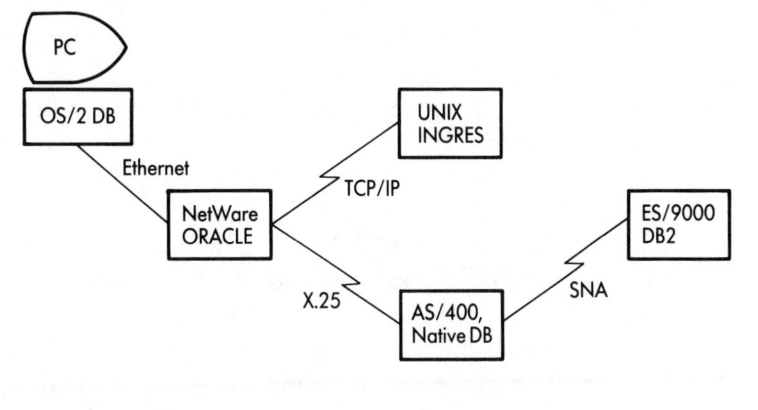

Figure 15.2 Date's concepts.

Database authority Chris Date specified a number of rules he thought should apply to distributed databases. In broad terms, the concept is transparency across all major system components, such that the user can retrieve or alter data at any site, local or remote, without being aware of either location or technology. When Date's rules become effective, the PC user in Figure 15.2 will be able to issue statements in SQL (either directly or via a package), and the data he wants will simply appear or be updated as if it were on his local PC. The fact that different operating systems, databases and communications protocols from different suppliers exist within the network will not inconvenience the user, as he will not be aware of them.

fall, but the development process here has been a relatively slow one. Prospective users are not advised to wait for great leaps forward in the technology, as they may not arrive.

Types of distributed information

In a local-area or client/server situation, some simple distribution of data is both inevitable and straightforward. Transfer of relatively high volumes of data, and recovery from corrupted files, are made easier by the rapid communications available. Such transmissions might be between two servers, or between a workstation and a server. Here, the close control offered by what is effectively one overall system helps to keep errors and malpractice in check. With powerful workstations now available, and with reasonable amounts of disk storage on them, it is feasible to hold many types of file within the workstation. If network or server performance becomes variable during the day due to heavy peak loads, one could copy, say, customer master information, price tables and common inventory information into the various workstations at the beginning of the day. In the ideal case, this would be treated as read-only information by the workstation, and actual updates to master files on the server would be done either during the day or at the end of the day, depending upon requirements and system loadings.

In either local or remote situations, the copying of a subset of a file to the distributed node may be feasible. If only active customers and items are sent to local systems, this will cut much transfer time and would shorten any recovery procedures. Distributing only part of a record is also feasible. Most information is static and required for reference purposes, and distributing such information may be simpler than sending whole records or files and then trying to reconcile updates at the end of the day. In other words, if item descriptions, shipping weight, and so on, are sent to local stations, and if all changes in quantities on hand are updated on-line centrally, then there is no danger of files becoming inconsistent.

Controlling distributed data

If fully distributed data really does need to be implemented, especially across remote communications links, then care in product selection and usage as well as in designing control procedures needs to be exercised.

Most database packages on the market now support what is called 'two-phase commit', which means essentially that the updating of a number of records at different sites can be done securely within one overall transaction. If an error occurs (such as a communications fault or a machine failure) during the multiple update, then the entire transaction is reversed at all sites involved so that the data across the several locations is logically consistent and as it was before that particular transaction was initiated. Some database products are longer established at this type of work (INGRES and the OS/2 database spring to mind), and this maturity is important in view of the technical complexity and the performance issues involved.

While the database software should look after the strictly mechanical side of things, care must be taken that end users and those operating the system know what has happened and can take remedial action if need be. While the database may be kept 'pure' from the database product's point of view, the failure of an important updating transaction may require re-running of applications or alternative procedures to keep the business on an even keel. In the rush of the end of the day procedures or during peak business activity, it is easy to overlook such problems, or to be unaware of the full import of what has happened.

Monitoring distributed data

15

Communications systems are by their nature difficult to monitor. Users can suddenly acquire expensive habits that were unanticipated, and various types of peak loading can overwork a normally under-utilized system. Distribution of data can add to these monitoring problems, especially if the data is distributed badly. Access and updates to remote files may be much greater than planned, adding to communications loads and to server or mini node activity.

Communications monitoring tools, though sometimes expensive to run and demanding a certain level of expertise to operate, can give insights into data activity as well as that relating to other types of traffic. While we have stressed the performance overheads of updating remote files in volume, simple but heavy-volume retrievals from remote databases can also overload the system. In other words, just because some data distribution is easier than other types, one should not assume that the effect on line traffic is beneficial.

One culprit with database systems in general, but particularly with distributed ones, is the SQL language. Taken beyond the very simple enquiry level, it becomes complicated to use, such that many users have absolutely no idea what they are doing to the system. The effect of this is often to request much larger numbers of records from remote machines than was anticipated, and this can tie up both networks and servers severely. Cases of several hours worth of

Table 15.1 The Distributed Relational Database Architecture (DRDA) standard.

- Remote request: one SQL statement accesses data at one remote site
- Remote unit of work: several SQL statements access data at one remote site
- Distributed unit of work: several SQL statements access data at several remote sites
- Distributed request: one SQL statement gathers information from several different sites

The technology to support distributed data is moving forward at a reasonable pace, though scarcely at high speed because of the software complexity involved. IBM's Distributed Relational Database Architecture (DRDA) standard represents one way of implementing progressively more stages of data distribution. The 'Unit of Work' (UOW) concept is effectively a procedure or task composed of several SQL statements, and the statements operate as a block at a given site (meaning that while operating at a remote site they would only process data from that site, then return the results to the requesting site). In broad terms across the industry, steps two and three in Table 15.1 are variously usable, depending upon which supplier one is dealing with. Aside from the actual functionality available with distributed database software, one should be careful about both performance and recovery issues, as with distributed data these can be involved.

heavy traffic spring to mind, simply because an SQL statement was coded in the wrong order or a 'not' was inadvertently omitted. Some database products or add-on products such as program generators anticipate this by allowing a limit to be placed on the number of records retrieved, or allow only so many records to be sent down the line at a given time, so freeing it temporarily for other users. It is vital that the system or data administrator in charge of a database sees that such limits are applied. It should be appreciated that where SQL is used badly, it not only ties up systems resources, it also wastes them and the user's time, as much has been wasted on a completely useless retrieval. Banning the use of SQL except in highly specific cases might be appropriate.

Key issues

- Encourage developers to appreciate the close link between distribution of data and communications layouts, and that the two together pose formidable system management challenges.

- Where an apparent need for duplicated data at different sites does arise, make doubly certain the need exists by modelling and costing such a system fully and in the longer term as compared with single-site alternatives.
- Where duplicated data is necessary, try to keep update levels from remote sites minimal, and preferably non-existent.
- Choose database products that have a track record in distributing data.

16

Designing downsized applications

One of the most important distinctions between the old and new IT worlds is their different approach to applications. The significance of these differences cannot be overstated. Most traditional IT people will miss many important points governing new-world applications. The result will be an only partially successful downsized system at best. At the worst, if complex, monolithic mainframe-style applications are imposed on small downsized systems, one will be faced with more expense and less control than applied in the old world.

Categorizing applications

The area of applications, though simple in many respects, still demands a reasonably structured approach. As a general rule only, downsized applications cover much more breadth and less depth than do their equivalents on the mainframe. Also, newer types of application are run on downsized systems, further broadening the application spectrum.

Downsized systems vary widely in what they are expected to do. Most, at installation, undertake relatively simple jobs, especially if the application is a new one (not converted from the mainframe). A cautionary point is that, as time progresses, the spectrum is likely to widen. A system that starts off, say, with some low-volume transaction processing may later need to move to information handling and office applications. Some forethought is helpful in considering into which new areas the range of applications is likely to expand. To keep this diverse environment manageable and within its budgetary limits, a number of complementary techniques can be employed:

- The use of applications packages, either generic or industry specific.
- Keeping designs for applications as simple as possible.
- Using the most productive development tools available and avoiding known low-productivity traps.

Most newcomers to downsizing do not spend enough effort in trying to categorize applications. This clarifying is useful, as the different application types both require different design techniques and assume different machine performance profiles. By quantifying efforts within each category, one can get a better picture of how both the people and the system will perform. A general list of application types might look as follows:

- Simple transaction processing.
- Complex transaction processing.
- Simple reporting based on predictable summary information.
- Heavy-volume and often unanticipated management information production.
- Word processing.
- Heavy document handling.
- Image processing.
- Voice and mixed media.
- Manufacturing process and machine control.
- Numeric-intensive work, including business spreadsheets.
- Housekeeping utilities - archiving, backing up files, consistency checks, and so on.
- Disaster recovery programs.

Where much work is being done within a certain area, it will be worth dividing the appropriate group into sub-categories in order to get a better picture of requirements. A marketing department, for example, might want to produce brochures, catalogues and price lists, all quite different in character and in length, and combining techniques from several groups (spreadsheet, image and text).

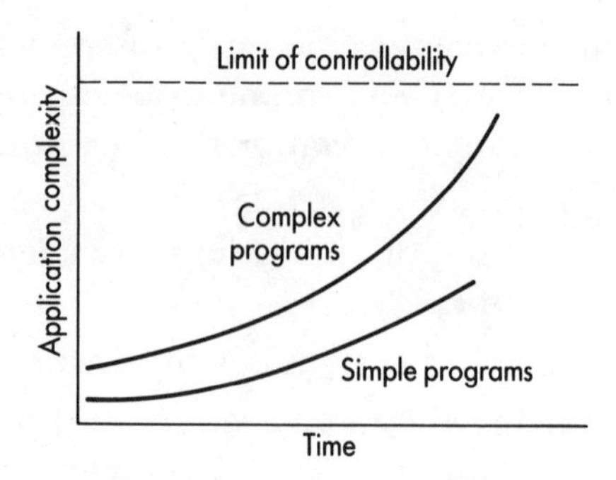

Figure 16.1 The need for simplicity.

The IT world is becoming ever more complicated. In many installations this complexity is near the limits of control. Only by simplifying applications wherever possible, is enough space created to render new applications feasible and to enable control to be maintained.

Assessing the application need

Most IT analysts, especially those of the 'give them everything' school, will ask what the user wants. The analyst will then go into the system design phase assuming that the application will be coded by traditional methods, using a mix of screen generators, third-generation (step at a time) languages and low-level database access to produce the programs. He will thus carry forward a complicated and unstructured request toward an equally chaotic solution.

Design in the downsized world should be of a broader scope. A wider variety of solution types is available, and the solutions vary widely in both character and cost. Moreover, such things as initial cost and ongoing cost can vary, depending partly upon how the product or program is treated.

IT goals in application design should relate closely to the general business goals of one's organization:

- The solution should be as cheap as possible, consistent with performing the business activity required.

- Part of the business activity is the training, motivating and encouraging of non-IT staff to use the system efficiently.
- Both of the above are long-term as well as immediate goals.
- The system should allow for change, with the least cost and disruption possible.
- The system should provide effective interfaces to other systems with which it needs to communicate.
- The system should be reliable. When faults do occur, it should be easy, quick and safe to re-start at the point immediately before the failure occurred. 'Reliable' here also means that the applications programs should be secure from either malicious damage or unintentional misuse.

As with all wish lists, compromises will be needed. The major trade-off in most designers' minds will be that between providing a high level of function and the simplicity that comes with a very basic core application. The trade-off applies whether packages are under consideration or whether the coding is to be done in-house.

In the chapter on project planning, some suggestions were made regarding packages and the use of generic packages (such as word processing and spreadsheet) to replace coded applications. By looking at the application's actual need, rather than how the system designer feels like meeting it, one can use these packages in a wide variety of situations. Many reporting systems can be put together very

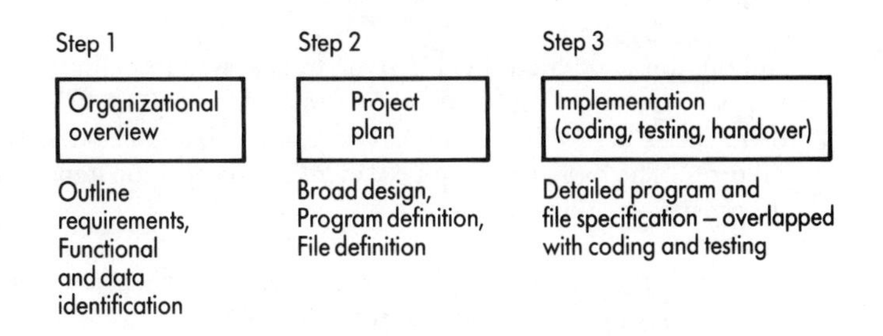

Figure 16.2 Applications and the project cycle.

The downsized project cycle is ambitious when it comes to designing and implementing applications. The process starts early and is progressed rapidly. It should be thought of more as a continuous process than one of start-stop stages. If the opportunity arises to jump the gun and begin work on the next theoretical stage, then it should be taken. Though there is some risk of wasted effort if the project is cancelled, the amount of time wasted will be small in relation to the rewards of having accurately defined the application in good time.

quickly by extracting the summary sections of a spreadsheet program and then including them into a document. In general, using text is a high-productivity technique anyway, as it avoids many of the inconveniencies and restrictions of using fixed-length character fields. By combining text usage with packages adept at handling such data, one is saving effort in two ways.

Similarly, spreadsheet programs can handle a wide range of accounting and reporting tasks, and they can do so better than many programs written by users. The packaged PC product is not necessarily inferior or more limited in function than mainframe-type in-house creations; in many respects (cost, function, presentation ability) it may be vastly superior. This is still another example of 'you don't necessarily get what you pay for' if one looks outside the downsized environment.

As a matter of design policy, when an application's needs come up for evaluation, generic and semi-generic packages (the latter including fairly standard invoicing and sales routines and similar applications used across several types of business) should be considered *first*. Such packages are well known and it should not take

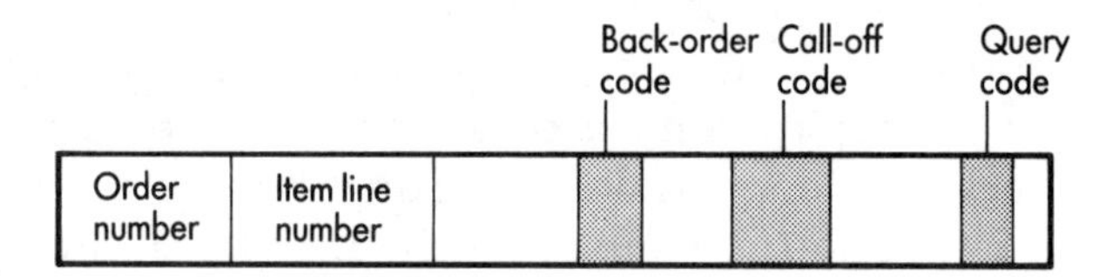

Figure 16.3 The role of identifiers.

Building in good identifiers is basic to any system definition. In downsizing, under the pressure to get results quickly, such work may not be done thoroughly, and any deficiencies here will undoubtedly cause trouble later on as the system expands and matures. The basic problem is to identify any specific item that may require it. Such items may include:

- Products, where individual items may need to be specified by a serial number or other positive identifier.
- Service agreements, including specific calls for service.
- Payments, especially where several might occur in a day.
- Errors.
- Customer or supplier queries.
- Changes to orders or item lines on orders.
- Documents, or parts of documents such as images or text special to that particular issue of the document (say, a special clause on an insurance policy).

long to determine whether they might fit a particular user need, however unconventional the context. A very large motor company recently put together a mix of generic packages to implement a highly functional reporting system for use across Europe. The implementation was rapid, economical, and did the job in hand well.

Simplifying application programs

Though packages provide simplicity, economy and a high level of function, they will still not fit every downsized need. In some cases, generally because of application requirements but sometimes also in order to gain acceptable machine performance, coding of some type will have to be done in-house. In these cases it is important to spend the right amount of time during the design phase trying to simplify the programs. This can mean a number of things:

- Reducing the number of programs.
- Lowering the size and complexity of programs.
- Organizing the inter-relationships between programs so that the system is easy to develop, understand and maintain.

The simplifying of applications often gets lip-service, but one also needs to push the concept aggressively in terms of *how* it is done. It is pointless to tell traditional designers to keep things simple when this is against their natural inclinations and when they have no idea how to do so anyway. To assist the cause, one can cite a number of techniques for application simplification that have proved effective over the years. The major steps in reducing an application's complexity are these:

- Reducing the size of the application overall by separating features that are not strictly needed but merely 'thought nice' by the user. A good designer will try to prevent these arising in the first place, as to reduce a system's scope can look like a broken promise. In other words, pre-empt where you can, and do not suggest extraneous items. If the user brings them up, 'consider without commitment' is the operative phrase.

- Postponing areas of the application that are not needed in the short term. It is characteristic of extraneous features that, however much people may say they desire them in the short term, many turn out not to be needed. Additional follow-on needs might be met in simpler ways or because a new solution type (say, a package) has become available. If the extra feature is usable across application groups, a commonly funded effort might take place when the need is perceived by several units rather than just one.
- Splitting up the application into a number of related sub-applications. This process has two benefits: it makes the overall group of programs easier to schedule and code, because modules of more manageable size are introduced; and it often makes it clear that certain modules can be either simplified or postponed.

Before the specification of programs begins, it is vital to attempt this last exercise diagramatically, in order to show users and other IT staff what might be possible. Figure 16.4 illustrates a convenient method for organizing components of a planned application. Specific examples should accompany each area, as these will help show users what is required and what is not.

The most important part of the dismembered application is obviously the core system. This should relate most closely to the business function in question. It will consist of programs which modify records on master files (such as customer and inventory), and it may create numbers of new records (order masters, item lines). With transaction-oriented applications, it should be easily apparent what comprises the core system. With other types commonly met in commercial computing, a general rule is that the core surrounds the essential record-handling functions – those where the designer has no choice. Where flexibility occurs, one should begin to get suspicious, as one is usually drifting away from the business purpose of the exercise.

One notes from Figure 16.4 that there are likely to be many 'extra' areas (this not implying that all are extraneous). The more areas that can be drawn, and the larger they are compared to the core application, then the more power one has in manipulating the components of the application. 'Size' might be expressed in number of programs in each area, the number of logical record accesses required or communications messages passed, or the number of user functions involved with an estimate of their complexity. If traditional coding techniques are used (say, in COBOL), then an experienced

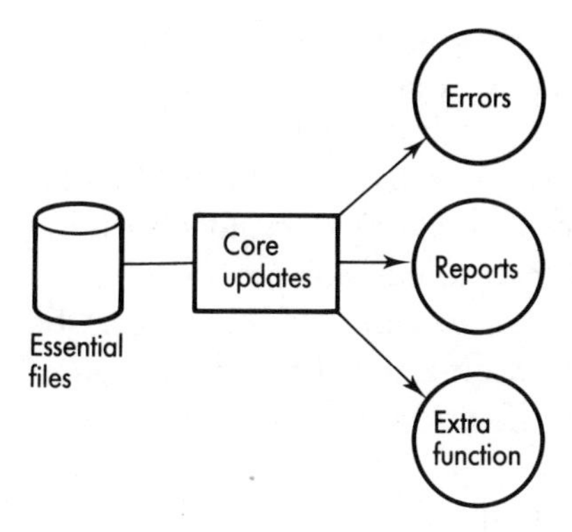

Figure 16.4 Splitting the application.

The modularizing of an application makes it easier to understand and helps to develop it over time in a smooth and consistent fashion. Most applications can be broken down broadly into the areas in Figure 16.4. Within each area, an immediate and a longer-term requirement should be evident.

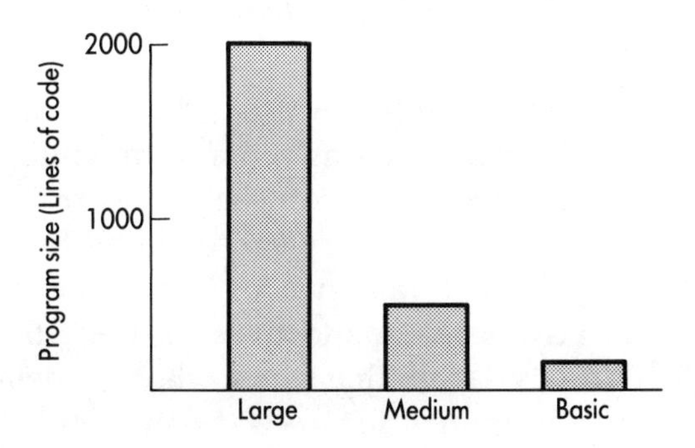

Figure 16.5 Estimating application complexity.

There are several methods for estimaiting the size of a program. Broadly, size is related to complexity, though for non-standard application types the relationship may not hold. Such measures as lines of code equivalent or function points are common. A function point is effectively a major file update, and will typically require nearly a day of a programmer's time to code. Where lines of code are used, 50 lines per day (including all testing) is about what most programmer's would achieve, though with a good program generator they could double or treble this (and productivity using function points would of course also go up by an equivalent multiplier). However, productivity in programming is not a linear phenomenon. The large 2000-line program shown above might take more than four times as long as the 500-line medium-sized one. The 200-line basic-level program, especially where a productivity tool is used, could take less than the theoretical 40% of the time needed for the medium one, and might require only 5% of the effort needed for the large program.

designer might be able to estimate the lines of code likely for each program and so provide a very accurate estimate of the effort required. Such estimates may be possible where program generators are used as well, if a 'COBOL-equivalent' estimate can be made, then translated into actual effort likely with the new tool.

Once the various pieces of the application are apparent, one can go to work on them. The core is likely to be relatively irreducible, though as a matter of course one should always examine it with a view to simplification. Because this is probably input/output intensive, gains in response time and machine overheads might be possible if it can be simplified at all. Advice in broad access techniques might be obtained from central database support, both to ease design and programming and to gain performance.

Any portion outside the core of the application may be subject to negotiation. There are three basic tactics:

- Postpone some of the features, either to a definite or indefinite future date.
- Agree with the user that some aspects are more important than others, and so politely agree to abandon the unimportant ones.
- Agree with the user which whole non-core areas might be implemented as separate modules not necessarily to go live at the same date as the core. If whole modules are not postponable, try sub-dividing the model and agreeing which elements are needed when the core goes live. This is not the same manoeuvre as the first one on the list, as it is envisaged that these slightly delayable items will only be postponed for a very short time (a few weeks at most), and only in the event of an unexpected problem. This strategy enables the core application to go live on the scheduled date with greater certainty, both aiding the business and preserving the system's credibility. Such areas as reporting, error handling and follow-on functions can often be postponed in part for a short time without impacting significantly the main application.

One technique for simplifying designs is to involve the user more directly in design. If the user can be persuaded to draw diagrams, or to provide a structured and prioritized list of what his application requires, these main benefits are likely:

- The requirement will be stated more accurately.
- The user will have more commitment to the design.
- The design is likely to be simple, partly because the user is not trained to think in terms of needless computing complexity and partly because he is doing the work instead of you and is therefore likely to do less of it, concentrating mainly on essentials.

One feature of users' outline designs which this writer has noticed is that, for simple online programs, they are often better in many respects than those produced by so-called professionals. There are several reasons for this. Reasonably IT-aware users are used to working both with forms and with simple screens, and tend to think of the immediate task which they need to perform using such media. Also, many IT professionals still think partly in batch processing terms, or in terms of relatively rigid block-oriented screens rather than more interactive types of terminal (such as conversational screens or windows). Those with batch or block-mode mentality tend to try to do too many things at once, rather than one thing at a time in a series of events. Even assuming one gets to the same place at the end, in programming terms it is undoubtedly quicker and cheaper to do the series of simple events rather than using the blockbuster approach.

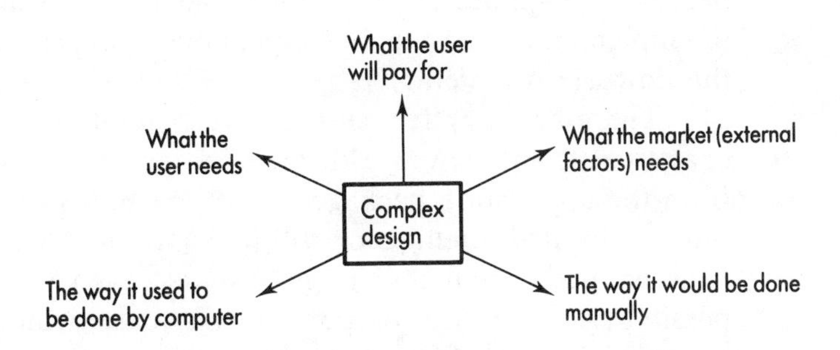

Figure 16.6 Techniques for simplification.

If an application design turns out to be too complicated in view of what might actually be needed, there are a number of related techniques that can be used to reduce its intricacy. All involve looking outside the application to other measures. The point should be made to whoever designed the application that he should have looked at these in the beginning, and so not wasted time by necessitating the shrinking exercise.

The complex-core application

Despite all the above pious hopes and simplification/postponement techniques, the designer will, more frequently than he wishes, come up against applications which are complex. There are two common categories of these:

- Applications which are already running on the mainframe. These may not *need* to be complex, but at the moment they are.
- Applications which really are inherently complex. Net-change materials requirements within a manufacturing context is one such. Applications which need to track components over long time periods, when groupings or definitions may have changed in the meantime, are also complex (these too can be found in manufacturing and many product analysis applications, and also in financial accounting).

In the first of the above instances, the complex mainframe application to be moved to the downsized system, the first question is: convert or re-systemize? The traditional IT person will instinctively opt for conversion, thinking in the back of his mind that, because the application took three elapsed years and fifty man-years to implement, it would be impossible to repeat the experience for the downsized system.

There are very few classic mainframe-type systems that can be converted to the new world, and the market is full of bad examples from the application package side of the industry. During meetings, those of limited intelligence will be heard observing that, if COBOL runs on both small and large systems, then conversion may be a possibility. The other components (database, windowing, transaction monitor) may be different entirely, or completely absent on one of the machines, but an amazing percentage of people forget to ask about them. The large application may also have a batch processing component which will not suit the small environment. Error reporting and operational procedures are likely to be much too complicated for the smaller departmental unit and, even if they are not, the IT support load for the converted system would probably be too heavy for the user's budget.

In some cases, where the mainframe application has been written

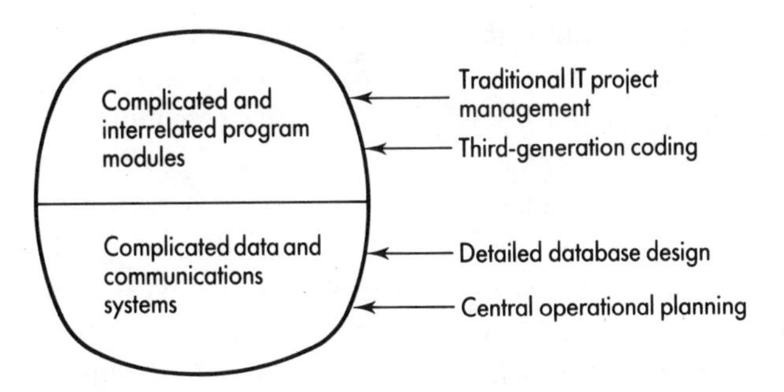

Figure 16.7 The complicated downsized application.

However much one dislikes the idea, there will occasionally be a need for a large and intricate application suite. The case for downsizing such an application may rest on cheaper machine costs or user proximity, though many other benefits will be lost. Here, one must revert to standard centralized ways of doing things, otherwise control will be lost. The logistics behind such projects are formidable, and so must be planned well in advance. However, if any downsized benefits are to apply, one should make certain that the traditional technicians do not get carried away and simply create another mainframe-type system. Downsized design and user-interface principles should still apply where possible.

in a modular fashion, and where the modules are relatively small (preferably in the hundreds of lines of code and not in the thousands), then conversion may be likely at least in part.

In the average case, however, one should be suspicious of any attempt to convert a mainframe system. Many such will be out of date anyway, and user dissatisfaction could prompt a redesign shortly after the costly conversion.

Windows and client/server applications

The two above concepts are both inter-related and new, and are of fundamental importance in the downsized arena. Most applications should place both items first on their consideration list, and only move to older and more unwieldy technologies where there is a clear case for doing so. Unfortunately, there is not a great deal of design expertise in either area. While tools supporting client/server (of which windowing is an integral part) are appearing on the market every day, there is a huge deficiency in experience.

There is a tendency to regard windowing as merely a workstation issue, and a simple one at that, to be isolated there while real designers turn their attentions to more important technology. The reality is that windows are a fundamental part of applications, impacting both the user's view of his application as well as machine issues far from the workstation. Bad screen design has been a feature of the online world ever since the first VDU was shipped. Regrettably, windowing design is following in its footsteps. In demonstrations of application packages, one sees a wide variety of windows designs. It is normally quite clear – to everyone but the designer – which are the good ones and which are the bad ones.

A basic point about screens and windows is that there is no one design style that will suit all user types; one has instead to look at the character of the job in hand. If a user (say, a foreign exchange dealer) does need a great deal of information instantly available (which means without changing screens or wrestling with a mouse and losing), then a full, intricate screen is justified.

However, the most common error in both screen and window design is the overly cluttered screen, with too many items, often too small, and too many different colours. For most commercial users, a small number of clear options, backed by lucid but non-irritating colours, are appropriate.

An overly complicated windows design is liable to result in many files and programs being open on a client, server, or both, and may on occasion also cause excessive loads on the communication system that links the two. Where complicated screens need to exist, extra care should be taken to simplify the underlying programs and file structures.

A basic problem with windows and client/server products is that one will rarely have much flexibility in the details of program design. Generators for programs are highly advisable in this environment, primarily because of the complexity of programming in low-level languages for any graphical interface, but also because of the economy and productivity in general offered by such packages.

Because of the limitations or specific characteristics of the actual program generator in use, one may be restricted as to feasible task structures. The desired general case is that each object within an overall screen design is connected to an object in programming terms, and that this object is open or operational for a minimum amount of time. Such modularities make programs – or objects – smaller and easier to maintain and also assist in achieving good performance. Otherwise, catering for numerous processing actions on both client and server can result in extremely large, complex and interlinked programs. Program maintenance and change, as well as development, will thus be difficult propositions for the small user.

Advantages of small programs

In considering matters of detail design, small programs are particularly desired where the updating (meaning change, modification or deletion) of disk-held records is done. If several programs or modules need to be active at once, perhaps because the terminal operator is on the telephone to the customer while an order is being entered and decisions are being made, then it is beneficial if only a few separate programs are handling master files in update mode.

An advantage of simple programs is that they are easier to understand by other programmers, and they are easier to document clearly. This is particularly an issue in the downsized environment, where many programs (typically several hundred) may be available to the user of a small system. If problems occur, the actual person who wrote the program may not be available (especially if the program is part of a package), and rapid action may be needed to amend or to bypass the fault. While IT support people should be available to maintain programs at short notice, the logistics of a few centrally located people and many programs out in the organization inevitably present a challenge. Designing programs for trouble-shooting and quick amendment should be a stated - and monitored - goal.

In virtually any computer implementation, there are great pressures to get things done quickly. This is likely to happen particularly with downsizing projects, as time-scales are short and any severe upset will, in percentage terms, postpone the live date substantially. When delays occur anywhere within an application project, it is the programming effort that is likely to be under most pressure. This is because programming is the final activity in the development of a system and is therefore likely to get most of the blame for the delay, whether justified or not.

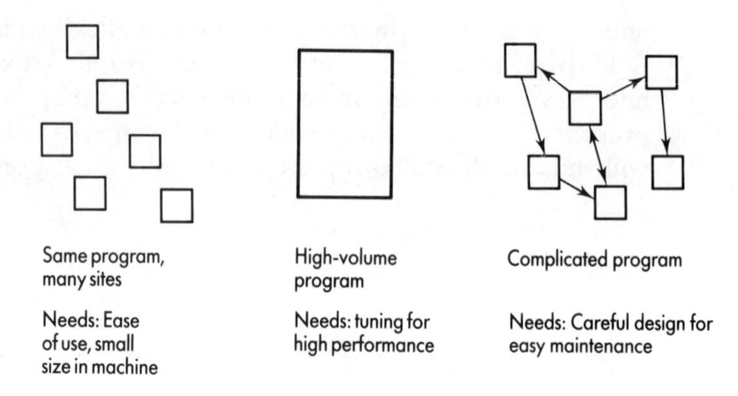

Figure 16.8 Different program needs.

The environment in which a program is to run is an important factor in downsized systems, as needs may differ. These environmental requirements should be thought of initially, otherwise the wrong types of program and file may be considered, and overall designs either changed later or not changed at all with consequent problems occurring. Three common categories are outlined above. Where a program fits more than one, extra care needs to be taken both in the design and in the coding.

Because programming is most likely to suffer under pressure, implying badly written code and inadequate documentation, it pays doubly to check that the outline design for the programs is as good as it can be. If most of the programs have been designed to be small and modular, this frees resources for any remaining complicated programs.

A point often missed regarding small programs in a small project is that they make the checkpointing of progress easier. Because each programmer will be writing a relatively large number of small programs, any delay will be easy to spot early in the project, whether it is a problem with the programmer himself or with the general approach to the programs.

Prototyping programs

A widely discussed technique in recent years has been the use of prototyping (also called protocycling) in the production of programs. The essence of the process is to involve the user in what is a combined design of the program and the actual programming itself. This is best done with a program generator of which there are many types on the market.

Prototyping is entirely valid for the downsized environment, as it speeds up development, gets the user involved in the details of design, and also trains the IT developer in the user's business. Like all techniques using advanced tools, it has its limits. Prototyping is generally suitable for small programs that are not performance sensitive. Enquiry and reporting programs in the management information area are one obvious target. What are sometimes called 'light-usage' systems are also generally suitable (classic examples of light-usage systems occur in the personnel area, where transaction rates are relatively low and a high rate of enquiry and reporting take place). Prototyping is also suitable in part for higher-volume systems. In most systems of any sort, windows or screen designs are a sufficiently important part to demand much attention from both user and designer. Tools which can set up, display and change screen layouts not only speed up design, they invite rapid feedback from the user so that a more appropriate design results. Speaking in generalities only, where most program generator tools fail is where complex disk input/output processes are required within a single application task. Programs performing more than, say, ten or fifteen straightforward record accesses, a third of them being updates, represent a cautionary boundary for high-volume transaction processing.

16

Key issues

- Application design is one of the key success factors in downsizing, and the best available analysts and designers should be assigned to the area.
- Classify applications carefully in order to obtain a concise picture of coding and performance profiles.
- Consider non-standard ways of implementing applications, such as the use of generic packages or standalone PC packages.

- Design for easy incorporation of change later on, as the demand for change is likely to be high in most downsized systems.

17

Management information in the downsized world

Among the more traditional application areas, that of management information has caused IT managers problems disproportionate to the modest results normally achieved. Downsizing can greatly assist the provision of management information in two ways. Indirectly, it furnishes an excuse to drop bad practices and to re-think requirements. Directly, it provides managers with the benefits which downsizing provides to other applications: concise results under user operational control, and at bargain prices to boot.

It must be recognized, first of all, that management information is a contentious area where downsizing is concerned. One has noted the role of the large information centre as a prime defender of the mainframe faith, and of the associated corporate database, which is assumed to be a monolithic entity that must reside on one large central machine. Not only the traditional hardware vendor, but also many IT staff defending careers and empires, can be expected to object vigorously to any proposals for change.

An initial point to establish therefore is that management information is inherently as distributed as any other type of application. No single user needs or even wants access to the entire pile of data on the information centre; the programming to handle it would be unfeasible anyway. Unexpected requests for management information – a prime justification for the information centre – generally relate to summary data within a particular user's area of responsibility. The desired data is generally of moderate volume, though in a disorganized situation much data may require examination in order to sort out the relevant records. Overall, management information obeys our primary downsizing rule: at a given time, a given user wants to do one fairly simple and straightforward thing.

The basics of management information

The reason why there is so much confusion about management information goes beyond the mainframe versus downsizing argument. The simple fact is that neither business managers nor IT staff understand the subject at all well. In the absence of any policy or guidelines, the natural tendency is to throw all of the data thought remotely pertinent to information production into one great pile (the information centre), then to close one's eyes and hope for the best. The information centre concept, now over ten years old, has been at best a mixed success, and a very expensive item for what it is. With planning and organization, things could be much better. Thus, to downsize management information successfully, planning and organization must take place, and admittedly in a more challenging area than transaction processing or office applications.

A basic problem about management information is that, as few understand it, no one takes charge of it. Both general managers and IT staff begin at too low a level - that of the actual data floating around an organization - and so fail to address the actual business requirements for information. Certain groups have been good enough about specifying relatively low-level reporting of information in their

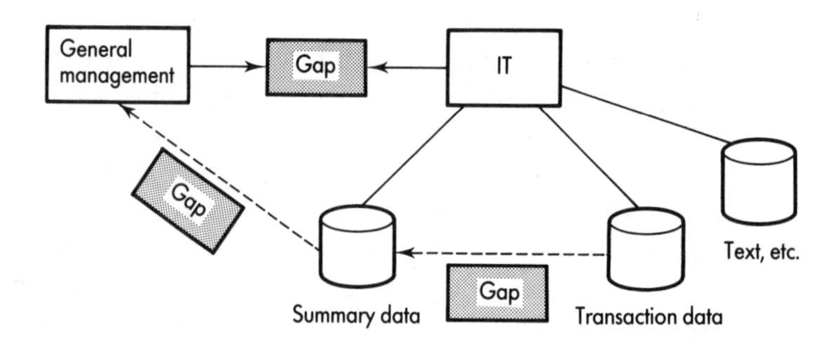

Figure 17.1 Management information and the management gap.

Management information has never been one of computing's happier areas, and the reason is simple. In most organizations there is no real management of the management information function. Senior managers are of the pre-computer era or are otherwise too occupied to concern themselves with information management. IT people rarely have insights into management mentality. While downsizing can help to solve management information problems in many ways, one still needs very astute and experienced business analysts to manage the management information function on behalf of both IT and the business at large.

particular areas. Accountants and production managers normally have a fairly good idea as to what monthly summaries they need in order to keep track of the basics.

It is when one gets to higher levels of management information, or meets requests that may span areas of senior managerial responsibility, that the problems start. One has seen several cases of senior managers, when baffled by the question 'What data do you wish to store?', simply reply 'Everything', because no other answer springs readily to mind. When one, perhaps tactlessly, points out that 'everything' will cost infinity and take eternity to implement, one may not be that popular, though one is approaching, however circuitously, the notion of the information centre.

The basic point we are making here is that, to be handled successfully in any environment, downsized or not, management information needs to be organized from the level of *specific* requirements downwards. Even *ad hoc* information requests can be predicted on a broad scale if one knows the business and the user's likely interests, though the specific query eventually arising obviously cannot be foreseen. Only IT staff can take the lead in forming information policies, as general managers do not have the data-organizing skills to undertake the task. It is entirely possible that a given IT department also lacks the data-reorganizing tasks for management information. If this is the case, then by all means forget about the downsizing of management information and leave it where it is.

17

Information

Laying out a coherent high-level management information plan is not as difficult as many think, though it is almost never done. The best way to start such an effort is to define what may be termed subject areas of the business, at first ignoring actual organizational responsibilities and specific departmental layouts. Such subject areas will normally include Customers, Products or Services, Sales, Purchases, Production, Costs, Personnel, Assets and Premises. These areas are rarely defined initially. Instead, one waits until a request is made and then scrambles around over the entire universe trying to find bits of data that might (and equally might not) answer the

Figure 17.2 Defining subject areas.

Defining business subject areas on a theoretical basis (without much regard to actual departmental responsibilities) is more justified with management information systems than it is with transaction work. This is because most genuine high-level management enquiries relate to such subject areas, and also because head-office management information units are likely to shift responsibilities, making detailed mechanization of departments difficult.

question. In other words, if one does not think up the questions in advance, then the answers become more expensive, chaotic and possibly incomplete or inaccurate.

Because the broad questions need to be formulated first, downsizing management information can take much longer than would other types of system. Obviously, those in authority in different areas of the company need to be consulted when one is arriving at standard definitions, or even the components to a definition. For example, an item such as production cost may have varying definitions in different national subsidiaries of an international company. In one case it might include shipping and insurance to the port of embarkation; in another, production cost may end at the factory gate, and all further costs be termed distribution costs. Until a standard definition is agreed, it is difficult to answer the question regarding production costs of an item, because the answer will depend upon the assumptions of the person asking it.

In the real world, one must recognize the incompleteness of definitions and build systems that can handle at least some imprecision. This is more easily done with downsized systems than with central ones, as one is close to the department using the information and can pick up most assumptions involved. If one knows where imprecisions lie, one can build models that have all likely components of the definition in them, and can thus include or exclude them as needed (see Figure 17.3, which deals with the question 'How much oil is in stock?').

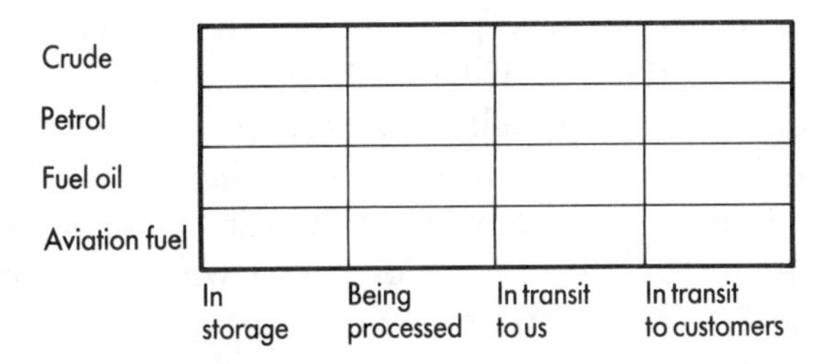

Figure 17.3 How much oil is in stock?

A senior executive of a large oil company asked his IT director the question in Figure 17.3. It took many weeks to answer, as no IT analyst had anticipated such a question at corporate level, however obvious. Had some pre-emptive summaries been put into place, the question could have been answered very quickly.

Distributing management information systems

The downsizer faces a number of options in laying out configurations of information-handling systems. The actual choices taken will depend as much upon organizational layout and practice as upon logical considerations. As management control is inherently a central function, one assumes the systems will be located near users in either international head offices or in more regional centres. Though subject areas, as suggested above, may be the neatest logical way of modularizing systems, the actual definitions of existing user departments may hold sway. What this means in practice is that financial controllers and accountants may obtain larger areas of control than departments such as marketing and customer service, partly because they know better how to specify information and partly because they have large and influential presences in most head offices.

However the physical topology of the management information actually turns out, it should not detract from the key activity of pre-emptive summarizing. While accountants do a certain amount of this, it is rarely done adequately in other areas. The tendency is to produce relatively rigid reports containing predictable topics, then to ignore the refinement of information not on such reports, however useful it is likely to be in dealing with unexpected turns of events.

In theory, distributed management information systems should be relatively quick to implement, once definitions are agreed. This is because of the fluid state of the program mix. Many information-handling programs are temporary or in a state of continuous amendment, and so may be replaced with little effort or disruption to the user. The limiting factor, as suggested earlier, is likely to be the scarcity of management information design skills. Topologies for distributed management information may not be as clear as for other applications. Also, pre-emptive summarizing of data is particularly important in the distributed environment, as otherwise one may have to access many separate servers in different locations with excessive frequency. The existence of a mature information centre within the business may enable some knowledge to be collected quickly, but even here some time will have to be spent in drawing order from a relatively chaotic situation.

Architectures for management information

The client/server type of system based on a local network is the most obvious solution to the distributed management information issue. Business analysts of various sorts typically work in relatively small groups on defined sets of data. Within virtually all medium to large companies, the PC is reasonably established as an analytical tool. The idea then is to establish a relatively small amount of summary data locally for the PCs to access, rather than have them offload from a larger and less exact mainframe pool. Once established, users should get much better overall response from the system. They will be dealing with an information analyst who knows both the user department's needs as well as the sources and meanings of the data on the server. Should other servers need to be accessed in neighbouring departments, this should be achievable easily and at low costs as well.

Distributing management information on client/server may frighten some people, especially if the risks are overstated by guardians of the old order. The concept of keeping all eggs in one basket, then watching the basket carefully, has a superficial emotional appeal. However, that is not what happens in practice. An excessively large

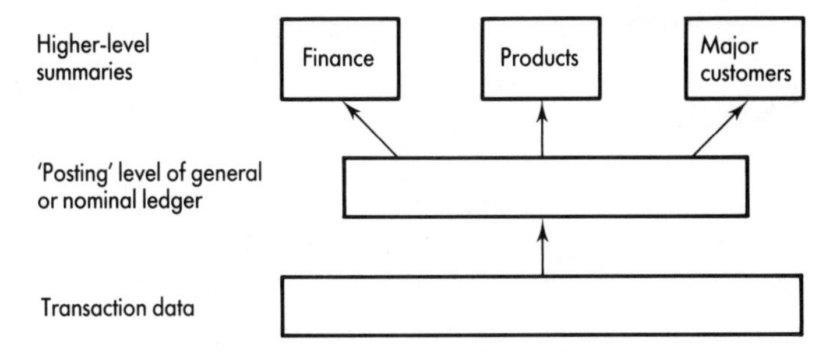

Figure 17.4 Accountacy ledgers and management information.

Many management information systems are dominated by accountants because the latter are the main body of numerate people in head office. Because ledgers are there already, there is a tendency for some designers and package suppliers to throw vast levels of detail into the basic, or 'posting', level of the general/nominal ledger. Both the data and the programs or packages to implement this approach can therefore be both complicated and disastrous regarding machine performance. Decentralizing and downsizing management information can make the modules more manageable.

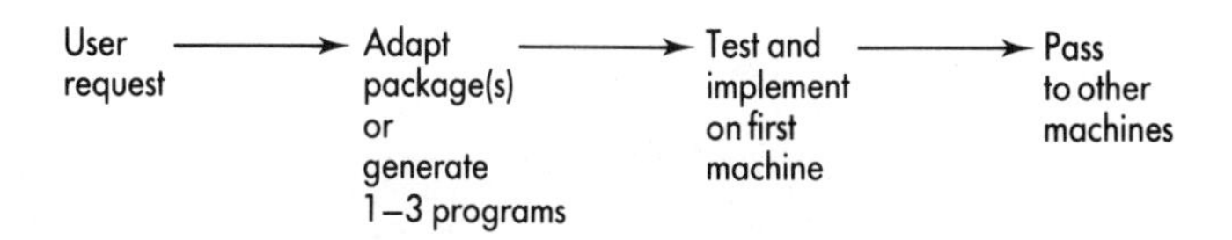

Figure 17.5 The one-day management information project.

The combination of local, simple data, packages or generators and a knowledgeable IT person in close proximity to the user enables downsized systems to achieve startling gains in development efficiency compared with traditional information centre approaches. We have seen many examples of the one-day (or even less) project diagrammed above. In the traditional environment, it might take a day or more simply to explain the issue to IT staff.

and centralized information centre simply becomes so disorganized that it defeats the purpose for which it was originally designed, and the cost of locating data rises sharply. By keeping data close to its owners, who understand it and can keep it organized, one, in fact, is increasing the security of good information. It should also be kept in mind that the data comes from decentralized sources in the first place (the transaction systems that created it), and this in no way impacts its security or credibility.

Key issues

- Try to bridge the gap between general management and IT by appointing a very senior consultant or manager to oversee management information as a single high-level area.
- Recognize that the information centre concept is only a partial (and by now largely out-of-date) answer to the management information question.
- Consider powerful PCs for management information wherever possible, as these give individual numerate users the independence they need. Complement these with local servers where large amounts of summary data are required.

18

The development environment and its tools

Early in the planning phases of downsizing, one should begin to think not only of the files and programs required, but also of the environment in which the application is to be implemented. This environment includes:

- The people from both user department and IT who will be closely involved in the project.
- Training and other preparation for both of the above personnel categories.
- Physical siting of the development effort, and how the people there communicate with their colleagues in either IT or the user area.
- How the project is monitored and controlled.
- What machines and software tools will be used for design, programming and testing, and for project management.

Older types of development tool still may be relevant to parts of the downsized world, particularly where a larger project on a minicomputer is under consideration. There are also newer items for newer products, such as windowing development products for the PC and UNIX workstations, and generators for cooperative programs on client/server systems.

Even in the old world there was much misunderstanding as to which tools suited which application types. Much of the confusion continues, both because people have not learned from experience and because people new to such tools may not make the fine distinctions required. Table 18.1 explains in approximate terms where some of the more common program generators and relational databases are targeted.

Table 18.1 Different tools for different applications.

Infomation handling	*Transaction processing*	*Some of each*
• AS	• ADABAS/NATURAL	• ORACLE
• FOCUS	• CSP	• INGRES
	• PRO-IV	• INFORMIX
	• POWERHOUSE	• SYBASE/SQL Server
	• RALLY	• BASIC
	• RPG	• MANTIS
	• USER LANGUAGE (MODEL 204)	

During the 1980s, on both large and small machines, many mistakes were made because users did not understand that high-productivity development tools were designed with very different goals in mind. Using an information-handling tool for transaction work may incur vast performance overheads, whereas using a transaction-oriented product for information handling will be unproductive in personnel terms. For the vast majority of downsized systems, the relational database is a good enough all-rounder. The big plus of such systems is that the databases are well integrated with the high-productivity languages and screen formatters included with the products.

Development tools are major items. They are complicated internally, require training in variable degrees in order to be used effectively, and their costs can be substantial. Sets of development software (sometimes including the relational database to be used for ongoing work) can cost in the tens to hundreds of thousands of dollars, depending partly upon the product and partly upon the size of machine at the user site. Even a PC product can cost twenty thousand dollars, especially if it is marketed by a direct sales force rather than promoted through dealers. Other PC products may cost under a thousand dollars, and these can be quite useful, if not the exact equivalents of the more expensive ones.

Developing with tools

Most old-world tools naturally presuppose the traditional IT environment, where developers sit in a separate location, well away from users, and talk with the latter only infrequently. Such tools require trained IT technicians, familiar with many details of screen formatting, programming code and database designs. The time taken to learn to use such tools, even assuming a trained IT person, is a matter of several months, though some products can produce simple programs with much less training.

Throughout the history of the downsizing movement, there is much evidence showing that most old-world tools do not migrate down the size scale that well to smaller machines, whether mini or PC. This is reflected in the collapse in sales of older fourth-generation languages (4GLs). The success of products such as ORACLE, INFORMIX, PROGRESS and others is based on their greater suitability to the smaller world. These are integrated products, combining the usability features of both relational database and fourth-generation program-generating technology, and are reasonably easy to use in relation to the functionality provided.

At a level down from the mini, development tools may be needed less or not at all, because of the aforementioned possibility of using packages. The various PC spreadsheets can in many cases compete directly with such items as FOCUS on the mainframe or ORACLE on the minicomputer. The essence of their superiority is twofold, and not simply due to the fact that no programs need be created. The second, often unrealized, benefit is that the spreadsheet organizes its information in a more comprehensible fashion than any earlier product type. Any accountant or semi-numerate marketing analyst can instantly recognize both problem and solution. This is not the case where more abstract data is being manipulated with an abstruse language, which is the case with most traditional program generators and relational databases. With the spreadsheet, one can actually buy the solution to the problem at a fraction of the price of even describing the problem in the first place – a trade-off still either not understood or stoutly resisted by many within the IT information centre.

Windowing tools

Software to assist in developing programs for the graphical interface (or windowing) environment is coming onto the market at a very high rate, such that by the time this is being read there will be

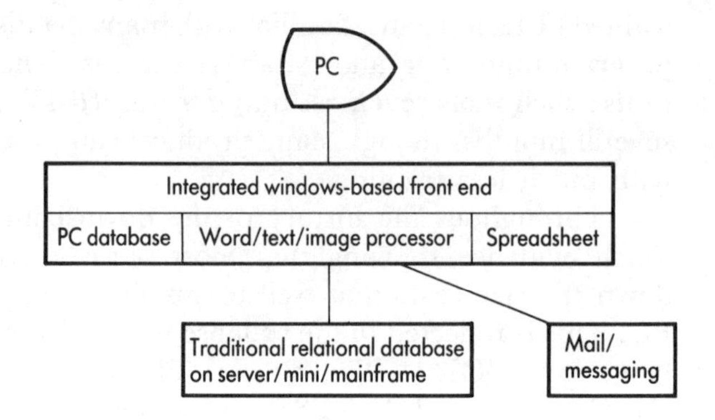

Figure 18.1 Developing development tools.

A rapidly moving area is the integration of generic PC products, such that the workstation user will be presented with a seamless front end for such facilities. This close integration will make more likely the development of application systems using solely generic products, where no actual program code is written. Even today, the use of generic products represents a powerful alternative to the detailed coding of systems, especially where text or information summaries play a high part in the application. The power of generic packages is much under-appreciated in the down-sized environment.

many new items worthy of evaluation plus improvements in existing products. Aside from adding new features and improving the machine efficiency of programs they generate, these products are trying progressively to cover a greater number of common platforms. The PC and one or more flavours of UNIX are common for a given product, the most common varieties of UNIX being those from Sun, Santa Crux Operation, IBM and possibly the two standards organisations (OSF and UNIX International).

With most new style development tools, especially for the PC and UNIX, support from the supplier is very thin. No software supplier can afford to sell products for a few hundred or even low thousands of dollars and provide the mainframe levels of support which many users still appear to expect. Aside from very basic support (bug fixing and telephone support for technical queries), users may have to look to outside organizations such as consultancies, dealers and training companies to get to grips with issues. Among the more current and difficult problems for many is windows design. As noted earlier, it is a rare skill, and with the high development speeds now available with window generators it is possible to create a baffling user interface with amazing economy.

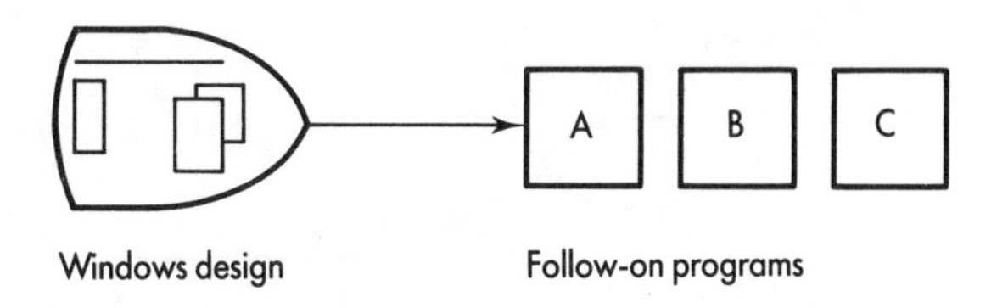

Figure 18.2 Development tools and project planning.

The use of small-system development tools enables task estimation and project control to be carried out more accurately and on a more dynamic basis than can be managed in traditional environments. A Windows prototype can give a good indication as to the complexity of the underlying application. The fact that the first few programs can be put together quickly will give a good indication as to how progress may be made during the remainder of the project.

End-user tools

In any downsized environment, the issue crops up as to which sort of tools are suitable for direct use by an end user. Depending upon which end user and which tools are being discussed, one gets a predictably wide variety of answers. In one sense, a lot of 'end user as programmer' nonsense has been going on since the dawn of computing (assuming, that is, that one believes the dawn has yet arrived). Because COBOL was similar to natural language, or because FORTRAN looked almost like real mathematics, it was supposed that end users could use these to program their own requirements. When this approach failed, the same expectations were trotted out when, in the 1980s, relational databases with the SQL language and a host of program generators entered the market. Such products were not so much an improvement on COBOL and FORTRAN, but instead they attempted to do different things. This was rarely understood by users and never by salesmen, hence the history of inappropriate use and the collapse once again of the end user as programmer theory.

The reasons for poor end-user experience with software tools demand some thought, as misuse and incorrect targeting blurred many messages that might be worth hearing. End users can in most cases do some things with tools, and a good downsizing policy will

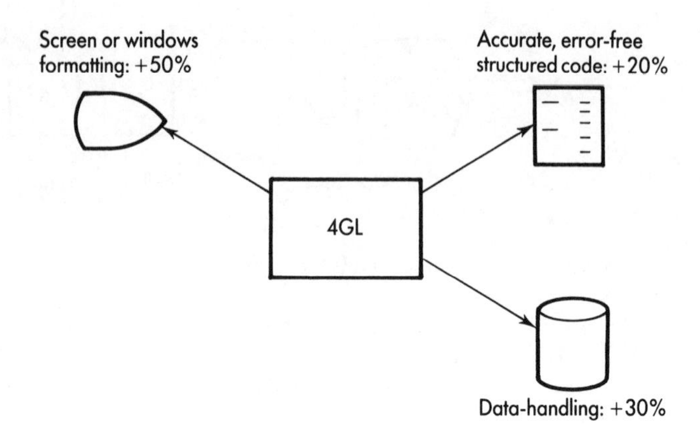

Figure 18.3 Productivity and the 4GL.

Though Fourth-Generation Languages (4GLs), also called program generators, have been around for two and a half decades, there is still a lot of misunderstanding regarding their selection and use. Most productivity gains come from areas other than raw coding, as illustrated in Figure 18.3 where one assumes that the 4GL delivers twice the productivity of coding on COBOL or an equivalent. The figure also illustrates why larger, more complicated programs are less suited to 4GL development. Generally, 4GLs cannot cope with intricate data handling, and the fact that actual coding is much the same in 4GL and third-generation languages means that productivity gains are less. Many downsized development products are well suited to very rapid development of small programs, but quickly lose effectiveness when applied to more ambitious efforts. A particular issue with small-system program generators is that many are very poor at self-documentation, again a minus where large, complex programs are required.

capitalize upon this and expand tool usage over time. There are several inter-related problems;

- No one, programmer or end user, can reliably write many lines of code, whatever the language. IT people, noting a user's difficulty with a product, generally forget that their own people cannot do much better. The point is that, once more than a few lines of code are written (few = 10 or 20), one has progressed from making a simple enquiry into the writing of a proper program. These programs require testing, because mistakes of several types will have been made (with the syntax, structure or data). When users test programs, they often complain and ask annoying questions of IT people, whereas when an IT programmer tests programs he either keeps quiet or else no one listens to him. Users who test programs may also use prime machine time, whereas the IT person may test in the lunch hour or work after hours.

- Users – and many programmers in fact – tend not to understand abstract data or metadata that well. A high percentage of a commercial program, no matter who writes it, will be concerned with data records, their relationships and the codes within them. With a program of any size, a high percentage of testing and debugging is due to testing the data manipulation aspects of the task. To a large degree, this is language-independent.

If end users are expected to program at all successfully, then there are four messages from the above experiences:

- Use the newer products, but those with a record established for end-user operability.
- Qualify carefully the end users who are expected to use these tools. He who uses a spreadsheet may not be able to use dBase or the SQL language. The SQL or dBase user in turn could probably not write a modest program in FOCUS or NATURAL. Even with substantial training, it is often impossible to make a programmer of any sort out of an end user.
- Keep the size of the programs or enquiry procedures within tight limits. Twenty statements is not an unreasonable limit for most end-user types. Programs over the established limit should be discussed between user and local IT analyst/programmer.
- Data should be presented as clearly and as simply as possible, 'simply' meaning, among other things, that it should be summarized in advance so the user does not have to worry about detailed extraction procedures. An enquiry or program handling more than three or four simple tables should usually be referred to IT.

There will be cases where the above rules can be extended, but in general one should not count on the sudden appearance of user enthusiasts capable of both writing and testing substantial programs. Users do learn over time, and the use of prototyping techniques, where the user sits beside an analyst/programmer actually using the tool, can speed up learning substantially. Certain aspects of programming, such as merely altering the layout of an

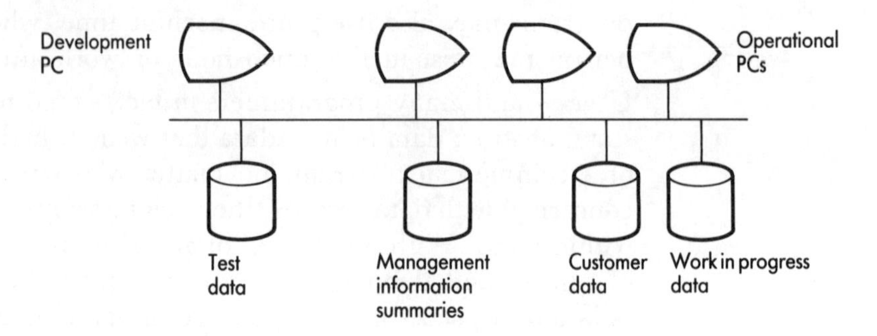

Figure 18.4 Development in the client/server environment.

Client/server architecture is ideally adapted to rapidly developing or changing environments, especially where management information systems need to be closely linked to transaction work. The layout in Figure 18.4 might apply to a section within a large organization, where high-value tailored products or services are produced for major customers.

enquiry screen or changing a detail within an existing windows screen, might be within the user's scope. Programs which only read data, rather than altering it, are clearly safer to leave in users' hands.

CASE and dictionary tools

While the software industry may be guilty of many things, understatement has never been among them. This particularly applies to the marketing hype put out by CASE, dictionary and repository suppliers during the late 1980s and early 1990s. Because the earlier tools such as the relational database and fourth-generation languages did not perform to expectations, the same vendors decided to add CASE and similar tools to their armouries to keep up the pace of attack (CASE means Computer Assisted Systems Engineering). This is again a typical example of the 'glue-on' mentality, where if the first product does not work then pile on another that might (or might not), so earning extra profit and filling up the hardware as well. As seen by most software vendors, the only alternative to gluing on the go-faster stripes is a fundamental reassessment of the foundation product, and that sounds too much like work.

The essence of the CASE tool is to act as a storehouse for systems design information. This includes codified descriptions of business processes, data designs and sometimes network details. The objective is to increase the productivity and accuracy of the design process and, by providing a central point of storage, one increases controllability as well. With some products, the data designs may be fed straight into the programming or enquiry process, thus speeding up these activities as well.

Some of the arguments for CASE-type products are sound. Because the downsized environment is both diverse and cost-sensitive, any automation of systems design and programming effort must be welcomed. However, CASE items come in a number of shapes and sizes, some of which are more relevant to new-world computing than others.

A main benefit of CASE is simply that it stores application-related information in one place, so providing a reference point for others within the implementation team. The tool is useful for maintenance purposes as well, as, long after the initial implementation, it can help to refresh memories on what the various application components actually do.

The choice of CASE tool depends in great part upon what other items have been chosen for the solution. If a relational database such as ORACLE or INGRES has been selected, then the CASE tools marketed as add-ons by these suppliers are an obvious choice (the tools offered by these two particular vendors are in fact quite reasonable). If development is based heavily on PCs, then a PC-based product such as EXCELERATOR would make sense.

CASE is still another area where new-world generic packages might replace more conventional products. Many CASE basics could be put into a text-handling package, perhaps with some quantitative information copied in from a spreadsheet. This would suit installations where most of the applications and systems were small and relatively unconnected, and where project budgets were on the slender side.

Key issues

- Choose development tools appropriate to the type of application being coded, appreciating that those who sell such products may have but an approximate idea of their applicability.
- Adopt an 'as little code as possible' philosophy. If packages are not suitable, use as high-level a programming approach as possible. Try to avoid any version of C, so-called 'object-oriented' languages and any direct coding of graphical interfaces.
- Where CASE or dictionary tools might look likely, consider simplifying the need so that generic text-handling packages can be used.

19

Implementing downsized projects

When a downsized project goes live and is handed over to the user, a number of points must be watched, as this is clearly a critical point in the system's existence. While the handover of a downsized project has much in common with going live anywhere else in computing, the very local nature of the solution and the fact that the user department may be expected to take charge of it focuses attentions mightily.

In a badly run project, critical faults may not emerge until the system is virtually live. Many of downsizing's planning and design activities aim to avoid exactly such situations. If an undue number of unpleasant surprises do crop up at the very end of the program writing and testing phase, thorough evaluation needs to establish why this is so.

What this usually means is that the application was not sufficiently known. Though in theory application knowledge is a joint user–IT responsibility, it is in practice up to IT to uncover and agree key details very early in a project (often before the detailed project planning phase actually begins). It is a very unusual user who either deliberately or mistakenly keeps the most important details of an application hidden. Where a disruptive change has occurred, then this should be evaluated as to its impact upon the project - whether to incorporate the change, delay the project until further implications are clear, or to ignore the issue for the moment. However, such business-driven changes are rare. A major objective of spending large amounts of time with the end user is to ensure that both needs and wishes are complied with. In the vast majority of cases where problems occur suddenly at handover, the analysts have simply not spent the time required with their users.

Key points to watch at handover are:

- Does the user understand the system as a whole, as well as the individual screens, programs and files?

- Can he handle interruptions, and resume work without losing undue efficiency or jeopardizing system integrity? This last includes not only data integrity but procedural integrity as well (the ability to complete without duplication any backlog due to the interruption). The sort of interruptions we have in mind may stem from the department's need to give priority to other work, a system failure, a switch in user operating personnel, the need to run work in an unexpected order, or the need to segment work because of unexpected volumes.
- Do enough individual users understand the system as a whole, as opposed to the bits and pieces for which they are responsible, sufficiently for them to undertake tasks in neighbouring areas in case of need?
- Is first-level management reporting data sent upstream for higher management understandable as expected? This is a key issue, as often such managers try to avoid getting overly involved in computing matters, with obvious consequences. If this basic-level management information is not clear, it could have an undesirable complicating effect on higher levels of information.

Obviously, all of the above should have been covered during the body of the development. But surprises will occur even in a well-run project, as no user or analyst can pay one hundred percent attention to his work. In a properly organized project, such items as emerge should be minor and able to be corrected at low cost. If more than, say, a few man-weeks are needed to correct faults in a basic project, then something is wrong.

Operational training and handover

In practice, operating a local system under day-to-day business pressures is more complicated than it may appear during the planning and coding-testing stages. This point itself should be made to users early on, in order to concentrate their attentions. If the application is necessarily complicated operationally, involving the running of many programs in set sequences as well as looking after involved backup and data communications procedures, then contingencies in operational training should be allowed for on top of a reasonable training budget.

For convenience in organizing the various tasks, operational issues might be thought of in two categories:

- System operation, where one is concerned with maintaining the basic machines, communications links and system software (database, operating system, and so on). This would include general backups and recovery of the system itself in case of failure.
- Application-related operation, where the aim is to deal with mechanized business-related procedures rather than those pertaining to the lower-level overall system. These would deal with procedures for end of the day processing, specific data transmissions and copies of data files needed for some particular business purpose. Application recovery would also be included within this group of activities – how actually to get the terminal user started again after recovering the basic system.

Where different people are carrying out the two different areas of operations, they must clearly cooperate with one another, especially in such closely related areas as system recovery and application recovery. The system proprietor will normally be responsible for system operations, either directly or via delegating it to a subordinate. Application-related procedures could be carried out by more than one person, depending upon how involved is the operational side of the application. It goes without saying that the person dealing with application-related operation should enjoy a high familiarity with the applications themselves, otherwise he will make mistakes under pressure which will be disastrous. In a small unit, one person (or the system proprietor himself) could carry out all aspects of operations. It still pays to keep the two areas of operations separate mentally, to clarify thinking and to facilitate both system and application changes. It may take some time for user operational procedures to sink in fully. Accidents are likely initially, when people are both nervous and unfamiliar with their system. They are likely later on as well, after people get into a routine which lulls them somewhat and when an unexpected crisis can catch them out. In such cases they will act without thinking, or will assume that someone else has done something, which in the confusion may not have been done.

As data transmissions are a particular source of trouble, it pays to test these well, and to refine or proceduralize steps which prove confusing. It is important to collect control information which is meaningful in application terms, though this may require extra work including additional programming. In other words, it is easier to spot faults if the user can see record counts by his definition of record, not just number of data blocks sent as the communications network understands them. Part-transmissions must be identifiable as such, and as quickly as possible otherwise the data to be transmitted may not be in a ready or otherwise appropriate state.

In a certain percentage of cases, a system will be installed which works satisfactorily in application terms, but which the user department cannot operate as envisaged. The initial tactic must be to try to teach the local personnel to operate the system, perhaps by leaving one of the analyst/programmers in the department for longer than envisaged. If after a week or two the problems still look severe, more drastic action might be considered. The options include:

- Moving the machine to an operational centre within the building or site. This might be feasible if there is already a machine room of some description on site. One assumes that it would be too costly to devote a single person full-time to operating the system in the user department, but in extreme cases this might be considered.
- Moving the machine to a location remote from the user's department. This might be feasible where high-speed communications lines already exist between the two sites, possibly with spare capacity. If the two communicating sites are close together, then an extra line should not be expensive – it would be much less than the cost of siting an operator in the user area.
- As a last resort, the application may have to be simplified. This may entail re-writing and re-testing many programs, and will obviously (and justly) lower the reputations of all concerned. This should be considered only where the alternative is to scrap the entire system. Cases such as this should be reviewed carefully, in order to prevent the same thing happening again. Complex operations are likely to have resulted from overly complex application design or not getting the initial topologies right – both very serious errors in downsizing.

One point which the IT staff supervising the handover should be encouraged to note is the rate of progress which users achieve in picking up operational matters. This will help establish how secure

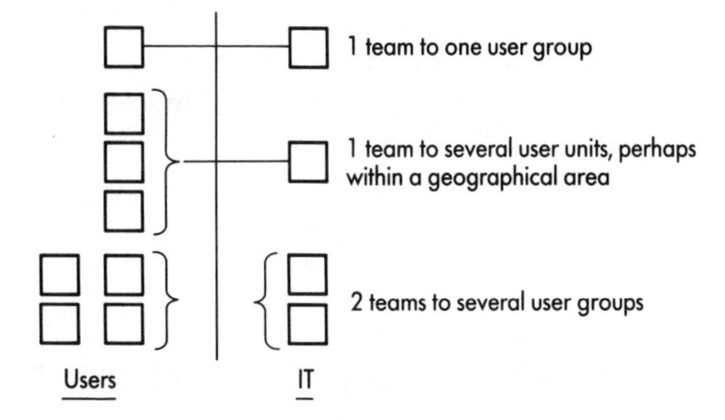

Figure 19.1 Setting up progress meetings.

During the later stages of the implementation phase, a system for holding ongoing progress meetings should be set up. Because of the need to economize in both user and IT time, several ways of holding these might be considered. Ongoing meetings are usually less intense and broader in scope than those held during planning and implementation, so it may be feasible to involve broader groups of users.

Table 19.1 Factors influencing support levels.

- Size (number of users and programs, capacity of machine)
- Complexity (size of programs, coding methods used, numbers of files)
- Homogeneity (one machine type and one software set, or several?)
- Activity (transaction rate, number of messages and documents processed and transmitted)
- Data volumes (in records or Mbytes)
- User types (how numerate, literate, experienced, neurotic)
- Location (distance, country boundaries)

He who has not downsized properly will pay a heavy price in the handover stage of the project and even more so when the system is fully operational. Even then, the users may not be particularly happy. If, nearing handover, any of the above items are much worse than expected, a two-pronged plan should be put into place, first to support the system, second to simplify it in the longer term if this is at all possible. Overweight systems, because of the dissatisfaction factor, tend to create more requests for enhancements (which may be disguised requests for simplification) than do their lean and mean cousins. Because users may identify development staff with some of the ills, changes in personnel either during handover or afterwards may be advisable.

and confident they are of their system, and the rate might be projected to estimate if they could handle more complex tasks in the future. One can use the experience to try to gauge more accurately the capabilities and learning rates of similar user departments within the organization. These estimates can then be used further to refine training and handover exercises, both saving costs and rendering later projects more effective and secure. It is very important that early operational experience in downsizing not be lost, but be noted and capitalized upon.

Altering people

At the end of any single project, it will usually be clear who was effective and who was not (in fact, to the observant eye much should be evident in the beginning). With IT staff in a small project, it is easy to see whose programs work quickly and how well any analysis homes in on the real issues. Difficulties arise when one gets higher up the IT chain of command or over into the user management area.

IT staff will usually have an accurate opinion of those with whom they work daily, but may not be able to form an opinion of user management. This is partly because project-level IT people may not have much idea of management anyhow, particularly in the user sphere. Regrettably, many managers, IT and non-IT alike, get where they are in large organizations simply by being elusive. This is a syndrome to watch for particularly where departmental managers and project sponsors are concerned. As a general rule only, when the project is under way it is unwise to try to force their involvement unduly, as it is often with good reason they steer clear of that which they cannot understand and may secretly fear. Such people, if forced into the project, may cause more damage and delay than is there in the first place. The project sponsor role is often suggested for a person because nothing better can be found for him at the moment – scarcely a recommendation for the dynamic problem-solver required in the role.

Within the IT area, the business analyst acting as project leader for the small project may not be that easy to evaluate. The systems development manager or project leader who supervises the business analyst should in theory be aware of what is going on and should examine the analysis and project progression taking place. In many cases this does not happen to the required degree, particularly where the project is some distance away from the central IT department. We suggested earlier that it is essential to keep the supervisor project manager overseeing the business analyst not too heavily loaded, otherwise he will not have the time and mental energy to devote to these projects. The business of evaluating the initial design boundaries and topologies does require intellectual energy and some time spent discussing matters with the business analyst.

Even where an IT manager has time and ability in general terms, if he is not used to downsizing he may spend his energies watching the wrong things. It is common for such people to get too involved in technical matters or too great a level of application detail in a particular area, so losing perspective. One should therefore be aware that mid-level managers within IT, as well as those at ground level, may require corrective training, and this too should be reviewed at the end of the first phase of downsized projects. Some such managers will not be able to adapt to the downsized world, and so may have to be taken off further projects.

So far we have suggested working structures for development and maintenance, and covered likely support ratios for different types of project. A further issue is how long staff should be left to be associated with a particular user or group of users. While one wants business analysts and analyst/programmers to identify with given groups of users, one wants also to keep them alert by offering a variety of work and also to keep them trained in current IT matters.

A reasonable time to leave IT developers associated with a given set of users is two years. Shorter than this, and they will not develop the in-depth knowledge or perspective they need for working in general with users and applications. They must see several systems go live, then maintain and enhance them, and also be able to observe operational and technical aspects of maturing systems. If they do not see this maturing process, they will not understand the full consequences of their own designs. One of the great flaws of the traditional IT world is that development and maintenance have generally been kept separate, a result of which is that developers rarely discover what they have done wrong.

There are exceptions to the two-year guideline. Very complex applications (say, manufacturing) and specialized areas such as management information may offer career opportunities to developers who wish to stay in these areas. The analyst/programmers' own feelings should be taken much into consideration – some welcome change while others may wish to become completely immersed in an application area they like. One should watch for boredom, demotivation and simply getting stuck in a rut. Even if a person likes an area, he may become less effective if he becomes too blinkered. Developers who stay too long in one place may become emotionally attached

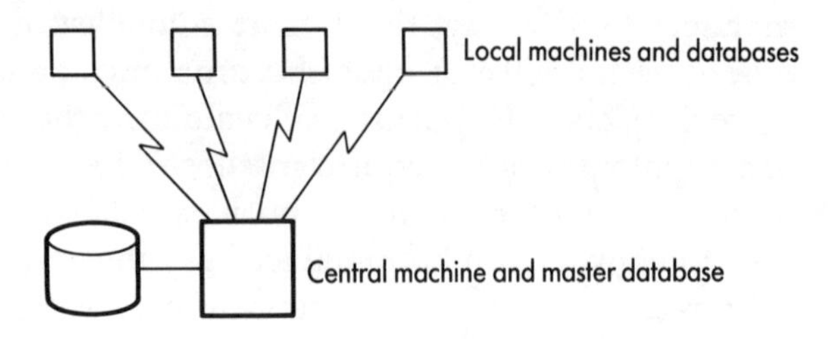

Figure 19.2 Coping with disaster.

What happens if all remote sites require recovery from central resources at the same time? Such an occasion might arise for a variety of reasons, including an operator's mistake (perhaps loading data in the wrong sequence to the remote sites, so corrupting all their files). The full system recovery could take a very long time and might require combined operations and applications staff to ensure that the recovery had been carried out properly.

to their users, and so side with them when politics rears its ugly head. Some such types will even initiate political intrigues, which user–IT relationships can do without particularly in the downsized environment.

Carrots and sticks for users

Dealing with users is like dealing with insecure beings anywhere. First of all, such people are inclined to be volatile, and a primary goal is therefore to minimize volatility in favour of stability. It is common for such users to swing suddenly from friendliness to animosity toward IT, and at what IT people may regard as minor provocation. The resentment can often take highly personalized forms, and so can damage working relationships. Such reactive incidents are just as likely after implementation as before it, especially if the system proves too complicated to operate or otherwise turns out to be not what the user had in mind. In conditioning one's own people to handle such issues, it is important first to warn them that such behaviour is likely, and that the analyst/programmer should not take it as an overly personal criticism. The second point is to encourage the use of carrot and stick techniques to bolster user morale and at the same time maintain a certain fear of failure.

In the use of such techniques, tact is of the utmost importance. Neither carrot or stick side of the equation should be overplayed. This is particularly a concern with analyst/programmers, as opposed to business analysts, as the analyst/programmer is rarely a trained diplomat and therefore may state issues too baldly. A sensitive business analyst or other manager should take pains to point out what may be an appropriate level of encouragement or warning in a particular user situation. If one is dealing with blunt, plain-spoken types, then any subtlety or gentle hinting will simply be lost. If too strongly stated matters are put before a department full of shrinking violets, then offence will be caused.

It is obviously the 'stick' side that may cause most reaction, as any warning of failure may be taken to reflect on the capabilities of the users themselves. Therefore, some attention should be given to specific phrasing of messages that need to be understood. These can often be stated in veiled, slightly positive terms, for example, 'we would like to see this department maintain its position' rather than the more negative 'if this department falls behind . . .'. If a given analyst/programmer is thought insufficiently skilled in providing tactful warnings, then he should be given a 'carrot-only' restriction (though tactfully, of course, and never calling it that to his face). He might also be cautioned not to overdo the encouragement either, otherwise he will wind up sounding like just another software salesman.

The inter-departmental meetings between downsized users can be used to promote positive attitudes as well as to cover details of good practice in maintaining and operating their systems. As always, finger pointing should be avoided, and IT should make it clear that it shares both blame and credit where due. The meetings between users are not only for user benefit, as IT can note where it has treated users differently and achieved either better or worse results.

Key issues

- Handover of a downsized project is a more critical activity than of a traditional system, so bears watching carefully.

- Allow for flexibility in finally assigning any system operation to the user department, in case more preparation is needed.
- During preparation for handover and at the actual event, try to measure the user's learning progress, both for immediate purposes and to extrapolate into the future.
- Once handover is complete, analyze the performance of the IT people involved in the project with a view to providing more training or re-assigning the people, as appropriate.

20

Ongoing application development

While implementing a downsized system is relatively straightforward, maintaining both momentum and control in a maturing environment is very much a challenge. A number of factors make life complicated:

- The growing and changing nature of most downsized application needs.
- The possible need to continue to run the mainframe.
- The requirement to update the technology and to introduce new versions of software.
- The consequent strain on IT people and budgets.

IT policy must be aimed at keeping risks down and maximizing the effectiveness of limited resources. One should appreciate that the two are connected: high risk sooner or later equals more money or personnel, as the cost of cleaning up a mess is generally greater than that of preventing it. Efficiency and low risks can be maintained only if the environment remains reasonably orderly. If such order is not maintained, a degree of chaos similar to that on the worst mainframe sites can be approached. Once IT management is drawn into non-stop fire fighting, it is difficult to marshal enough resources to retrieve the situation.

Controlling development

While some IT people may regret the independence and volatility of the downsized user department, one should keep in mind that this is the result of downsizing policy in the first place. The static, unimaginative user might just as well have stayed tied to the IT department's apron-strings. Policies should aim at maintaining the legitimate momentum of further development, but doing so under agreed monitoring procedures. The stringent cost constraints surrounding most downsizing efforts impose problems. Depending upon its size, an individual downsized system may have only a fraction of an IT person (business analyst or analyst/programmer) supervizing it on a day-to-day basis. Even a large minicomputer unit may have only a handful of analyst/programmers minding an inventory of over a thousand programs and many hundreds of users. While such types of system are meant to be supported by small numbers, it is vital that the IT people there do not get distracted by extraneous matters and instead spend their time watching what they are supposed to be watching.

In many downsized situations, it is academic to divide program maintenance from ongoing application development. In some of the larger situations, where relatively stable transaction processing is offset by more volatile information-handling and office systems, there is a theoretical split, but except in extreme cases it is doubtful whether support efforts should be divided between maintenance and development.

A common fault with downsized systems is to assume a support load more or less proportional to what is installed already, and to assign IT people to departments or groups of departments on this basis. Many downsized components, such as generic packages, themselves have a highly variable support load, depending partly upon the specific package but more perhaps upon how it is being used. Management information systems usually have high support loads, best calculated on a 'per awkward user' basis rather than just on the amounts of data stored or on the number of enquiry/reporting programs in use.

Transaction processing systems, once installed, should have a very low overall support requirement, however important they are in the scheme of things. However, such systems can have a sudden large requirement for change, which, if not foreseen, can mightily disrupt other efforts. Because of its proximity to the business core, a change in transaction-processing needs can be both unexpected and labour intensive. Close planning between users and IT can sometimes prepare the ground, but even then there are bound to be surprises. A sudden reorganization or a merger or takeover can upset any planning process.

Table 20.1 Ongoing charges for users.

User's own costs	*Directly-related costs*	*General overheads*
System operation Liaison with IT Enquiry tool testing Space, power, cooling, and so on for local machine	Business analyst, analyst/programmers Direct operational or technical support Hardware and software products, plus maintenance Communications Outside consultancy, training	IT management and non-attributable technical and operational support Shared and non-attributable machine, software and hardware costs Space, power for machines and central people

We stress continually the need to charge users fully for IT services in the downsized world. The most difficult of the categories in Table 20.1 is the 'General overheads'. One can follow examples from the supplier side of the industry to arrive at possible methods. While no single method is entirely fair on a theoretical plane, one does not want to have different methods applying to different departments. Any overheads which cannot be identified as belonging to a particular user might be pro-rated according to the following:

- Size of the user department in people (whether or not all are users)
- Number of terminals attached
- Number of terminals busy (say, in average terminal-hours per day)
- Transactions processed
- Power or disk capacity of local servers or minicomputers

The difficulty of charging general overheads can be solved partly by keeping such overheads minimal, and attempting to identify mainframe, communications and personnel usage by user department.

Parallelism and continuity

20

The essence of supporting the smaller system is to provide two components which are not always compatible:

- The right level of support
- Continuity of support

The conflict between the two is that, in stressed situations, managers may compromise continuity by directing support personnel to this week's crisis, such that the people with knowledge of a given system may not be available when needed. As with all ideals, sometimes compromise is necessary, but there should be established limits to such compromises (perhaps a policy stating that the relevant person could be returned to his native system within a specified time period). A small, installed system that is also stable might be left for a few weeks with no contact from its analyst/programmer, with some contingent procedures outlined for emergencies.

The type and the amount of support a system requires are closely inter-linked, as with downsized systems there are fewer central pools of support from which people can be dragged at random. Existing pools containing mainframe people will in most cases be inapplicable to downsized units, possible exceptions being those covering communications and database. The range of support functions for a given user department needs to be thought out from the application design stage. The ideal is that the business analyst or analyst/programmer in charge of application support can also provide at least basic levels of operational and technical support. This simplifies IT contact from the user's point of view and also simplifies IT management's planning of support. Much fault diagnosis and recovery is in part application-related, so having one person knowing both areas increases reliability and security of the system. A system that is overly complicated operationally or technically cannot enjoy this single-person support.

Generic packages lend themselves to a degree of centralized support, and many PC support groups within otherwise mainframe sites already provide such assistance directly to users. Generic packages are getting more complicated as they mature, and they are developing relationships to other generic packages (for example the typical text–spreadsheet–mail/messaging combination). A central support function for such packages will gain wide experience as to the many different ways in which packages can be used, and they will also develop good fault diagnosis skills for the packages.

Where many locations run the same application program, central support may or may not be likely. If the application is basically a simple one, with most nodes running it being of the same approximate size, then there may be no great need for a central pool. Such systems are diverse geographically to a greater or lesser degree, and it might make sense to have support staff grouped in convenient user locations but able to travel quickly to surrounding sites should problems arise. Such systems often use communications heavily, and where possible support for both application and technical/communications items might be combined.

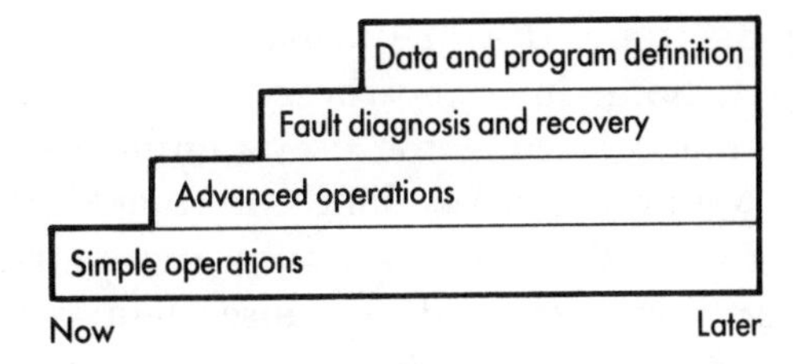

Figure 20.1 Encouraging the user.

As a downsized system matures, the user and IT should have a flexible plan in place that allows the user to take over additional system responsibilities. This will lower costs overall, and also will transfer costs to the user budget from IT-related expenditure. As a user feels confident with one stage of operations or system definition and planning, he should be encouraged, never pushed, to advance to the next stage.

Whichever support and development mode is chosen, management efforts must try to maintain the 'parallel' approach in one of two ways. Either one person must be able to balance the several threads within one system (these being the application, plus the communications and machine technology). Or several people must support a group of systems. Whether the parallel threads are represented by several activities within one system, or by one activity over several systems, the important thing is not to lose sight of one element or system in favour of another. If monitoring is not done, then inevitably the support person's attentions will drift to the area or system of greatest interest or convenience to him.

20

Relocating data

Data location and the concept of data ownership play a great role wherever systems are distributed and linked together. In the ideal world, data and application groupings look much the same on the trial diagrams drawn during the planning and design stages of a project. Sometimes, however, we get it wrong, or else changes have to be made because the user's emphasis has shifted.

Wrongly placed data can make itself felt via a number of symptoms. Perhaps communications traffic between machines is higher than expected, because data records are not at the most convenient place for the user. Faults in the day-to-day operation of databases may occur because the user either does not care about or does not understand the databases for which he it nominally responsible. For whatever reason, it may be decided that data should be either removed to another node, or duplicated so that several parties can use the data effectively as if it were solely a local database.

While it is tempting, and looks easy, to move a database from one location to another, it is in fact a significant step and should be carefully reviewed. The effort and commitment from all concerned is major, and the risks are also high, as one might either duplicate the original mistake or even make it worse. There may be a chance of overloading the new owner, or of giving him a database which he does not fully understand. When one is doing this to an operational and changing system, life is necessarily more complicated than when such things are being planned in the design stages. If it is suspected that data may be in the wrong place, the following questions should be asked:

- Will both old and new data owners be happy with the new location of the database and their altered roles?
- What machine loading and communications traffic will apply? In fact, are these likely to be predictable?
- Will programs and enquiry procedures need significant alteration?
- What data security, integrity and recovery procedures will need to be changed? Will the system still be recoverable within a reasonable period?
- How might IT's support role change, and will it be at least as effective as it is now?
- Is distributed data in fact the right answer at all? Should we consider some degree of centralization (perhaps, putting the database on a minicomputer commonly and equally accessible by all departments that need it)?
- Does the data location problem point to something more

fundamental that might be wrong, and how might those problems be solved?

If data relocation is the required course of action, one should be sure to use as advantageously as possible any features within the database software or in its associated dictionary. Some products support distributed databases well, and it may be possible to run parts of the database in more than one location. As always, response and recovery times should be checked when such features are used.

The problem of growing complexity

With any system, things tend to grow as time progresses. More programs are written, generic packages are used in more complicated ways, extra data fields and records are incorporated into the database, and features are added to hardware items or to system software.

Much of this growth is beneficial, and an indication that the initial implementation was successful enough to provide a base upon which to build. The issue is to control and direct this growth, such that it assists the basic business purposes of the department and does not instead lose direction and dart off into side alleys. Apart from this functional view, the growth must not render the system uncontrollable, either from the user's or from IT's point of view.

Regular planning sessions with the user will help to ensure that the most useful tasks are installed earliest on the system. Less essential or technically difficult items can be left for consideration later, unless there is an overwhelming need for the latter type. Part of the user's basket of responsibilities is housekeeping, and this should be reviewed on a regular basis.

Periodically (perhaps at a monthly or bi-monthly progress meeting), the user department should agree among itself a list of objects in the system that are now thought to be less important than they used to be. The objective of naming such items (programs, enquiry procedures, data records, documents or images) is to downgrade them in stages. Users, like everyone else, either do not like

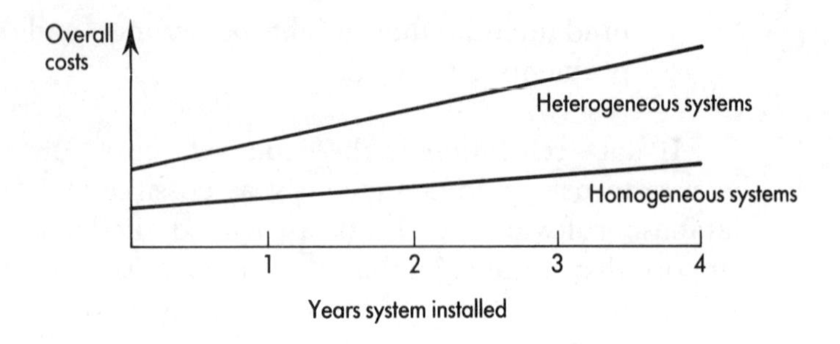

Figure 20.2 Maintaining homogeneity.

The longer downsized systems are installed, the more likelihood there is of incompatibility entering the system. For a variety of reasons, users will decide they need to do something differently or buy something different, so creating extra complexity and costs in the overall system. Good monitoring policies can keep these digressions minimal, and ensure that any incompatibilities are justified on business grounds.

to throw things away, or they simply do not want to be bothered with thinking about housecleaning.

IT's main objective should in the first instance be to get the inactive or duplicate objects off the live system, perhaps storing them on a backup tape or diskette. If the item is not wanted for a set period (say, six or twelve months), then it might be disposed of or sent to more distant archives such as an out-of-town warehouse. Users should be occasionally reminded of the high costs of keeping items online as compared to storing them in more passive locations.

When it comes to applications themselves and their possible complexity, encouraging concepts of modularity will help keep them manageable. IT will normally need to take the lead here, as users have little idea as to how programs and data are structured. If modular programs mean an extra step or two, or a few seconds extra response time, the user may not care so long as countervailing cost savings are illustrated. Because of pressures existing in the small, demand-driven environment, it is usual for quick fixes to be applied to programs, without thinking of better and more structured ways of organizing. If users are willing to wait a short while, or if they can help to anticipate requests, the broad benefits in doing so should be pointed out.

System security

In virtually every computer environment there are opportunities for unwholesome activities, whether fraudulent or simply malicious. Prevention of these rarely gets more than lip-service in the early stages, partly because everyone is too busy doing other things and partly because the full ramifications of the system are not understood.

Some types of business have well established inspection functions (for example, banking and insurance). Others may rely on outside accounting and auditing firms to provide a modicum of security awareness. Unfortunately, too many of these generally seem unacquainted with or interested in computer-related aspects of security. Where auditors and inspectors may have built up some expertise and interest is in the mainframe environment, as they have been dealing with these for some years. With downsized systems, it is rarely possible to engage the watchdogs within the short time periods applying. IT often has to make basic security decisions itself, and then must try to encourage interest and participation from auditors/inspectors over the longer term.

Prevention of unauthorized access to files, knowing who has tried to log on to a network, and who has last changed a program or file (and what the change was) are all basic to system security. Network management software and operating systems of most machines will provide such facilities, but often at a low and very detailed level such that one may have to spend time summarizing or otherwise making sense of the detail. Where one is using mixed systems, some gaps are inevitable, and a skilled technician will know how to exploit them. In other words, watching one's own people is very much part of the security equation.

In recorded cases of fraud, computer users within the organization account for a very high percentage, though often their attempts are quite basic. Applications that deal with shipping goods or money either into or out of the company should receive attention, particularly where facilities exist to make amendments to basic documents such as invoices, payments, returned goods invoices and payroll records. Dishonest administrators may slice small amounts from many accounts belonging to customers, suppliers or employees, hoping to conceal discrepancies that are minor in each individual case. Such people may feel more able to do this when using a local computer system, thinking that such systems escape the tighter scrutiny of the centralized machine. It is therefore important to give users a certain watched feeling, making the point to members of a department that they should be alert and should be on the lookout for odd behaviour by either user colleagues or local IT staff. Such a state of alertness will deter at least some attempts at fraud or malicious damage.

A particular hazard in any PC or similar environment is the introduction of a 'virus' (a maliciously intended program that destroys data and other programs). Anticipating viruses as well as combatting them once they have appeared should be part and parcel of any downsized security policy. Viruses are commonly introduced via insertion of an infected floppy disk into a particular PC, and some may then spread their way around a network to other machines, so corrupting an entire installation.

There are a number of anti-virus packages and services on the market. At least one product is in the form of a plug-in card, so being incorruptible by normal virus software. Software packages use a variety of techniques (not all of which may be published for obvious reasons). They cannot provide complete protection, as they may search only for known viruses or may be run periodically.

Protection against viruses and similar forms of malicious damage must be multi-faceted, with three main elements dominating the strategy:

- Encouraging users of PCs and other types of workstation *never* to insert into their machines any diskette of unknown origin.
- Use of anti-virus packages, and possibly the employment of specialist security consultants.
- Designing procedures to shut down portions of a network that may be infected, or to isolate that segment from the healthy side of the network.

The most important thing to understand about security where small machines are concerned is that more issues are in user hands than would be the case with a centralized system. Encouraging vigilance on the part of unrelated parties, and engaging in spot checks at unpredictable intervals, will minimize many security risks.

Core and 'extra' applications

As applications grow on a given system, continuing distinction should be maintained between core and non-core tasks. Otherwise, there will be a tendency to keep adding bits to the core system, whether or not they should belong there. Either programs will be made more complex than they need to be, or extra files and programs will be appended to the basic files and programs, such that a large interlinked suite of programs is involved. This may lead to unsavoury practices such as having to run too many housekeeping jobs to keep files synchronized, or having a screen update several files all at the same time, both complicating recovery and causing poor machine response.

It bears keeping in mind that it is not always clear what systems run mainly core applications and which do not. Many head-office departments, or those running office packages, may not clearly fit the pattern. Office systems in particular would normally be thought of as non-core, though there may be some departments where there is an urgent business need for their maintenance and enhancement. In today's highly diverse world, the old distinction between the transaction processing that was supposed to represent the base of the business and lesser breeds of application may not hold true. While IT may have its own thoughts as to which systems belong in which category, the voice of the business overall should hold sway. This means that the steering committee governing the whole IT effort might occasionally be called upon to agree a list of priorities, as to which areas might be slowed down in case of need. IT people are understandably reluctant to raise such topics, as it may imply ineptitude. Tact is of course necessary, not simply asking in effect 'which plane would you rather see crash?', but specifying instead which are the most important to keep in the air should the unexpected occur.

As downsized systems develop, it is usual for much work to drift away from the transaction processing core (assuming that the core does involve transaction processing). Such more remote application areas might include management information, or processes that make the department's work easier (say, document preparation and messaging). Because of the less critical nature of many such applications, the user might be encouraged to look after these to a greater extent than he would the basic business-critical system. If the user can do some development of such systems, perhaps by changing

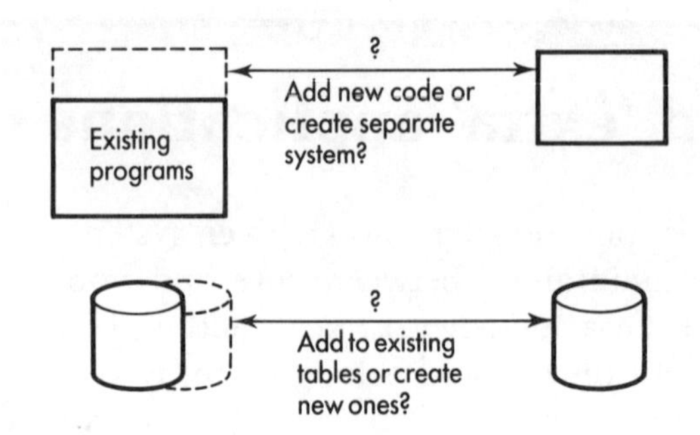

Figure 20.3 Add or modularize?

Whether to add to an application or to segment it as it grows is one of downsizing's more difficult questions. For manageability and low-cost maintenance, it is better to create new programs and files rather than just gluing more bits and pieces onto existing systems (the latter being the normal tendency, especially when motivated by panic and constrained by tight time-scales). However, too many separate modules may confuse the end user and created operational complexities. The trade-offs between the two policies should be discussed with the user in each specific case.

parameters or reformatting screens or reports, then he can do this at his own speed as well as removing effort from the IT department.

Key issues

- In a downsized system, there is often no meaningful distinction between development and ongoing maintenance. Plan resources accordingly.
- Cost ongoing development/maintenance as carefully as one would the planning and implementation phases of a project.
- Where complicated application packages are installed, try to anticipate changes to these and to match contingent resources to the possible requirement.
- The possibility of supporting generic packages centrally can lower costs and therefore increase the desirability of this type of solution.

- Where systems grow over time, try to handle the extra function by adding on programs and files rather than making the native system larger and more complex.
- Do not neglect security issues as systems mature.

21

Hardware suppliers and their products

When we turn to the selection of products for the downsized environment, it is appropriate to remind ourselves of the basic principles that are driving the effort:

- Lowest possible risk
- Cost-effectiveness
- Ease of use and flexibility

Where product evaluations are given to traditional IT specialists, there is an understandable tendency to look at the more fascinating technical features that are thought to be state of the art. Not only at the beginning of the evaluation, but also during meetings with vendors, one should try to look beyond these technical niceties and ask oneself: how does this product or service advance the above three goals?

Today there are numerous suppliers in almost every category of the hardware and software markets. If one includes business along with product criteria, most can be dismissed out of hand before one even approaches the specific requirements of one's own organization. Many computer companies owe their existences to aggressive salesmanship, buyer ignorance or ineptitude or simply being a warm body in a fast growing area. One need only look to the past to gauge the futility of the average computer supplier. The also-rans of the mainframe 1970s were superseded by the minicomputer non-starters of the 1980s. Today, the majority of these two categories are lying dead on the battlefield or else they wish they were. The errors of the previous two decades are being repeated in the PC market. What one needs to do is spot the most probable survivors – the IBM or the Hewlett-Packard of the client/server world if you like – and deal only with these. Spending time with unlikely suppliers simply to fill out the short-list is done more frequently than the honest reader might expect. It wastes time and creates a certain danger that one will wind up dealing with such a supplier.

Like all extremely simple models of the complex world, the above thoughts require refinement given the nature of downsized markets. The basic problem is that a very successful company today can be killing time in the mortuary tomorrow. There are several reasons for this, the two most prominent being that blinding success blinds companies to dangers inherent in changing competitive markets, and that one-man companies have great problems the moment the one man loses his mental composure. One may therefore be willing to take a risk with such a company, so long as there is an escape plan and so long as major benefits compensate for a defined and limited risk.

The other modifier of traditional vendor-viability policies is the commodity aspect of many downsized markets. If one buys a PC clone or an inexpensive server, benefits of much lower price against very limited risk apply. If worst comes to worst, a PC can be thrown away and replaced with another, obviously with some loss of money and face but with little interruption to the business of the user.

21 Old and new mentalities

One of the main differences between company cultures lies in their attitudes to new events. A good company will be controlling events within its area, and will be doing this by initiating products and services, not through heavy handed sales tactics or via defensive lock-in policies. Such companies are rare, but they are often easily recognizable. The 'me too' company, of which there are a vast number in computing, will come rather late onto the scene, often with not very impressive products and not quite knowing how to sell them. They will typically copy superficial features without understanding the underlying rationale of the product type in either business or design terms. The UNIX and PC camps are both full of such suppliers.

Many companies that now look staid were in fact leaders of

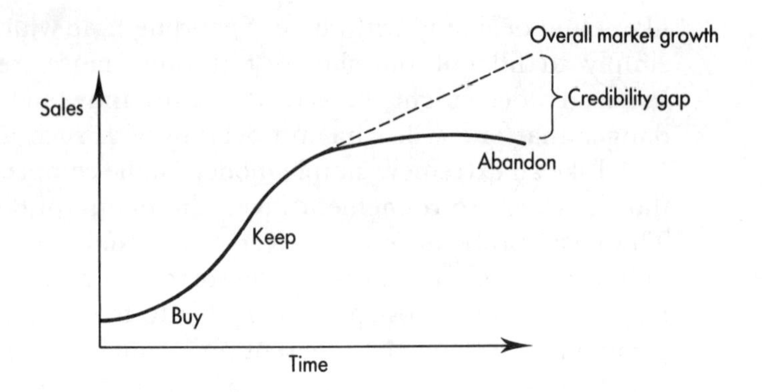

Figure 21.1 Buy, hold or sell: investing in suppliers.

Acquiring a small system is much like any other investment decision. One should try to estimate where the vendor is on the 'S'-shaped demand curve, and then also try to estimate how accident-prone the company is. While all computer companies make mistakes, the small growing concern has less padding in the financial regions to insulate it from a crash. The conceptual 'sell' point occurs when major problems become evident. These are often associated with loss of relative market share, when competitors keep growing at a higher rate than the afflicted company.

the market early in their history. It is not accurate to view IBM, DEC and Unisys as organizations that made their fortunes coming late into the market by copying the ideas from others. Such companies provide a lesson in industry watching which prospective users should try to apply to today's organizations: there is some point at which the innovator loses sight of his own philosophies, and this turning point marks the beginning of a long-term decline.

A good new company will bear certain characteristics, not all of which may be desirable in theory, and some of which may imply risk:

- It will often be a one-man show. IBM and DEC were thus in their primes. Alternatively, it will depend upon the efforts of a small team of highly imaginative people.
- It will have philosophies behind the product which are valid for their time. In other words, the product is not a happy accident, but instead is a thoughtful answer to a large-scale market requirement, whether or not the market knows in advance of such a requirement.

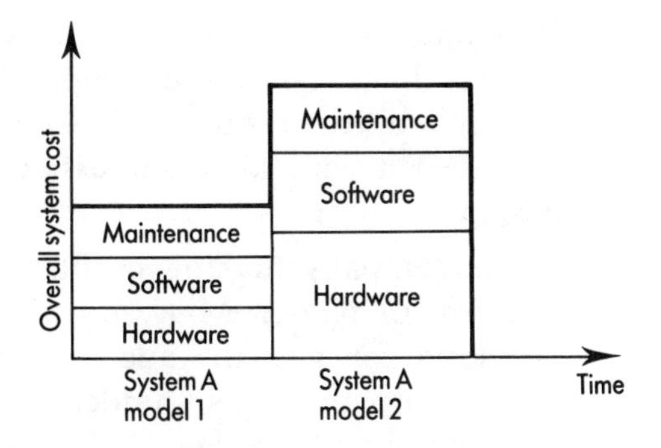

Figure 21.2 The forced upgrade.

One of the main reasons users should beware of the proprietary system is because of the lock-in and consequent forced upgrade should needs expand. This is particularly an issue in the downsized world, as growth in installed units is normal and needs may change suddenly. Proprietary suppliers often offer a low entry price to entice the beginning user into the range, then impose steep additional charges for upgrading to more powerful models. The cost of these upgrades may include much more expensive software and maintenance as well as the actual hardware. In open, competitive markets, suppliers cannot get by with such stunts.

- A high degree of enthusiasm will be evident among the employees. They will understand the company philosophy and the product's rationale. They are effectively converts to a new religion, and are even more of a pain in the neck on that score than their founder.

With downsizing products, most of the best come from such a background. Sometimes a good product comes from a sub-group within a larger and otherwise inert organization, the sub-group displaying many of the above characteristics. When one looks at such companies, there are a few questions one can ask to assess viability at least approximately:

- Does the company know how to extend its basic idea? (Wang, Olsen and de Castro, of Wang, DEC and Data General respectively, did not.)
- Does the company have separate but related ideas that will help to keep it going? (Microsoft, Lotus and Borland do.)

- If an anarchist sub-group within a large corporation produce the product, can these people fight off the bureaucracy imposed by their supposed betters? (IBM's AS/400 people managed it with some success; Unisys's UNIX people also did so.)
- Is the company making profits and retaining control in its fast-growth phase? Many do not ('just cashflow problems, investing for growth, and so on, nothing fundamental'). When growth stops suddenly, such organizations find themselves with neither profits nor excuses.

Many users are understandably put off by the obvious risks associated with innovative companies, and indeed we have made much of risk issues here. Our main overall point about risk perhaps bears revisiting: by all means look at the risks involved in dealing with new areas, but equally look at the risks inherent in staying with obsolete technology or in doing nothing. Measuring risks, as suggested in Chapter 6, will help to clarify and quantify such issues.

General hardware considerations

In the two major downsized areas, PC and UNIX, we are largely into the commodity markets touched on earlier. This is good for the customer, as he is guaranteed reasonably standard, known, compatible products at competitive prices. In such add-on areas as peripherals and communications gear, 'commoditization' is especially effective, as a small, specialized vendor can enter a market and expand quickly.

Because hardware is both a minor portion of the system, and because it is well-defined, the user is freed to turn his attention to the more critical areas of software and services. With the PC, by far the most commodity-like market, we see this very pronouncedly, as the brand of PC itself may be less important than the choice of even a single software package, let alone a combination of applications.

It should be a conscious policy to buy commodity products, where a choice exists. Such a policy naturally links to open or standard systems, as these areas are the largest and most competitive. However, even with proprietary but fairly standard systems (such as VAX/VMS and AS/400) one can participate in the commodity mentality where add-on hardware is concerned.

In dealing with commodity hardware, one should be aware of the quality issue. Both UNIX and PC boxes vary in design goals, sturdiness, reliability and durability. Many of those that are built down to a price may offer less reliability and durability than expected. We are not saying one should automatically buy the high-quality item, as it may have a high-quality price attached. The point is to know what one is buying and why. The cheap PC clone may enable extra features or more capacity to be obtained within a given budget, and users may be very happy with the equation. This writer's experience is that most PCs even within a given brand vary widely in quality, so the user who pays more may not necessarily get that much more.

In theory, most users will recognize that a multi-user system (whether mini node or server) requires greater reliability than does a desktop machine. However, years of small-machine experience on our part do not support this view. While some users are reliability conscious, many seem oblivious to the issue. While some minis and similar are well-built and reliable (Hewlett-Packard's, Tandem's and IBM's to name a few), many others are not, especially if one includes disk drives, software and communications add-ons in an overall definition of system reliability.

Even IT professionals often think little of system reliability, failing to measure it properly and preferring to think of technically glamorous features instead. In fact, measuring reliability of distributed systems takes some effort, and one may not always get reliable answers. We have seen cases where minicomputers were collapsing once a day or so, yet were supposed to be enjoying 99% uptime. By some definitions, they were, as the user just switched the machine off after a failure and then switched it on again, and in most cases it would work. The fact that data might have been corrupted or that twenty or thirty users had to re-enter all of that day's transaction data did not worry the supervisor in the least.

A broad expectation of hardware reliability might be in the region of a year or more before a central processor falls over. When one adds failures of disk drives, communications items and software, the overall system reliability drops sharply. Small-machine reliability overall varies considerably, and depends as much upon how well the system is configured and run as on other factors. It is not unusual seeing a badly run mixed-mini site experiencing periods of substantial downtime several times a month, which is far too often.

Hardware architectures

There is a case today for choosing product architectures over suppliers. In commodity markets, this defines which commodity one is aiming for, whereas in proprietary systems by choosing the architecture in most cases the supplier is chosen by the same move.

In terms of units installed, Intel platforms dominate the scene by a wide margin, with perhaps a hundred million or so boxes out there somewhere. While Intel is thought of mainly as a PC architecture, there are UNIX options. If one is committed to UNIX, one might consider the Intel platforms both for their cheapness and because of the reasonably easy-to-use UNIX packages put out mainly by the Santa Cruz Operation (SCO). With Intel boxes, one can swap them around between architectures and locations as departmental requirements change, say using a given system for NetWare for a time and then moving it to another department using UNIX (though such mixing of software is certainly not advised for its own sake).

When choosing architectures, one should keep in mind that they are designed to do different things, and that software sets commonly available with given hardware types reflect these design assumptions. UNIX products are still aimed much at scientific/technical work, and the majority of software suppliers and distributors of UNIX are still so based. Even in a commercial UNIX market, many people may have come from the technical applications side, so it is always worth checking their assumptions if one has commercial requirements. The PC market still is based around the desktop office product, despite much recent publicity given to transaction-oriented client/server systems. Some types of small commercial machine are aimed at commercial transaction processing and little else (examples being IBM's AS/Entry and AS/400, and the MUMPS and Pick systems).

In many cases, people do not think out these architectural issues clearly. One has seen AS/400s purchased for batch processing and Pick systems for complicated transaction work rather than the basic tasks for which the system was designed.

The traditional proprietary minicomputer is now for all practical purposes obsolete, as UNIX can do whatever its predecessors could

Table 21.1 Best-fit architectures.

Product type	*Application environment*
PC	Text-handling, spreadsheet, small database, simple packaged industry-specific applications, mail/messaging (assuming basic communications available)
Client/server	Medium-volume transaction processing, heavy text/document/ image processing, medium database, rapid development, management information
UNIX	Scientific/technical work, high-powered graphics workstations, large servers, large database, manufacturing and process-control applications

In today's downsizing world, there are only three 'best' choices, as in Table 21.1. While other respectable solution types can be made to fit (for example, it is still worth considering IBM's AS/400 for commercial transaction work), their proprietary or otherwise limited designs make them less likely for most prospective users. All three of our top choices are open or standard architectures, so protecting the user's investment and offering a vast choice of both hardware and software options. They are also lower in cost than most alternatives, and are eminently capable of doing the jobs specified.

do, and probably do it more cheaply. Unless truly exceptional circumstances apply (in reality they almost never do), one should accept UNIX for the technical or broad scientific–commercial capabilities that the mini is suited to. By 'traditional' mini, we mean such products as DEC's VAX, Hewlett-Packard's 3000 and Data General's Eclipse ranges. These machines think in much the same way, using bus-based interrupt-driven basic designs to handle highly interactive work, whether the application task is a commercial transaction or some form of process control.

UNIX hardware is at the moment stronger than PC-based servers at the larger end of the market. UNIX also has a reserved role in the high-powered scientific or engineering workstation area. Intel chips cannot currently match the performance or the numeric-processing capabilities of the very fast chips from Sun, Mips (now owned by Silicon Graphics) and DEC. Whether server or workstation, one generally pays a high price for the UNIX product. However, if one is thinking of a multi-user machine, then UNIX products are generally somewhat cheaper per user than a traditional minicomputer based upon proprietary designs.

Supplier choices

Despite the emergence of commodity markets, it is still important to consider one's choice of main suppliers. Unless very basic systems are being installed, the character of the supplier and his attitudes to support will be a major success criterion.

For those with long memories, the 'which supplier' problem is an unpleasant one in some ways. Stringent production and distribution economics, plus changing and diverse markets with a recession thrown in for good measure, mean that no supplier can offer the high levels of support that applied with mainframe systems in the old days. While hardware support is satisfactory from most major vendors, software support is not what it should be to solve the sorts of user problems that are actually occurring. Even where one pays large extra sums for non-standard support, all too often one gets the bored amateur at the end of the telephone line flicking through the pages of a manual apparently for the first time.

The single-supplier option is still an attractive one, as it enables a single point of contact to be maintained between IT and the main supplier. Volume discounts can be negotiated, and problems are easier to sort out than if a number of vendors were involved. Administration is easier as well, as in a diverse environment this can take up a surprising amount of managers' time.

Over most of the world, and for the international company, IBM remains the most logical choice for the single major supplier. Despite redundancies, the company employs approximately 350 000 people and so has the logistics to cover the ground in terms of support. The company appears to have partly stabilized after a sharp decline in the 1980s.

Other single-supplier sources to consider occur mainly in larger European countries where there is an installed political supplier (for example Siemens in Germany, Bull in France). Here, if systems are to be run mainly within the country, one has a reasonably sized presence to provide support. The growth and productivity records of such suppliers have been lacklustre, but the basic technical competence offered by support staff should be satisfactory. These suppliers often try to tie UNIX or PC sales to proprietary products, which may not be appropriate. They also seem to think all customers are in government or manufacturing, which in much of Europe is at least partly true. One assumes that in many cases these suppliers will be thrust upon the decision maker for political reasons, and that one must therefore be prepared to make the best of the inevitable.

For many users, supplier policies have to be determined with regard to substantial installed positions. If one is, say, a large DEC or Unisys user already, one is obviously tempted to remain with the devil one knows. However, many users remain with declining suppliers simply because of inertia. One must therefore be careful not to be in a position of allowing existing problems to escalate. Our general recommendation is to avoid giving large lumps of new or replacement business to a supplier one thinks may be dubious, and instead try to create a strategy that will progressively move one into more secure supplier and product areas.

IBM's AS/400

If we look at proprietary products before open or standard systems, IBM's AS/400 must qualify as one of the most likely such items. The product was technically announced in June 1988, though much of the system is very similar to the older System/38 which AS/400 superseded. The product is thus middle-aged by computer-industry standards, older than the PC family but newer than UNIX, most proprietary minis, mainframes and such niche products as the MUMPS and Pick systems.

Many people selling AS/400s do not understand the fundamentals of the machine, which are very specific (the machine is sold by a variety of third parties as well as by IBM itself). They may thus mis-apply it, either targeting it at the wrong broad application type or else not designing appropriately even within its intended area. The best environment for AS/400 is for order entry or similar types of application, where transactions which are not overly complicated in nature are fed into the machine at a not excessive rate ('not overly complicated' meaning that perhaps ten to fifteen logical records are accessed within a transaction).

Though the initial System/38 design started life small, being little more than a PDP-11 equivalent in power, the system has grown in high-end capacity and is now reasonably 'scalable' (meaning that one can run small and large AS/400s using compatible software

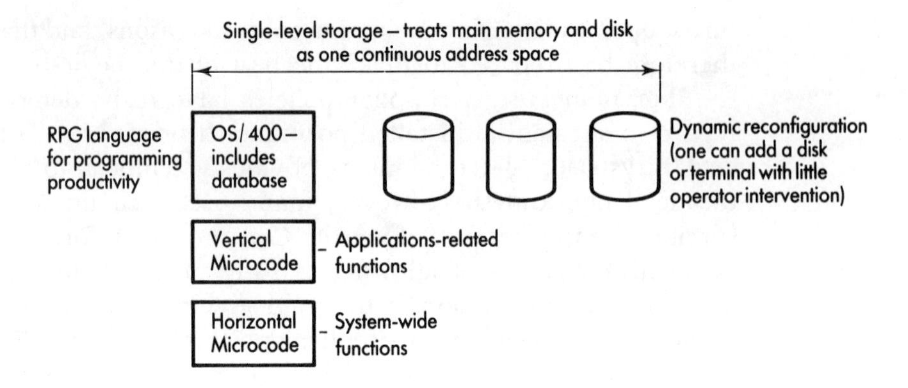

Figure 21.3 AS/400 concepts.

IBM's System/38 and AS/400 designs have a number of well-packaged components which help to 'future-proof' the machine and make it easier to use as well. Because System/38 started life as a very small machine and grew slowly, its successor (the AS/400) is less proven at the top of the range than elsewhere. Larger models use multi-processor architectures, and for this and other reasons are very expensive. A major plus for IBM is that competitors never understood the machine, and so were unable to compete against it effectively.

and operating procedures). IBM's claims of over 2000 attached users for the current top-end model (the E95, with four central processors operating in parallel) should be viewed cautiously.

Larger models of AS/400 are very expensive, but one might expect more price falls as the design ages. IBM has recently introduced cheap disk arrays using RAID technology, and this should keep prices moderate for storage. One of AS/400's strongest features is its relative ease of use. More on this is covered in Chapter 22 on software, as such benefits are conferred mainly by the OS/400 operating system. Where a number of machines are run throughout an organization, the savings in technical support staff would compensate in part for the high system prices.

The AS/400 add-on market is a large one. Something like 150 000 systems are installed already, and around 40 000 are selling each year world-wide. Third-party disks, memory and communications equipment are all available in wide variety. Around 10 000 application packages are now available, mainly in the commercial and manufacturing areas. When POSIX compliance is implemented, even more packages should migrate over from the UNIX camp.

DEC and VAX

Aside from IBM's AS/400, DEC's VAX running the VMS operating system is normally the only proprietary system one would take at all seriously. Though at first the two products might appear to cover the same territory, in fact they are quite different. In this writer's opinion, only very rarely should they appear on the same short-list.

Before one gets into the fine detail of VAX, one must try to get to grips with DEC as a company. DEC has always been a self-contradictory affair, now very much more so as its founder has recently departed. At the moment the vessel is foundering - a fascinating sight for the industry watcher but perhaps too fascinating for the prospective user.

Over its first two decades (1957 to 1977), DEC was a very successful company, growing steadily and rapidly as the arch-exponent of the minicomputer (the PDP-11 being the best known of the type). The product was underpinned by a sound philosophical base that was widely expounded by DEC's founder, Dr Kenneth Olsen, and equally by his employees. These philosophies involved interactive and user-friendly machines, openness, power to the people and much else that one recognizes as key messages of the downsizing movement. DEC then forgot its philosophies and began moving up-range with the more cumbersome VAX computer, and missed totally both the PC and UNIX movements. The larger VAX models, including clustered and mainframe-competitive models, were not popular with users, as they were both very expensive and difficult to use.

DEC has a very wide installed base in manufacturing companies of all types, and in such technical areas as universities and defence agencies around the world. The vast majority of these use the VAX with VMS software, though an increasing percentage use at least some of DEC's UNIX (called ULTRIX). While some VAXs are installed in commercial situations, most observers do not see commercial work as a mainstay for the future.

Within its longest-established territory (that of the very small mini), VAX is still a very effective proposition. Like many small machines, it quickly loses its attractions once dragged off its home territory. VAX is a good example of the 'tiger' machine - one that is tame when small but becomes progressively more vicious as it grows.

VAX scalability has long been a strong point, as the same VMS software can run on the full span of machines. This, plus effective

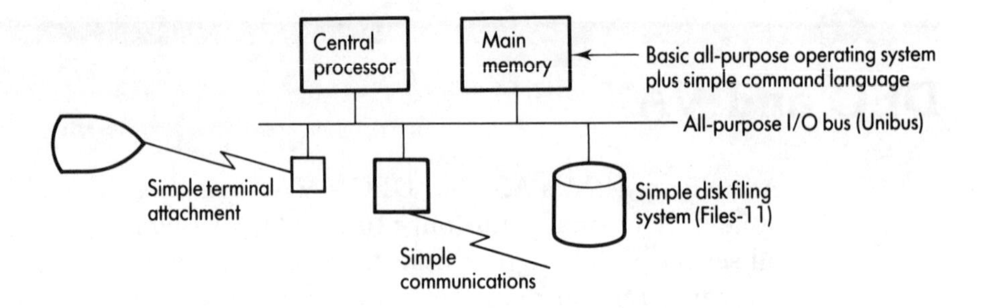

Figure 21.4 The classic DEC mini.

DEC's basic mini, best embodied in the PDP-11 and microVAX product designs, set the standard for what a small interactive machine should look like architecturally. UNIX and PC designs are much like the above, as the essence of a simple design is that anyone can copy it. DEC itself failed to realize this, and instead of consolidating its hold on the small-machine market it tried to turn VAX into a mainframe competitor when the last thing the market needed was still another mainframe. As a result of DEC ignoring both the PC and UNIX for so long, it lost control at the small end of the market while failing to do much up-range either.

communications, make VAX a possible proposition for networked environments with many different sizes of nodes. If one must use larger VAXs, the advice is to keep them unclustered, keep designs simple, and to buy plenty of hardware (particularly main memory); such a configuration will be easier to operate than an overloaded one by a wide margin.

UNIX system suppliers

Hardware that runs the UNIX family of operating systems varies widely by virtually all measures (quality, price, design goals, standardization). Where UNIX is concerned, one obviously accepts the architecture before moving to specific hardware considerations.

RISC (Reduced Instruction Set Computing) hardware is much an issue in the UNIX market, as many vendors use such architecture. RISC machines often target one application type (say, graphics for technical workstations) and build very fast instructions for such into the hardware. If the system is then used for, say, multi-user commercial record updating, performance may suffer. Also, some workstations were designed with single users in mind. If one tries to use such a system for multiple attached users, again performance may suffer. As there are a vast number of UNIX hardware constructors, one's initial job is simply to weed out the pack. Viability, quality, fit with existing hardware, support and the size of the third-party markets for a particular machine are all pertinent. Where third-party software is a consideration (it almost always is, as nobody buys UNIX for its inherent charm), care should be taken to buy as common a hardware platform for the application as is possible (assuming there is a choice). Because implementations of software vary across UNIX products, one is likely to get a better database or application package on a popular product. Software suppliers typically try to operate across too many platforms, inevitably becoming overstretched, so understandably they will spend most effort keeping the major hardware groups happy.

Because of the preponderance of scientific/technical applications running UNIX, most hardware is targeted on this type of work. The Sun, Hewlett-Packard, IBM and Mips products are in this camp, as is DEC's emerging Alpha chip. Intel hardware, on the other hand, is aimed more at general applications, though its numeric capabilities are improving.

There are a number of quality vendors offering UNIX. The most stable and viable are IBM and Hewlett-Packard. One also might consider vendors with a high commitment to UNIX, such as Sun, AT&T/NCR, ICL/Fujitsu and the larger European suppliers.

Overall, UNIX hardware is more expensive than it should be at the moment, with the exception of Intel systems. Prices should come down for two reasons: competition from within the UNIX camp and from the PC world; and the lower costs per unit capacity that will come from the new generation of 64-bit chips. These high-speed chips will lower costs in their own sector (high-capacity workstations, larger servers and multi-user systems), and should also drive down prices down-range, as the market will insist on a differential.

UNIX systems generally assume the presence of several layers of distributors and dealers, and so have been priced high to allow for the resulting distribution costs. Such costs are half or more of the published retail price, so a prospect for a purchase of any volume should negotiate carefully. One might get a third to a half off the retail price, depending upon the number of units purchased and the age of the product. Older products can be especially cheap because in a fast-moving market suppliers are desperate to clear inventory before the next model is announced.

Larger UNIX boxes using multi-processor architectures are still extremely expensive, costing in the many hundreds of thousands of dollars. Design and marketing costs are high for this type of product, and because of software limitations one may not be buying as much capacity as one supposes. Faster chips and better input/output systems should make obsolete many of these complicated designs in favour of the much simpler and cheaper 'single-component' systems outlined earlier. Prospective users should wait accordingly.

PC and client/server products

The PC is undoubtedly the industry's most standard piece of hardware, and the question frequently arises: does it really matter who makes it? The answer is: probably not, at least for most situations. Where a PC is to be used as a single-user workstation, price and cosmetic features will determine most situations.

Where servers are required, more circumspection is required. Reliability is essential, as is good performance in many cases. The Compaq SystemPro is the most widely understood server, and offers the traditional Compaq blend of reliability and performance.

In general, server prices should fall because of more competition and newer technology. Within Europe, the Apricot/Mitsubishi series of servers is probably the best-known range after Compaq. Apricot has made an issue of security features such as lockable cabinets, card keys to initiate the system and removable hard disks. Many other suppliers are plunging into the server market, as it now seen as a fast growth area. Most industry analysts believe that the percentage of LAN-connected PCs will rise from around 35% now to perhaps 70% by the mid-1990s. For both existing and new systems, there will be a high demand for servers.

Performance issues with servers invariably revolve around the disk subsystem. While many servers have effective features here, it is not always easy to uncover them. Brochures put out by marketing people and local distributors for this type of product vie in their intentions to keep users ignorant. It is doubtful if many dealer salespeople understand the issues anyway. Prospective buyers may have to make substantial efforts to find out what capacities are actually

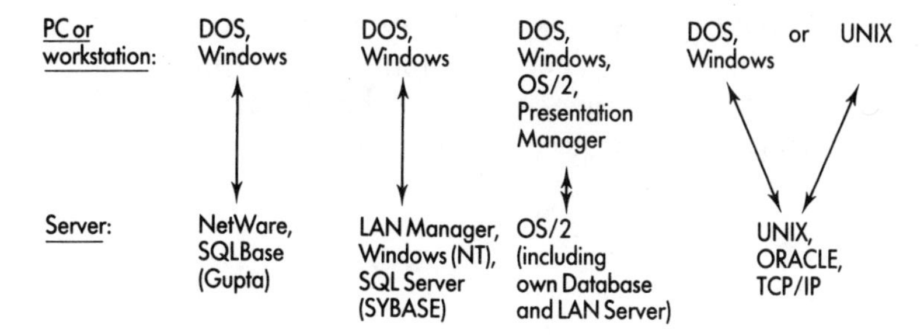

Figure 21.5 Server combinations.

The most likely software combinations for client/server are listed in Figure 21.5. On the hardware front, one has an increasingly wide choice, both of workstations and servers. Large-capacity servers are provided by: Compaq, Apricot/Mitsubishi, Sun, Dell, Tangent, IBM, ALR, Powerframe.

available, and for different types of work such as transaction processing on the one hand or large-document retrieval on the other.

There are other market-related issues aside from dealer ineptitude. The server market is a new one, and it has yet to settle down into defined product types. There may thus be a lot of chopping and changing by suppliers as they attempt to uncover categories of the product that are easily recognized and most wanted by customers. Most server suppliers are weak on marketing, so the process may take some time. In very general terms, servers can cost from around $5,000 for a simple model with two gigabytes of storage to above $30,000 for higher-performance models. Disk storage can go up into the tens of gigabytes, but this does not mean that the user can expect good performance on a single database this size.

Client/server systems have other items on them than PCs and servers. In most offices, printing and possibly the scanning and storing of images are important. Several types of printer may be needed, ranging from high-quality colour products to low-priced items for draft-quality printing. The main point we would make here is that printers often get much higher rates of use than expected, and false economies should not be practised. This writer cannot count the times he has seen a flimsy dot-matrix printer disintegrating into tinfoil only weeks after being installed, as no one had taken the trouble to estimate print volumes.

In distributing printers and scanners as well as PCs and servers in our downsized environment, one should consider the physical security of all such devices. Printers and scanners cost more than many PCs and as much as most servers. A midget on steroids could walk out the door carrying a server under one arm and a printer under the other, much to the detriment of the user's budget and high-flying concepts of data security.

Hardware: preliminary conclusions

People have a variety of objectives in downsizing, and it pays to review them before actually signing a purchase order. One assumes that the architecture desired has been chosen for business reasons and not technical fashionability. Users vary much in their cost sensitivity. Some will want a cheap item with extra power to drive their large spreadsheets or whatever; others will insist on robust, reliable systems. In certain cases, one might consider buying near-obsolete models or second-hand machines, so long as maintenance costs and software fit are not problems. The main message remains: do not spend excessive amounts of time looking at hardware, however fascinating it may be. Such infinitely less reliable and more trouble-some components as software, applications, end users and one's own IT colleagues all deserve much more attention.

Key issues

- Demote suppliers in favour of architectures, choosing the latter before specific suppliers are considered.
- Formulate long-term plans to escape from failing suppliers, especially if they are weak in PC areas or open systems.

- The traditional 'IBM versus the others' choice still applies to the downsized world. Pick one or the other, but not both (noting that the IBM world includes many compatible products supplied by other vendors).
- Spend less time on hardware acquisition in order to examine software products more closely.

22

Software for downsizing

Though hardware items are obviously important in downsizing, they are rarely as crucial as the major items of software in one's chosen system. Most rewards - and mistakes - relating to product selection today centre on software. In a highly packaged environment, the operating software (meaning operating system itself, database manager and communications drivers) is almost as significant a factor in achieving success as the application programs which it supports. If the operating layer is wrong, then high costs, low reliability, slow change and lack of manageability will be evident in varying degrees.

Software prices - and pricing policies - vary widely in the different sectors within downsizing. The common thread is that, if many items of a particular type are being purchased, much pricing flexibility can be expected, especially if the additional items are likely to require little support from the vendor. In general, the PC market is the simplest as well as being the cheapest (on a per unit basis). Some products that have separate run-time and development versions may give run-time elements free, especially if the supplier is pressured politely.

In the UNIX market, as well as with proprietary minicomputers, many suppliers try to price software on the assumed power of the central processor, or on the number of users likely to be attached to one machine. In some cases the prices escalate steeply, as suppliers are eager to extract high profits from software sales even where they are selling the hardware as well. IBM's AS/400 and DEC's VAX are both cases in point, as software costs much more at the top of the scale than at entry level, even though one is buying exactly the same product in most cases. Again, negotiation is called for.

Operating systems - overall issues

There are three rough categories of operating system in the downsized market. The most common is the traditional mini system, epitomized by UNIX, VMS, PRIMOS and Hewlett-Packard's MPE. IBM's VM system for its small and medium mainframes is a close relative. These are all relatively complicated to set up, operate and change, unless one is dealing with very small pre-configured packages for entry-level machines. In return, one can do a fairly wide variety of things with such systems, running different types of application task and with widely varying workloads. On a large single machine with many user types logged on, it is an appropriate enough product, though one pays in terms of training and personnel costs, and in both risk and sluggishness where changes are required.

In such a large-mini environment, many related products are also complicated, as it is assumed the user will have the expertise, money and willingness to tune systems using many low-level parameters. Database managers typify the philosophy. The issue of scalability presents some related problems, for both operating and mid-level software. While scalability is a fine thing *per se*, it is asking much of a software system to be able to support both tiny and very large minis with the same design, and stresses tend to show at both ends of the spectrum but in different ways. At the small end, as suggested, the product may be overly complicated for the user to operate well. At the large end, not only great complexity but also loss of machine performance may result. Mini software, perhaps even more than mainframe, is best somewhere in the mid-point of the supplier's hardware range, offering a blend of facility, performance and reasonable ease of use given the ambitious broad design goals.

If mini software is one category with recognizable traits, the second of our groups contains only one entry: OS/400, the operating system for AS/400. In theory some other older operating systems such as MUMPS and Pick might be included here, as they follow some of the same design concepts. However, these systems are not thought to have long-term viability by most industry observers.

OS/400's design target is simple transaction handling, which by many downsized users is seen as their high-priority core application. The software is both efficient here and reasonably easy to use, though as with all small machines matters become a bit fraught as one moves up near the top of the range. The software is not designed for

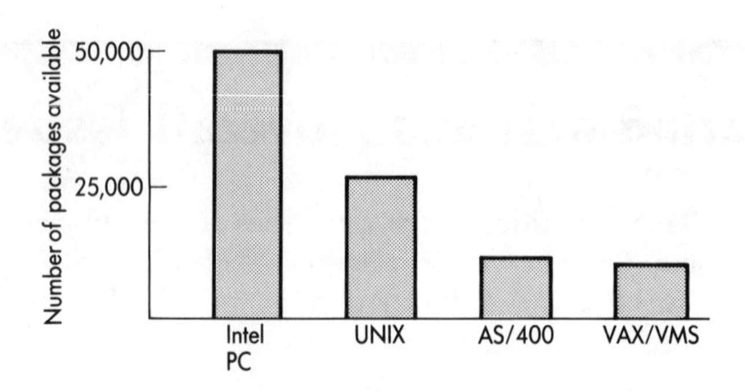

Figure 22.1 The fight for applications.

Small-system suppliers are desperate to show the largest possible number of application packages for their systems. The above numbers are approximate, and vary depending upon what is called a package and who is doing the survey. Both PC and UNIX categories are growing at a high rate, while VAX and AS/400 are relatively static. The number of packages and the growth rate are good indicators of a system's viability.

numeric-intensive work, so for scientific/technical work on any scale it must give place to the mini. For word processing and office applications in general, it is about as good as most minis (which is to say not very good, as most office work is better handled via attached PCs). OS/400 is easier to set up and use than most mini systems, though at the very bottom end of the range one would be comparing it to a shrink-wrapped mini or UNIX system, and there would be very little difference between OS/400 and its competitors.

Our third category of operating software includes PC operating systems, including those items that are targeted at PC-compatible servers. In the latter group, one includes Novell's NetWare (which was discussed in Chapter 14 on communications and networking).

So far as standard operating systems for the PC of the future go, OS/2 is the main item of interest at the moment. Microsoft's Windows (NT) will be of equal interest when it arrives, and the presence of two major broad spectrum products in the PC market should enhance that side of the industry substantially.

The above comments are not meant to diminish the obvious importance of the existing variety of DOS systems on the market (from IBM, Microsoft and Digital Research, the latter now linked with Novell), or of Windows 3.1 and onwards. However, the DOS family (which logically includes Windows as an extension) is both old and limited. While DOS machines will be around for many years to come, more ambitious offerings are required for the large and busy workstation and for the server alike. NetWare, OS/2, Windows (NT) and PC versions of UNIX all look viable here.

While much remains to be seen, given that Windows (NT) is not yet fully in the market, it is expected that the combination of OS/2 and Windows (NT) will sell at a rate of several million units per year, sufficient to tie up a large portion of the corporate market as well as of the small company client/server sector.

The recent success of IBM's OS/2 effectively gives it a lead in the corporate market (it roughly doubled its installed base to approximately two million copies during 1992). The product has been around for over five years, and by now it is reasonably known and trusted. Many of the larger software developers are bringing out products for OS/2 and Presentation Manager, whereas earlier they were hanging back and watching the direction of the market.

OS/2 is more resource efficient than many competitors, and it is reasonably easy to install and use, given its ambitious design goals. At this writing it is the lowest-risk operating system for the PC server area, though if one wishes to mix DOS or Windows products into the system then NetWare appears an equally safe bet.

UNIX

Among the traditional mid-range items, UNIX is by a wide margin the most important. It has already established itself as a standard in scientific, manufacturing, academic and many public-sector areas. It is the only significant operating system for high-powered desktop engineering or graphics workstations.

It is important for prospective users to understand what UNIX is, and equally what it is not. Most have heard by now the story of how it was invented – as a single-user operating system for playing games on an old DEC mini. To many cynics, this remains the product's only suitable use.

During the 1980s, UNIX was confined mainly to the manufacturing/scientific environment, and was used by software houses to develop packages. Until near the end of that decade, commercial users rarely saw the product. UNIX usage varies much by country. Within the UK, usage of the system began early, and for commercial as well as technical work. Within the USA, UNIX is still seen as mainly a scientific item. Much of Europe generally is somewhere between the UK and North America.

UNIX usage is expected to grow in most market sectors, meaning over the range of users and applications, and in both small- and large-machine territory. However, it will probably lose market share to OS/2 and Windows (NT) because of the combined PC and client/server thrusts. UNIX should grow particularly at the expense of the proprietary operating systems from traditional minicomputer suppliers such as DEC, Hewlett-Packard, Wang, Data General and others. It should also replace many of IBM's older mid-range offerings, on both the mainframe and the small systems sides.

An area of much interest is how UNIX will perform against PC server products such as Novell's NetWare, OS/2 and Windows (NT), both indirectly (mounted on a mini box) and directly (as a driver for the server in an otherwise PC-based network). Software developers of add-on products tend to jump onto the fastest-moving bandwagon at a particular moment, and this in turn reinforces the strength of that particular movement, creating a snowball effect. There is a significant possibility that the PC server software set will dominate the centre of the market, much at UNIX's expense. Much depends upon what specific software suppliers do.

In terms of what it is today, UNIX is a family of operating systems but with a reasonably common base. This commonality is

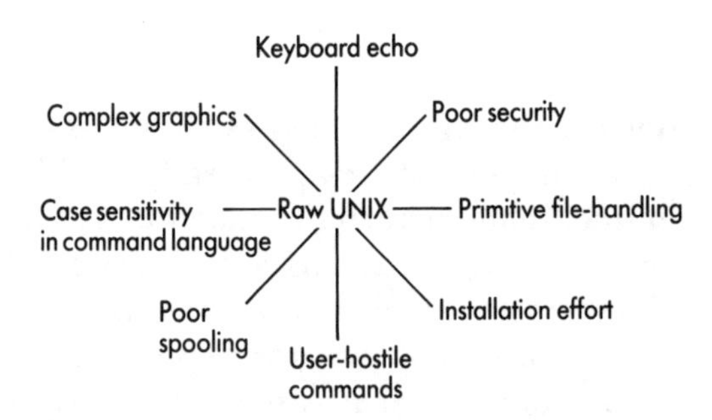

Figure 22.2 Insulating and enhancing UNIX.

For commercial users, UNIX requires concealment and enhancement to be even remotely suitable. Rapid progress is being made, primarily by IBM, Santa Cruz Operation and Sun, in packaging the product. Aside from wrapping the hostile portions into invisibility, use of good complementary products (especially for database management) can make a big difference in usability.

established by the low conversion cost of porting one UNIX application to another. This is not to say the application will run ideally on the new platform, but at least the functionality will be there. There is still a fair amount of variability in conversion efforts, even where different versions of the same supplier's UNIX is concerned. IBM's PC version of AIX (IBM's UNIX), for example, can require more effort than converting to AIX on the RS/6000 (the latter being an easy target for UNIX conversion). Users should therefore not make too many positive assumptions about converting between UNIX products.

The UNIX operating system will normally have a number of add-ons or 'extensions' provided by a given supplier. UNIX requires these, because in many respects it is a very raw, low-level operating system, especially for commercial users. It has no significant record-handling capabilities, and therefore requires a database package (though newer UNIXs are getting indexed file facilities). The database package is also required to provide file journaling, for recovery in the event of failure or corruption of data. Other UNIX shortcomings include case sensitivity in the command language, keyboard echo (meaning that a character keyed into the machine is not shown on the terminal until it arrives at the central processor and is sent back – a slow and cumbersome way of doing things), and poor security. This last item has several dimensions, from the danger of hacking to file corruption (this latter occurring when a machine is switched off before files are closed in an orderly fashion). Anyone used to a reasonable commercial system such as an AS/400 or System/36 will inevitably regard raw UNIX as an appalling affair, suitable for the technical marketplace and nothing else.

Suppliers, especially for the commercial market, must therefore enhance UNIX significantly if it is to be a contender against such friendlier items as NetWare, OS/2 and OS/400. While most large vendors do cushion the user from some of the sharper edges of UNIX, one should still check on the state of play with any given product at any specific time. Security is generally at C2 level (according to the US Department of Defense scale), meaning that passwords are required and auditing facilities can identify attempts to enter the system. One usually has the option to switch off the key-echo feature, as with a remote screen on a sluggish line the keying can be well ahead of what is appearing on the screen, so confusing and annoying the user as well as leading to unnecessary errors. With a buffered terminal, such as a PC, this of course would not happen in any case.

A more recent, if long overdue, development in the civilizing of UNIX has been the appearance of so-called 'shrink-wrapped' versions of the system for desktop and other smaller machines. This makes the product more competitive against small OS/400 systems, PC servers and DEC's desktop versions of VMS. While packages vary, this category of UNIX includes products from Sun, AT&T and Santa Cruz Operation.

In comparing UNIX against competitors, its resource usage has been cause for comment. Against some very lean systems, it is indeed hungry for hardware. However, as hardware gets cheaper this becomes less of an issue, and direct hardware consumption causes less concern than it used to. The more serious side of heavy hardware usage is that it can cause unexpected performance problems. Where much main memory or many disk channels are suddenly required due to peak loading, a small system short on these items can grind to a halt with very little warning.

It should be appreciated that UNIX performance is often not as bad as it looks. Suppliers are hoisted with their own petards when they boast of artificial hardware speeds, only to have to face apparently astronomic consumption of central processor instructions by the operating software. A variety of benchmarks on UNIX suggests that a standard transaction as defined by the Transaction Processing Council might consume approximately one million central processor instructions. However, if one reduces the claimed central processor speeds to more earthly levels, then UNIX is not that bad. If one divides the claimed instruction rate by three or four (life being very approximate in the world of hardware marketing), then we come up with more likely figures of between 250 000 to 300 000 instructions for a single transaction. This still does not compete with some of IBM's more efficient products such as the AS/Entry (formerly System/36), AS/400 or the VSE-based small mainframes, though it is broadly in line with most traditional proprietary minis.

Aside from central processor usage, UNIX is also hungry for main memory. Broad configuration guidelines for a multi-user machine suggest half an Mbyte per user, this in addition to several Mbytes (say, four to ten) for operating software, including a database and a windowing package.

Many of UNIX's more publicized features such as the file directory structure have more to do with the super-technical or developer's world than with user concerns. One area of UNIX strength is its interprocess communication, of which there are three flavours available, depending on the volume and urgency of data to be transferred. This makes UNIX suitable for complicated applications (as occur in manufacturing), where many different programs need to talk to each other. It also fits the client/server environment, as UNIX does not

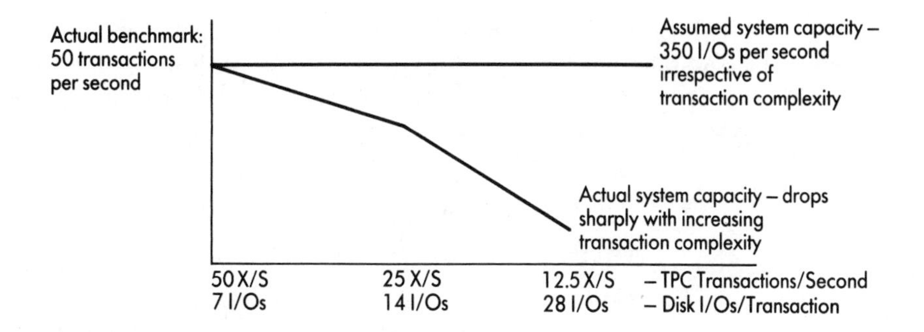

Figure 22.3 Extrapolating benchmarks.

Software suppliers have now gone as benchmark crazy as hardware vendors, filling advertisements and brochures with figures that are at once impressive and absurd. As the Appendix on benchmarks suggests, these claims need to be treated with care and should be related only in the loosest possible way to the real world. A particular hazard, stressed by Figure 22.3, is the use of the oversimplified benchmark to gauge capacity for other types of work. Depending upon how far one strays from the original assumptions behind the benchmark, the figures claimed by the supplier may range from the mildly relevant to the entirely meaningless.

mind particularly if the separate processes are on separate machines.

UNIX on any but the simplest machine requires more expertise to set up and maintain than many competitors, but it is not so different overall in this respect from, say, DEC's VMS or Hewlett-Packard's MPE. Users who are used to coping with traditional minis will need training in UNIX, but they will otherwise find it much like the systems they have been used to. A new user, on the other hand, or one coming from a genuine commercial machine, should exercise care in approaching UNIX. If the product must be used, then configuring all system components as simply and homogeneously as possible and then undertaking the right degree of training are both required to lower running costs and risks. Such a user will probably need to recruit trained UNIX technicians from outside the company as well, in order to bring skills on board within a reasonable time.

One aspect of UNIX is the POSIX movement, meaning that systems which are not UNIX aim to provide a core of system functions that are compatible with UNIX (and hence with each other). Systems which are expected to be POSIX-compliant within a few years include DEC's VMS (which is already), OS/400, OS/2 and Windows (NT). Because these otherwise proprietary systems have different extensions and performance characteristics, one should not expect too much from such supposed compatibility. The main advantage will be that it cuts the cost of software conversion, most of which will be done by suppliers of packages, not by users.

To put a bottom line on UNIX, its pluses are several and meaningful:

- It is here to stay.
- It offers wide third-party markets.
- It offers the wide application spectrum of the traditional mini, meaning that though it may not do everything well it at least can do it.
- It offers some inter-operability, both between other UNIXs and with proprietary systems.

The minuses of UNIX, detailed earlier, lie mainly in its costs, complexities and inadequacies, though for many situations these drawbacks can be minimized. For a medium-to-large installation with substantial needs for technical computing, UNIX has no disqualifiers *per se*. For commercial work, however, there are many competitors, and the fact that UNIX is theoretically 'open' should be balanced against a lot of less theoretical advantages of competitive offerings.

Database software

Database software, along with the operating system itself, represents a major focal point of any commercial installation. Here, the user has a happy choice before him, as there are a number of mature, well-defined products on the market. Many run over a wide range of platforms and over wide capacity bands. The market leaders are true relational items, and so are viable into the future on that score. Most are efficient enough for both transaction work and information handling, and the SQL language they use is at least semi-standard.

ORACLE is the best known of the database products, and is available on most platforms (though, like many wide-spread products, it may not be the best performer on a given platform). Most implementations are under UNIX, and the OS/2 version uses UNIX-like 'processes' rather than the more efficient OS/2 'threads'. In this consultant's experience, there are very few users who dislike ORACLE,

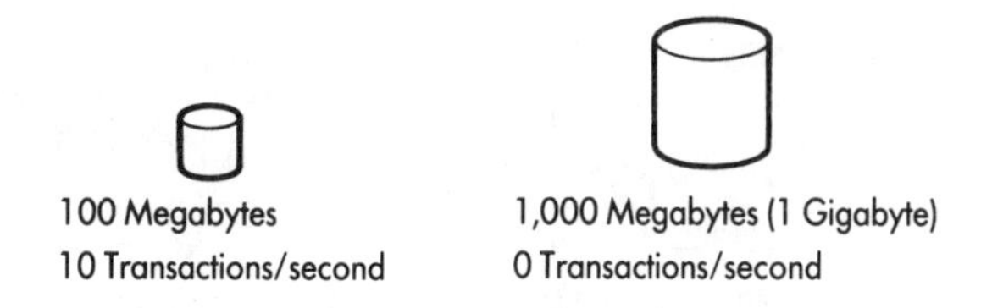

Figure 22.4 Database managers and the size issue.

The example in Figure 22.4 is an extreme one, but only slightly less disastrous situations are regularly reported. The point is relevant to downsized systems, as many database management products started life small and have not yet grown to very high-capacity systems. With most database products, one cannot run the same transaction rate against a database much larger than the one initially used, but with minicomputer and PC products one should be especially careful. In the mid-1980s, many UNIX-based database managers could only handle 10 megabytes or so of data gracefully. Now most are much better, but it is still asking a lot to handle databases several gigabytes in size. Even some of the so-called UNIX 'hot-boxes' cannot handle data in the tens of gigabytes, as they were designed to handle high transaction rates but on much smaller amounts of data. If the downsized user has a requirement for a large database, he should see it running in a like environment before he investigates further.

as it is functional and easy to use for this type of product. The most common objection is the price, which is high. The combined cost of ORACLE and its CASE development tool can be $20,000 per developer workstation, a much higher figure than would apply to PC-based products.

Newer versions of ORACLE support distributed databases in the form of the now virtually standard two-phase commit, guaranteeing the integrity of related databases across remote sites. The product has long included basic program-generation tools which are par for the course (that is they will generate simple programs but are not up to a complex monolithic application).

ORACLE's presence in the market is so pronounced that one should have a good reason for considering any other downsized database product. ORACLE gained its presence by being a reasonable product in the first place, but also by virtue of much better marketing than broadly similar products were able to undertake (for example, INGRES). The viability of ORACLE is higher than that of most or its competitors, often by a wide margin.

SYBASE is probably the second most viable third-party database product in mid-range. Much of its success in the future hinges on the

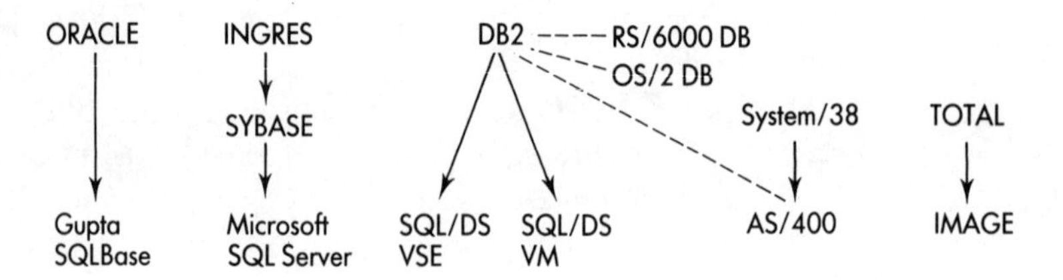

Figure 22.5 Database product relationships.

Database products have various types of relationship with one another on occasion, and it helps to know this to place products accurately. Related products may share, say, SQL compatibility, as is the case with IBM's, or good performance, as with the INGRES-SYBASE-SQL Server group.

Microsoft arrangement (we pointed out that Microsoft's SQL Server is in fact SYBASE, but properly adapted for the OS/2 Intel platform). Particularly, if Windows (NT) takes off as a server product, then SYBASE will benefit both directly and via its reputation, as it will be seen as a viable, successful product for other platforms aside from Windows (NT).

IBM and the Novell-Gupta combination are both offering PC server databases closely linked to the operating system. The close coupling of such products enables good performance to be enjoyed, as each can be tuned to fit the other. Also, the combination should be easier to use and enjoy better support. These two product combinations, plus the Microsoft-SYBASE one, are likely for client/server situations because of their probable stability. The two non-IBM combinations claim substantial performance advantages over the OS/2 Database Manager for basic transaction work.

For the scientific side of the UNIX market, INGRES has had a presence which varied over time. The company initially had acute problems, as it was run by narrow technicians with little business flair. It was recently taken over by Ask, so its future depends upon what this new owner does with it. INGRES has recently been dropped as a preferred option by DEC for its UNIX, though it remains a credible option for both DEC and IBM UNIX (the latter on the RS/6000). For scientific users, INGRES offers the QUEL language, which is more suitable than SQL for technical work though it can be extremely inscrutable.

The UNIX database market has a number of other entrants. INFORMIX and PROGRESS are among the better known. The former's strength is performance for transaction handling, whereas

PROGRESS has a more functional data-handling language than is usually common with program generators attached to such products.

We mentioned Gupta above in the context of the Novell alliance. The database manager is called SQLBase, and it has become a standard of sorts for client/server work. Gupta is noted for its aggressive benchmarks on Novell Intel systems. Figures of well over a hundred TPC transactions per second have been quoted on a Compaq System-Pro. To put such figures into context, one is talking about performance levels equivalent to those of a large UNIX or proprietary minicomputer - and at a fraction of the hardware-software cost. With continuing falls of hardware prices, one is approaching the $1,000 level for a transaction per second - compare this to DEC's boast for around $8,000 for the same on a microVAX.

Application packages

We have stressed already the importance of using packaged application software in order to lower costs and to ease ongoing running. Packages, as with much else, represent both opportunities and hazards, and it is often the latter that receive insufficient attention. Bad mistakes continue to be made simply because the majority of users do not know how to evaluate a package.

The most common way of looking at packages is to concentrate on the functionality involved, ignoring many other aspects which, especially later on, might damage the installation's health. In other words, attention is paid to *what* the package does, but not *how* it does it. This 'how' might be interpreted very broadly to include not only the way the package has been designed and constructed, but also how it will be supported by its supplier in the future. Even at the functional level, many errors might be made. This is especially likely if, as often happens, much of the evaluation is undertaken by IT people supposedly acting on behalf of their users. In such cases it is inevitable that some misinterpretation of requirements will occur and that the package will therefore not be investigated properly.

One has seen unbelievably bad examples of this in the marketplace, and where all parties involved were supposed to be professionals. One of the worst concerned a hospital management

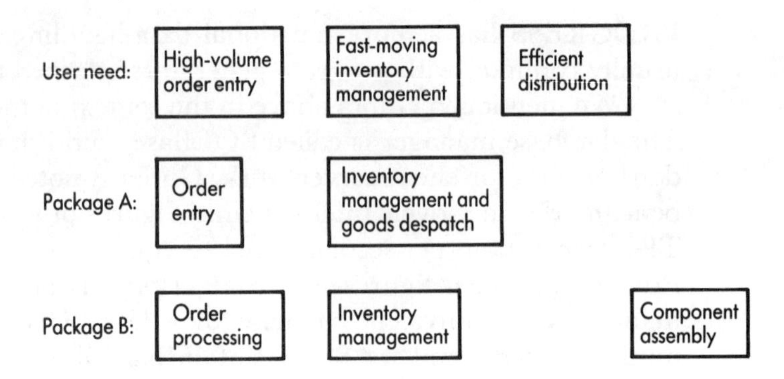

Figure 22.6 Broad application package fit.

Looking at the broad areas covered by an application package can warn of possible shortcomings in view of a particular user requirement. In Figure 22.6, Package A has been designed with a broadly similar application range in mind as the user requirement. Package B was aimed more at a manufacturing environment, and may or may not have a strong enough order entry front end to satisfy our particular user.

package, the origins of which were in the US. When bought by European health agencies the product was found to be virtually inoperable, and the reasons for this were simple. Many US hospitals, including the ones the package was designed for, are small private concerns, with no more than a few hundred beds each. The large, centralized European hospitals were many times this size, and also had more complex links with ancillary services.

The package could not handle the extra volumes efficiently, in either machine or personnel terms, and was also inappropriate in much actual functionality. Yet, no senior user or IT representative involved in the evaluation had thought to look at the most obvious design goals. They were too amazed by the high-pressure sell and the colourful screens presented by the hardware vendor's sales team, who were selling the package in order to sell their brand of hardware. A number of glowing references for the product were produced, all from the US of course where the product was perfectly valid.

Because most industry-specific packages represent a long-term commitment going well beyond the mere purchase price of the software, it pays to invest time looking at them. This in itself is an issue, as the more time spent looking at a package, the greater the delay to implementation and the greater its cost. Merely evaluating a complex package can take a number of man-years, if one includes both IT and user time. Simple packages should require a small fraction of that effort, perhaps as little as a few man-weeks to look at a few major alternatives.

As a starting point, an application package should be matched against topologies or application groupings defined by initial planning exercises. A package that maps only part of what an application does, or one which spans two or more groupings, is much less likely than one that fits. One should then look at further design goals, such as what size organization or user group was envisaged, and whether the package had a particular country's specific needs in mind.

The base system platform is also relevant (meaning hardware, operating system and database at least), as mistakes are frequently made here. One recalls a recent widespread incident, where a number of public-sector organizations were shown a demonstration of a package running on machine X. The distributor of the package was also an agent for machine Y, and glibly promised that the package would be converted to machine Y if the customers would only please sign up for the package. Surprisingly, many did sign up, and the conversion turned out to be a disaster. Machines X and Y had very little in common, being totally different designs and with very different ways of using their respective databases.

Though only IT personnel may be qualified to look at technical aspects of a package, user staff should be willing and able to spend much of their time assessing their side of the package. They should look at not only the base functionality, but also at how error conditions, interrupted procedures, enquiries and reporting are handled. The overall time taken per day to set up and close down the package should be estimated, as there are often unpleasant surprises here. One recalls the daily 25-hour overnight run, which any right-thinking package evaluator may understandably wish to avoid.

With a package designed for small machines, one sees two different ways of handling so-called extra or add-on functions, meaning anything that does not have to update master or key transaction files online. Older packages tend to do only the minimum updating when a transaction is entered, leaving extra updates (to ledgers and history files, for example) until after close of business. More recent packages, designed for machines with more capacity, may update all positions at the time of transaction entry, avoiding the need for the end of day runs. In general, the fully online approach is to be preferred, so long as adequate machine capacity exists to perform the add-on updates. The traditional notion persists in some places that fully online updating is somehow more dangerous than the plodding overnight approach, but in a well-run installation this should not be so. In fact, it is more likely that operational mistakes or abuse of the system will

Table 22.1 The application package.

User	• What functionality is not included? • Is unwanted functionality included? • Are both transaction and data volumes similar to requirements? • Is the sequence of operations appropriate for this business? • Is it easy to operate? How flexible is operation? • Are error reports easy to understand and handle? • Are management information reports appropriate, and is good summary data available for further queries and reports?
User and IT	• How easy is the package to evaluate? What time-scales and effort are involved on the parts of IT and the user? • Are there meaningful alternatives to the use of: - this package? - any industry-specific package (say, using generators to create one's own code, or using a generic package)?
IT	• Can the package be maintained easily, in terms of both code and data? • Could it be adapted to new software or hardware if the need arose? • Is it unduly tied to a proprietary system or to proprietary software, so presenting traditional lock-in risks? • What are the main machine overheads in terms of central processor, disk space, disk input/output operations per second, main memory and networking resources? • Is it supported in this geographical area by the native vendor or by an agent? If an agent, does he have a good understanding of the insides of the package? • Is the package easy to extend or change? To what extent can one do this without impacting support agreements or losing the ability to upgrade to the next version which the supplier plans to bring out? • What are the total costs of ownership likely to be, including hardware and personnel costs, over the expected period of use?

In the average evaluation of an industry-specific application package, too many of the above questions never get asked. One must be prepared to make strong representations to both users and IT people that an application package is a key investment, not a frivolous add-on to more fascinating bits of the system. Time saved by undue short cuts during evaluation is likely to be paid back several-fold later on when the predictable little surprises turn up.

take place during late-evening running. It is a point worth considering, because virtually every salesman plugging an out-of-date package will cite 'security' as a supposed benefit.

On the technical side of package evaluation, database usage should be examined carefully, as this is important in its own right and can give insights into other potential problems. Packages that have been converted from one database system to another almost always have severe problems unless the vendor has totally re-written the software for the new data-handling mechanism, something suppliers are reluctant to do in view of the high cost and uncertainty involved. Packages which are old or which have their origins on small machines are particularly to be watched. A conversion to fully relational database from either the old networked style of database (IMS-DB, DL/1, IDMS, TOTAL, IMAGE) or from the simple inverted files or multi-key indexed systems used on small minis is bound to cause major problems for the package supplier. Such problems will show in poor performance, undue maintenance effort particularly with regard to the database, and perhaps in a general awkwardness in adding new functions to the existing database due to the inappropriate design.

No matter what data-handling system is used, evaluators should always look at the basics of data access. Per transaction, one should estimate how many different files or tables are read, how many updated, how much access is done by secondary keys, how often secondary keys are changed, how many consecutive passes of the files are required (either for processing transactions or for housekeeping and utility functions), and how files may be recovered in the event of corruption or system failure. Many package suppliers will resent these questions and will be unequipped to answer any detailed questions, especially if they are acting as agents for a vendor outside the country.

Most packages are not designed to be extended or modified. Where modifications are suggested, the vendor will often suggest

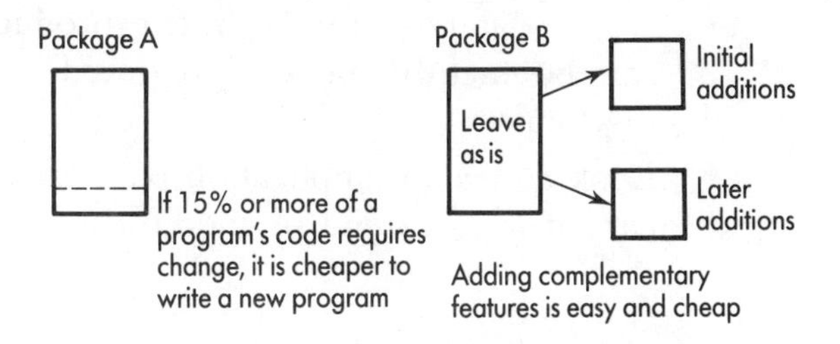

Figure 22.7 The application package – change or extend?

A common occurrence during package evaluation is to discover that 'just a few small changes' are required to meet the user's needs. It makes a big difference where these changes need to take place. It is not unusual to find users rewriting a package over time, at much greater cost and inconvenience than they would have incurred coding their own system. Modular add-ons, on the other hand, may meet requirements in an inexpensive manner and without damaging the vendor's ability to maintain and upgrade the core programs and file designs.

doing this himself, at great cost and with loss of compatibility with new releases of the package. If modifiability is thought to be a significant issue in package use, the costs and other inconveniences should be gone into as thoroughly as time and evaluation budgets permit. If satisfactory answers cannot be obtained, meaning that known costs and risks cannot be arrived at within a fairly small margin of error (say, 20%), then the long-term risks may outweigh short-term benefits. Because the internals of the package are not known by one's own IT staff, maintaining a package with its extensions or modifications can be more expensive than maintaining code written in-house. The better a package is, the fewer modifications it will require. The downsized world has increasing needs for *good* applications, and package suppliers are gradually meeting this need.

Key issues

- Where UNIX is chosen, pick as standard and widespread a version as possible.
- When choosing higher-level software, pay attention to how well it has been adapted to the underlying hardware-software platform and how long it has been established there.
- Avoid database management products if the requirement can be met by better integrated or simpler types of file mechanism.
- Look at *how* an application package does its work, and how easy it is to extend or modify.

23

Personnel and structural factors

In moving to downsized systems, virtually every existing assumption about IT must be questioned. If one answers these questions honestly and to the point, rather than trying to defend existing positions, then alterations are almost always necessary. The inconvenience of the likely changes puts many off from asking the questions in the first place. These are often the very people who refuse to perform capacity planning on their existing mainframes, because they know in advance how dreadful the results will be.

Downsizing, if the exercise is to be carried out to its most beneficial extent, does require shifts in roles and responsibilities, nowhere more so than in the IT department itself. Because of the time needed to carry out these reforms, one should plan well in advance and begin thinking of the issues as soon as one starts to consider downsizing.

Like most of downsizing, the problem is not a difficult one intellectually. It is more an effort to make certain the right steps are taken at the right time, and also to ensure that the effort is not derailed by pressure groups or individuals with existing interests. Company philosophies regarding employee treatment play an important - often constraining - role, and inevitably must be reckoned with. All the more reason for bringing the issues to management's attention in the early stages of the game. One should pre-empt any excessive personnal relocation or redundancy costs being charged to the downsizing exercise (as some mainframe defenders have suggested in certain situations). Such costs should be charged to the glorious - or otherwise - past, as is normal business practice.

Downsizing personnel requirements

The building block of the downsized IT department is the analyst/programmer. The most important point about such a person in this environment is that he really must be an analyst/programmer (note which word comes first), and not just a coder or recycled technician wearing the label. Across a large IT department, it is usual to see people called analyst/programmers performing many types of job and with differing skills and personality attributes. Of these, only a portion will normally be suitable for the project work located in user departments.

Though a given IT department may be short of the right type of person, the point must also be made that analyst/programmers are not an overly rare commodity. Highly skilled and expensive people are not needed in most downsized projects. Instead, a recognizable type of lower middle-class person earning perhaps $40,000 to $50,000 in most industrialized countries will be perfectly adequate. Such a person will be motivated by the job in hand (more elaborate types of people may not be), and will be pliable enough to train and condition. From within this relatively large pool, some sorting out needs to be done, as the person must be able to work easily with users as well as with IT types, and he needs to have the capacity to understand the particular application under consideration.

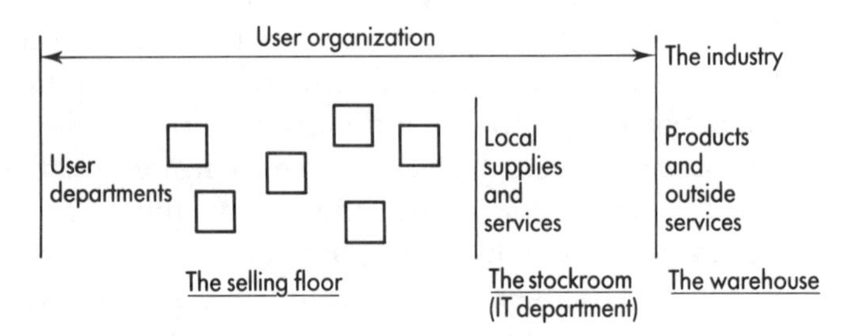

Figure 23.1 Downsizing as a retail business.

In order to break many of the 'set-in-concrete' ideas of existing IT staff, it is useful to picture the downsized world as a retail establishment. Business analysts and analyst/programmers are the customer contact people, effectively taking orders for whatever may be in stock (not, one notes, anything in the world they ask for). A good retail establishment is not pushy, but will spend time finding out both what the customer really needs and what he will pay for.

If applications are grouped into logically coherent areas, and if they consist of smaller modules that are easily understandable, then there should be no barriers to our analyst/programmer type's grasping of the application. The point we are making, and with no discourtesy intended, is that simple applications and simple people go together. A basic person, with some guidance as to what is expected, will be able to create a basic application adequately. Over a certain threshold of intricacy, the same person would find the application not merely difficult, but impossible. The mismatch of personnel and application strategies is a common fault throughout IT, and it certainly shows in downsized projects.

Aside from the analyst/programmer, who is the day-to-day interface to the user, the business analyst is the other key person linking the user to IT. Good business analysts are not that common, a fact which tempts many IT managers to fill the slot with the wrong type of person. It is common in the computer press to see recruitment advertisements specifying such things as 'Business Analyst – INGRES Experience Essential'. Often the advertisement will compound the felony by specifying a particular release of a product. Predictably, the advertisement draws responses from INGRES – or whatever – technicians, and the IT manager then wonders why his project loses sight of business objectives and instead gets bogged down in technical minutiae.

A business analyst for the downsized world should have a broad appreciation of technology, including specific design issues relating to the system platform and communications system being used. However, knowledge here need not be extensive, especially if acquiring it would detract from more important activities. Key product information should be able to be gained within a small number of days, assuming the business analyst is already competent in broad IT matters. A good business analyst will know what high-level questions to ask about technological capabilities, though he will be anything but a super-technician in personality and preferences. To expect him to acquire technical knowledge beyond a certain point is to miss the issue of what business analysis is about. Many IT managers recruit overly technical business analysts because the managers themselves are former technicians, and they feel comfortable with technicians. They think that the basis of IT is technology, and not people. If such an IT manager is wise enough to recognize his own limitations, he should try to get some assistance from more business-oriented IT people (not users) in selecting suitable business analysts.

The business analyst's primary function is to change the user's business need into a description of the application which IT people can understand. In the small to medium downsized project, he will also monitor the detailed design, coding and testing of the programs, and will have a continuing supervisory role once the system is running live and being altered and maintained.

Aside from general suitability for the business analysis activity, one is therefore looking for people with some leadership ability as well. This is common in proper business analysts, as opposed to wrongly labelled technicians, as the business analyst is inherently equipped to deal with multi-dimensional problems and those which require dynamic reconfiguration.

Another issue that arises with our business analyst is how specific the application experience ought to be. As with technical knowledge, a common mistake among IT recruiters is to look for overly specific application experience at the expense of general capability. Again, to the more 'bits and piecey' IT mind, the very specific items look both safer and easier to evaluate. One can simply check items off a list to see if a person is suitable; this is much less of a strain than actually thinking about the problem. Some refinement of what constitutes application knowledge might be in order. Certainly the business analyst must understand the general nature of the business areas he encounters, as to why they exist and how procedures may be carried out. He should also understand concepts of data underlying the

Table 23.1 A rough guide to user-contact people.

Yes	*No*
• Sociable	• Introverted
• Analysis experience	• Technical or coding experience
• Presentable	• Shower shoes
• Interest in business	• Wants to write own operating system
• 4GL and screen design experience	• Philosopher
• Upwardly-mobile social group C (lower-middle or skilled working class)	• Downwardly-mobile anything
• Moderate salary	• Over-priced plumber
• Methodical	• Chaotic but creative

Because of their high profile within the user's area, analysts and analyst/programmers, require selection on general business as well as technical skills. Those who view the organizational world as a gross infringement of personal liberty should remain locked in central IT with the rest of the semi-functional hardware. With most downsized systems, high intelligence and much imagination are not necessities, though they are nice when they do appear. Practical types who get on with it are the essence of good downsizing personnel.

business processes, and an analyst with some database experience or orientation should be substantially more capable here than one without such knowledge.

It bears keeping in mind that some businesses are more specific and complicated than others, and in such one should look at least for experience within the particular industry. Manufacturing and financial services are such areas, where handling of intricate products has a follow-on impact on application and file design. In the general heart of commercial data processing, where relatively simple record-keeping and office systems characterize most user needs, broad experience is good enough. Any slight lack in a particular area should be more than compensated for by the extra quality one obtains by paying more attention to the proper selection procedure.

Along with the analyst/programmer and the business analyst, the manager of the development team or teams is of obvious importance. Most medium to large IT departments have reasonable mid-level managers covering such tasks as project management or project leadership. Though the basic skills are important, especially with many concurrent downsizing efforts, such people may not be familiar with the more specific needs of new-world projects. Good project managers should be encouraged, and if necessary trained, to concentrate or minimize some more traditional activities (such as large and long progress meetings) and to direct their attentions more toward business-related items. Also, the need to adapt quickly and certainly to changes or other unexpected conditions should be stressed.

The key management role in downsizing is that of the systems development manager. In a small organization, he may be the project leader or project manager outlined above. In a large organization, he will be insulated from some projects by perhaps one or two layers of management, though for larger projects he may be directly in charge, perhaps supervising several business analysts and their teams of analyst/programmers. It is very important for the systems development manager in charge of downsizing to be separate from the person in charge of any traditional mainframe development and maintenance. In many IT departments, this could be a highly political issue, as it may mean splitting the systems development function in two.

If such separation of systems development management is not done, it is almost inevitable that one half of the installation will receive insufficient attention as well as getting the wrong sort of attention. We have made the point many times that the old world and the new world are very different places, and to expect one manager to carry on the very difficult task of developing and maintaining two such separate environments is asking a great deal. If for any reason this separation of roles is not possible, then it might be better to put the downsizing or the mainframe portion directly under a more senior manager (possibly the IT director himself). The systems development manager proper should be left to deal with whichever half of the installation is deemed more important over the next few years. If a small, static mainframe system will remain after downsizing, then the systems development manager is better off looking after the new distributed world. If, however, only a small number of downsized projects will be attempted, and if the mainframe is still to do the bulk of the work, then the systems development manager should remain here and let the downsized projects report elsewhere. The downsizing work should be left separate both to maintain its identity and to ensure that the work gets done properly.

Knowing the business

It was stressed that the two types of people involved directly in development (the business analyst and his analyst/programmers) should have application capability. It is essential to make certain this is so, and to correct any overly apparent shortcomings *before* the people are sent out to face the user (recall our earlier diagram regarding asking stupid questions in front of the end user). This rule, while obvious, is honoured more in the breach than in the observance in traditional IT as well as new-world projects. It represents still another instance where downsizing represents an opportunity to start doing things properly again.

Even with good selection procedures, business knowledge is more likely to be missing in analyst/programmers than in more senior people. The reasons are two: the people are more junior; and they are by nature partly technical, and so may not be fully adapted to the business world. There are two levels of knowledge that should be checked for:

- Knowledge of the business problem in general (for example does the person know what a goods received note is and what it contains, who uses it, and so on?).
- Knowledge of how this particular organization carries out the more universal business activity.

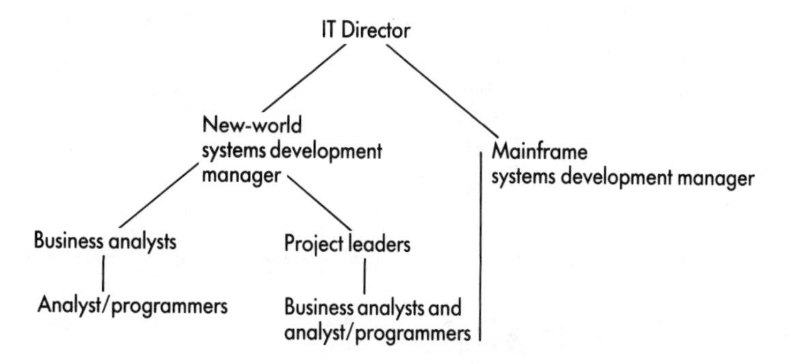

Figure 23.2 Separating downsizing project management.

Wherever possible, it is desirable to have downsized projects under a separate IT management structure. On the 'New-world' side, two alternative ways of managing projects are shown. The use of the project leader directly supervising both business analysts and analyst/programmers would be suitable for larger or more complex downsized projects. Where a number of smaller and more basic projects are concerned, the business analysts themselves could be responsible for their specific units, reporting directly to the systems development manager.

Many managers will try to economize in assessing and preparing people in the above areas. Often, they leapfrog to the second topic at the expense of the first (yet another example of fine detail before the more important principle). This is dangerous, because the analyst/programmer's lack of in-depth understanding may become obvious to the end user. Equally importantly, by knowing little of the real purpose surrounding the business area, the analyst/programmer may miss exploring alternatives that may represent a better solution to the overall business-IT problem.

The first step in dealing with the application knowledge problem is to establish what such knowledge is needed for a given project. The second is to evaluate those people who are aimed at end-user territory. Where the manager performing the evaluation knows the area, this should not be a problem. A few leading questions plus some informal discussion as to how the main problems might be handled should establish both knowledge and attitudes.

It is essential for managers to keep their own information updated. They may gain some inkling of what is going on in the heat of development, then get distracted into other areas once pressures have shifted. We have noted that a characteristic of the downsized world can be sudden and unexpected demands for change. For mid-level managers within IT, this will be very disconcerting and disruptive unless actual application details are monitored on some systematic basis. Sitting in on occasional progress meetings, either those within IT or where users are present, and where application issues are specifically on the agenda, can help to lower the shock factor.

Application training

Where development staff are not thought secure within an application, then remedial action must be taken. The most obvious move is to look for other people with better knowledge and the required level of IT skills. Where alternative people are not available, then training must be given. Depending upon one's location, there may be outside concerns that are willing to organize brief events (normally only a few days are needed). Accountancy bodies and those societies dealing with banking and insurance can often suggest likely sources. For manufacturing, universities and technical educational institutions often are interested in small amounts of consultancy, which might include informal training by a knowledgeable lecturer or postgraduate student.

With any such outside training concern, it is important to explain the objectives clearly, and to suggest an organized approach to the subject. The area to be concentrated upon is how the application is approached today, what are its major controls in terms of information handled and what are the necessary interfaces to other internal functions as well as to the external world (customers, suppliers, legal authorities, and so on). Excessive background and theoretical material, and undue levels of complexity, should be avoided, unless it is clear that the latter may impact the implementation (in manufacturing systems they often do).

In general, knowing about an application's essentials is more important in the early project stages than more specific appreciation of how the details apply within the organization. So long as the principles and the bare processing necessities are understood, then the missing minor items can be filled in during detailed analysis. This later-stage tailoring should not take much time. What does take time is to try to teach analysts or analyst/programmers both application basics and the techniques of systems analysis in a live project environment. This writer has seen it many times, and it invariably resulted in very low credibility of IT personnel as well as projects that were late and unsuccessful.

Table 23.2 What support ratios?

Analyst/programmer:	200 (generally basic) programs within one system *or* 50 programs each in 2 or 3 separate systems
Systems programmer: (machine-specific software technician)	5 medium-sized UNIX or proprietary mini systems if separate, more if similar (say, 10), *or* 2 to 3 times that number of servers
PC specialist:	100 to 200 relatively independent PCs (meaning not part of a closely-coupled mini-based or client/server system)
Business analyst:	3 to 6 developing systems, *or* 2 to 3 times that for installed, of 20–30 users, *or* 1 medium (50–100 user) system under development
Project leader:	1 large (200–500 user) system under development, *or* 3 such under moderate rates of ongoing development

The ratios in Table 23.2 depend on many variables, including end-user characteristics as well as application and technical complexity. These ratios been achieved by many users exhibiting good practice and where conditions were not overly difficult. Prospective downsizers might use Table 23.2 for initial targets, modifying them appropriately as conditions change.

Analytical skills

There are numerous organizations that purport to teach systems analysis, often under the umbrella of some all-encompassing methodology. Such courses can take a long time to get through the basics, and they may not cover some important issues at all (such as how to prioritize between conflicting requirements). They normally deal with very simple business or systems issues, and rarely recognize any sort of machine constraints, even in the most general terms. While the downsized project in its early stages does not worry too much about narrow technological issues, it is still vital to appreciate broad machine limits. The application group has been drawn with a certain type of (perhaps imaginary) machine in mind. If the analysis process does not recognize this from the first, then wildly inappropriate solutions are likely to be designed.

One meets very few concerns that are equipped to teach the art

Table 23.3 Mathematics for beginners.

Utilization:	50% - 2 × service time 90% - 10 × service time
Compound probability:	10 dependent components of 90% reliability mean overall system reliability of around 33%
Exponential complexity:	A system twice as large and complex might require four times the development and maintenance effort

A basic level of numeracy should be encouraged among those configuring systems, whether their concern is the application or the technical components. For most downsizing work, the concepts are good enough, as the object is to avoid making large mistakes.

of simplifying applications, as opposed to making them overly complicated. As with application training, much will depend upon what organizations are available locally, but in general one should avoid the large, expensive consultancies for this type of training. People who know how to get straight to the core of an application might be found in small software houses used to dealing with small machines. IBM's AS/400 agents or distributors generally have such skills, as should many of the larger PC distributors (regrettably, small PC dealers are rarely geared to any type of application development, as they are mainly package oriented). A commercial UNIX dealer might have the required orientation, especially if he is used to coping with small and medium UNIX systems for small businesses (larger UNIX solutions are often tailored, so basic, unelaborate design skills may not be applied).

Whatever training in systems analysis is given, some preparation in-house should also take place before project work is begun. This is partly to ensure that the training process is complete, but also to condition the analysts and analyst/programmers for the specific users they are to meet.

Longer-term training and relocation

If downsizing is to be done on any scale, and over a long period of time, then the relocation of more narrow and traditional IT types will have to be faced. For the downsized world, the usual IT department has far too many of these. The most obvious and pressing question is: how many of these can be reconditioned into suitable analyst/programmers, to fill the existing shortage? Possibly quite a few can, but the selection and training of these second-line people needs to be handled much more delicately than was the case with the first wave. More mistakes are likely to be made, however good one's intentions, and the consequences are going to be more serious.

The observant reader will have noted that we only mentioned analyst/programmers in the above paragraph, not business analysts. Bitter experience had shown that the business analyst cannot easily be recruited from unlike job slots even in the long term; as a short-term exercise it is a non-starter. The person who has come from elsewhere and has served his time as an analyst/programmer ('time' meaning a few years) might reasonably migrate up the scale into the business analyst's position. However, a narrow technician, however senior, is unlikely to turn into a business analyst ever – the odds are something like ten to one against. This 'instant business analyst' syndrome is much more common than the more innocent reader might suppose. There is a pressing political need to keep surplus senior people happy, and to many of these toying around with end users for a few years sounds like a mildly interesting proposition. The excuses indulged in include: 'well, he understands computers well, and they're more complicated than that business out there somewhere'; 'he's clever, so he should learn quickly'; or 'he might be upset and cause trouble or even leave the company if we don't keep him happy'.

The voice of experience is clear: unless he is exceptionally able *in business terms*, and unless he is exceptionally motivated, our technician turned analyst will be a flop. Software houses often try it, as do the more technical hardware suppliers (DEC, Prime and Hewlett-Packard were notorious for such unsuccessful experiments). A point to note is that an appearance of interest (which may be partly due to a fear of redundancy) is not the same thing as real interest, and even interest is a long way from ability. Technicians, if they claim business understanding, should be able to demonstrate such, either through a period of experience in their pasts or via a prolonged discussion with more than one person able to evaluate these issues.

The senior technician who is no longer needed has some legitimate choices: he can move to the supplier side of the industry; he can move outside IT, either with his present employer or with another; or he can retire, perhaps with some financial assistance.

Aside from technicians and analytical types, the most common

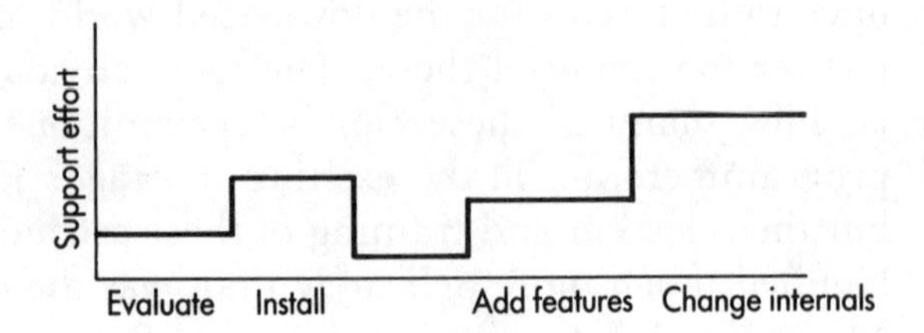

Figure 23.3 Supporting an application package.

Planning support levels for an application package poses specific problems. Especially where evaluation has not been thorough, one can get sudden requests for additions or changes. Where the package is complicated, both the number of people required and their quality may need to be higher than expected. The basic analyst/programmer whom we postulated for most downsized projects may not be able to cope with an intricate package, as one has to find out what it does, how it does it and what the implications of any changes might be before one actually effects the changes.

category of IT staff to be considered for the downsizing world are programmers - or coders - of one description or another. A certain percentage of these will be able to migrate to analyst/programmer work, and for many junior coders this will be seen as a promotion. Some junior technicians may also be trainable as analyst/programmers. Being at an early stage in their careers, they may decide that the narrow technical world is not for them and that they would prefer more business interest and human contact.

For selection, training and 'conditioning' purposes, the program coder and the junior technician may be treated alike. Few will have any understanding of either business issues or the broad scope of application development, though some application knowledge gained by the programmers will be useful. Junior technicians from the database area also may have gleaned some application-level insights.

Selection of these more junior people need not be as rigorous as that applying to system development managers, project leaders and business analysts, as the tasks they perform are simpler and under supervision. One way to cut the risks involved with such people is not to use the individual as the sole analyst/programmer in a small project, but first put him in as the number two or three (or lower) in a larger group, working alongside more senior analyst/programmers. Ongoing supervision is essential for these new people, and it is important to observe their rate of learning.

Interest, motivation and personality are the main things to look for among these new entrants to the analytical world, as their experience to date may be insufficient to form an accurate opinion. A relatively high failure rate (perhaps one in three) must be anticipated, as is usual with all categories of younger employees, as many will change direction or otherwise not adapt to the work.

The project manager gap

In our personnel scenarios so far, we have mentioned the project leader or manager in the broad context of mid-level IT management. There are two situations frequently encountered in downsizing where one should give much attention to the specific skill of project management in its own right, rather than merely thinking of it as a side-line for a systems development manager.

In many typical situations about which we have been writing, the project manager role in its traditional form has not been required. Where a business analyst himself is leading a team of a few analyst/programmers, and is reporting straight to a systems development manager, a trained project manager would be overkill and might even get in the way. However, where there are many such small projects, perhaps working to a common deadline, then standard project management may be needed to coordinate matters and to progress the laggards.

The second instance where traditional project management skills are essential is in the large downsized project, one with perhaps many elements of both application software and technology interacting (a large number of different items on a network would fit this description, even if part of the same application group). Even though we are talking about a single nominal project, its size and complexity would usually be beyond the business analyst's capabilities or interests, his leadership potential normally being limited to the small individual project. Within a given organization, there should be very few of these large, complicated projects, as among other things they contradict many of the philosophies of downsizing.

More senior project managers may be able to undertake some aspects of the systems development manager's role, especially if this

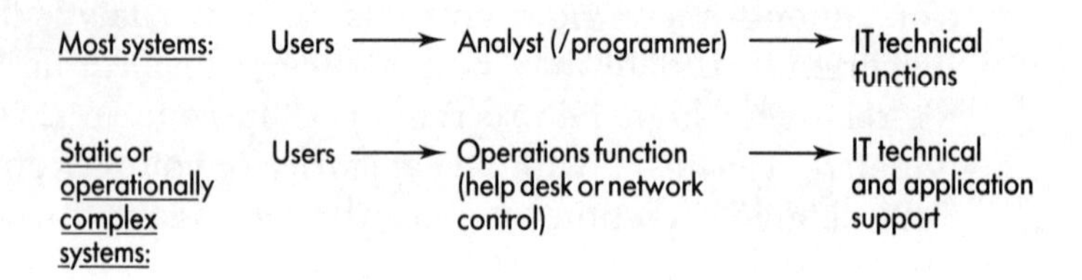

Figure 23.4 A single point of contact?

The ideal number of contact points between an end-user department and IT is one. Where this is not attainable, there should still be as few as possible and responsibilities should be clear. In all but the most static environments, the person with ongoing project responsibility (the business analyst for a large department or an analyst/programmer for a small one) should be the main contact point. Where simple systems are installed, such an analytical type should be able to serve as the first point of contact for *all* matters, not just those dealing with the application side of the system. Any single person will require backup of some sort, either an alternative person or a help desk facility.

is to be split between mainframe and downsized areas. Certain types of project manager may also be able to play a role in operational management, in the event that there are skills shortages here. One has in mind the ongoing management of operations over a large networked system containing many downsized nodes, a challenging and essential job where the downsized units cover essential business services such as branch-level customer contact.

Technicians

The need for technical staff will vary in the downsized environment, and not only according to the technology chosen and application complexity. In larger organizations, as every operations manager knows, a lot of problems can occur suddenly within a short time frame. Much of this is due to random distribution principles; at certain points in the year a number of unpleasant instances will occur simply because the laws of probability are looking gleefully over one's shoulder.

Other occasions may require substantial technical support, such as the need to implement new features on a number of systems at once. A hardware upgrade or new software release for several hundred machines is a formidable logistical problem even in the unlikely event that there are no complications. For reasons of homogeneity and ease of ongoing support, it is ideal to have the various systems broadly in step. However, the logistics to support this ideal policy can be formidable, substantially raising the overheads of the downsized systems. Also, when little is happening, technicians may become idle, as there is little alternative work this type of person can do. Here, once again, we are in trade-off territory. The most economical approach is clearly to stretch out changes over a longer period of time, such that the end of one installation process virtually coincides with the beginning of the next. While this means longer periods of incompatibility between systems, upping fault-diagnosis costs and causing a certain amount of management effort to keep the resulting confusion away from users' eyes, the cost savings overall can be substantial. A skilled technician costs somewhat more than our analyst/programmer, perhaps commanding a salary of $60,000 to $70,000 in most western countries. A saving of several such people is therefore meaningful.

Managing IT staff

We have so far discussed types of people, their training and preparation, and longer-term issues for getting some more traditional IT staff out into the downsized world. Thoughts ought to be given as well to working practices during development and ongoing maintenance. The better these are, the lower IT-to-user support ratios can be.

Some sensitive topics are involved. While some advocates of downsizing argue that the business analyst and the analyst/programmers should actually belong to the user department, we have already suggested that this is not usually the best course of action. Career structures, motivation and evaluation of performance all present problems. Even in the downsized world, the user is a user and the IT professional is what he is. If the twain are meeting on friendlier and more productive ground, this does not mean they are the same quantity or that they belong in the same unit. During the project planning and development stages, it is advisable for IT staff to spend large amounts of time actually in the end-user department, whether or not they are actually talking to users at the time. Sixty per cent, or three days per week, is the recommended figure. If this is done, application-related work will get done more quickly and accurately, as people will offer informal comments which may not come out in occasional discussions. By making their presence felt, the IT staff will become more closely identified with the department's goals. The traditional IT approach, where the systems analyst may spend less than a day a week talking to users (including time spent on the telephone), with the rest of his time spent dealing with bureaucratic and technical matters back in the IT department, will not work in the downsized world and should be consigned to the past. Wherever space can be afforded in user departments, IT staff should have their own desks.

Once a project has gone live, the ongoing maintenance of the application should be subject to the same approach as development, if on a reduced scale. Aside from progress meetings (normally every second month or so), the person responsible for a particular department should make short visits as questions arise. For highly distributed scenarios, location and travel time will be a problem, and substitution of some visits by telephone calls should be considered.

Formal progress meetings should be accompanied by minutes, including any action that needs to be taken by any of the parties involved, whether the project is in development or maintenance mode. Overall, the ongoing management of downsized projects and their people follows the pattern set during development, but on a reduced scale.

Operations managers

The large centralized IT department inevitably employs a large operations staff, with numbers of former operators in management jobs. These may be in actual system operation, or in related areas such as network control, database administration and advisory or planning functions.

In general, operations managers are among the more meaningful assets of an IT department, though often they do not get sufficient recognition for their services. Theirs is one of the most difficult jobs in computing, a consequence of which is that many managers have developed good trouble-shooting abilities and the ability to react

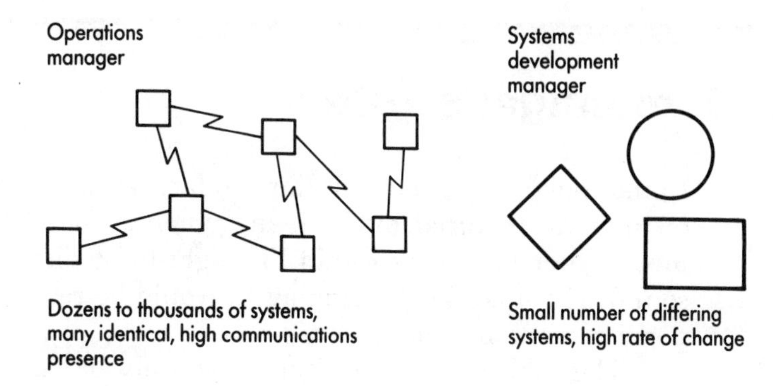

Figure 23.5 Who oversees downsized systems?

The ongoing management of implemented systems, as with much else in downsizing, should be straightforward and unambiguous, with not too many fingers in any given pie. For the highly distributed situation in Figure 23.5, a good operations manager could oversee limited systems development within his sphere as well as coping with the more fiendish communications side.

quickly to unexpected situations. Many such skills are exactly what are required in the downsized environment.

When an IT department decentralizes, there may be surpluses in both operators and their managers. A minority of the operators themselves, with training, may eventually be deployable as junior analyst/programmers under similar conditions to those of other junior staff (program coders and beginning technicians). Other operators will not have either the intellectual qualities or the personal attributes to cope with such work, and they may lack interest as well.

The operations manager himself deserves some consideration. The normal operations person in a large networked company may already have some technical understanding both of communications and of general machine matters. Where large amounts of networking are involved in the downsized scenario, such people are obvious candidates to manage a substantial percentage of the ongoing effort. How their role is structured *vis-à-vis* other managers depends on the size and complexity of the networking component and what else is going on. In many very intricate and large-scale cases, a manager with an operations background could oversee the entire collection of downsized systems once they have been developed. If sufficiently broadminded, he could include some amounts of development and enhancement under his authority, though very large developments would still remain under separate management.

The IT manager's role

In the course of our deliberations so far, we have noted the new types of thinking required by IT management. The changing role of the more senior managers within IT ought to be discussed as well. With so much around them changing, it would be remarkable if their own position remained unaltered.

The new-world IT manager can only be effective if he mirrors the values and the structures in which he operates. In our new environment, this means:

- Proximity to the actual business activity as personified by the end user, not merely as personified by senior general management.
- Control of application quality.
- Strict supervision of the technology used.

To achieve such objectives to the degree one would wish is impossible. However, in order even to get close, much restructuring will usually have to be done. Existing IT management structures are often deep, with many managers or supervisors having a relatively small number of people reporting to them. In a large IT department, there can easily be five or six layers of management sitting above the analyst or programmer. In this situation, not only the top IT manager or director, but also the next couple of layers below him, are going to be out of touch with what is happening on the ground floor. A common defence of this deep management structure is that it helps to effect changes quickly. In this writer's experience, much flatter structures have also shown the ability to change rapidly. Much depends upon the actual people and the issues involved in the change. Top-heavy managements, in the eyes of many observers, may be too isolated to decide on which change is required, and in this case changing to the wrong type of solution quickly is clearly of no benefit. Also, time may be wasted coordinating different groups of managers. In the downsized world, it is vital for the *right* changes to be effected quickly, and to do this one must be close to users, senior general managers and the rapidly changing computer market itself.

Closeness to the action level of the organization can only be achieved by organizing along the following lines:

- Having the least number of management levels possible, meaning that as few people at as few levels must exist, consistent with the maintenance of control.
- Encouraging managers to spend most of their time maintaining contact with essentials, rather than talking to each other overmuch or getting enmeshed in trivial administration and bureaucracy.

The two above reforms go together. By reducing the number of levels, each manager will be taking more direct reports, so getting a wider variety of feedback. By a simple process of subtraction, one can only spend more time with one's own people if one spends less time with colleagues, however pleasingly insulating the latter might be. A further benefit of this 'flat, active' model is that it makes highly visible those who are not performing.

Such structures have their hazards, and they should be recognized. It takes much administrative skill to slice time such that each individual person reporting to the manager is monitored, motivated and trained to the right degree. Techniques for improving productivity in these areas include group meetings where feasible (say, to obtain feedback on common types of project or technology), and combining meetings with different types of people where there are no undue risks involved in doing so (one has in mind some meetings where both users and one's own staff are involved). The most important thing is to keep the objective in mind: the maintenance of short but frequent periods of contact. The means by which this is done is secondary.

Key issues

- Select very carefully all IT personnel who will spend significant time with the end user.
- Look for analyst/programmers with fourth-generation or prototyping experience.
- Train developers in application basics before sending them into end-user territory.

- Be prepared to use traditional project managers where large, complex applications are necessary. Similarly, consider using operations managers to oversee installed systems where intricate communications networks are present.
- Generally keep narrow technicians away from the user's view.

24

Case studies

Downsizing has by now progressed far enough for there to exist many real life examples of how to do it properly. By paying attention to these, we not only gain confidence that the overall idea is sound, we can also derive rules that might apply to one's own situation.

Vernons' pools

A well-publicized instance in the UK is that of Vernons' Pools, a large lottery operator. The characteristics of this business suggest that downsizing, but in a centralized rather than distributed context, should be a reasonable alternative to a mainframe solution.

The most elemental processing requirement at Vernons' is to handle very large volumes of relatively simple transactions. The bulk of these transactions are in the form of betting slips or coupons returned by post. Vernons' receive two and a half million such coupons per week, which implies a transaction rate of 20 per second on average, and short turnaround times are required. At first glance, and especially if one were to allow for peaking and recovery workloads, this, at the time (the late 1980s), appeared ambitious for a downsized solution.

However, other characteristics appeared more favourable to downsizing concepts. The transactions were discrete and basic in nature. Moreover, the size of the database was moderate (two million customers, or a small number of gigabytes), and its structure was simple enough to permit a basic relational design.

Aside from the fundamental transaction-processing workload, important requirements lay in accounting and in management information. However, these needs were less awe inspiring than those of the core application and could in theory have been offloaded or at least partly separated from the main system.

The existing position

Vernons' computer installation at the start of the downsizing evaluation consisted of an old IBM mainframe that was very heavily utilized. Not only the central processor, but also the disk subsystem, were obsolete, so the whole hardware core of the system required replacement. The mainframe was based on the old VSE operating system, so any significant expansion in capacity would most likely have to be accompanied by an upgrade to the more expensive and troublesome MVS software set. While in theory it might have been possible to remain with VSE, Vernons' regarded this as unattractive because of the suspect viability and ongoing support of that system. Also, even the VSE software rentals would have been relatively expensive.

At application level, many programs were written in the IBM Assembler language, and thus were very difficult to extend and amend. Most were poorly documented. It was therefore clear that software problems figured perhaps as prominently as hardware issues in Vernons' deliberations. A main objective in choosing a new system was to enjoy rapid development and ease of use in comparison with the old mainframe system.

The alternatives

Vernons' initially looked briefly at over a dozen vendors across both mainframe and minicomputer areas. A short-list of three was then produced, the surviving entrants being IBM, Sequent and Pyramid. Two systems were to be proposed by each, to cater for resilience and for a separate development environment.

Because the AS/400 was then of insufficient power to handle the transaction load, IBM was forced to propose two middle-sized mainframes (4381s). This increased IBM's cost significantly, much of the high cost being in the software. Pyramid and Sequent proposed multiprocessor UNIX systems, Pyramid's being based on Mips chips and

Sequent's on Intel's. INFORMIX and INGRES databases were proposed respectively.

Though all three vendors would have been able to handle the requirements ably, there were marked differences in price, as might be expected. In particular, the Pyramid bid was one-third the price of the IBM offering (when software costs were included), and it was this system that was selected. A pleasant surprise for Vernons' was that, though the Pyramid system was cheap, the personnel involved in sales and support were as professional as those of any of the other vendors, IBM included.

Aside from the Pyramid-UNIX-INFORMIX central system, Vernons' ordered a 24 terminal Altos UNIX subsystem for accounting, and 10 PCs for management information. The two subsystems were connected to the main processor via an Ethernet local network. A total of 135 terminals (including the PCs) were to be connected to the two machines, either directly or indirectly.

Implementation and results

Though there were some unexpected problems with the large UNIX system, these proved to be relatively minor compared with the benefits experienced. Probably the most significant negative aspect was UNIX's poor print spooling. Standard UNIX spooling lacks space compression and is relatively primitive in some other respects. It cannot split a large print job across two printers, nor can it re-start an aborted print run part-way through. Vernons' solved these problems by writing their own compression routine (which took approximately one day) and by acquiring a third-party package to address the other problems.

Otherwise, the system proved successful, unexpectedly so in the eyes of observers who had been trained to think of UNIX as a non-commercial offering. Vernons' considered their new system flexible and easy to use, and well suited to rapid application development. It must be kept in mind that Vernons' were an experienced IBM shop, and therefore were familiar with technical matters in general even though they were new to UNIX.

The basic system (hardware and system software) also proved robust, offering mainframe levels of reliability. Broadly, the new system was accepted by Vernons' IT staff, though two IBM loyalists left to continue their careers elsewhere.

Vernons' pursued an aggressive time-scale in developing their replacement system. The main system went live less than a year after re-design started, and some eight months after the delivery of the first Pyramid machine.

The key elements in Vernons' Pools' downsizing exercise were in line with many established rules on the subject. The organization was well-acquainted with its application needs and understood the topology required to meet those needs. It was not afraid to look to the best technology at the time, and was not overly dissuaded by its established position and previous experience. Vernons' were willing to take a few limited risks in order to achieve benefits which included quite substantial cost savings (well over a million dollars at the then current rate of exchange). Finally, they got on with the job in hand and quickly overcame minor obstacles.

Decentralized cases

While Vernons' Pools was a reasonably straightforward central mainframe replacement, there are many other cases where large central machines have been either partly or completely replaced by much smaller solutions. A sign of the times is that many of these large central machines are minicomputers (typically VAXs or Hewlett-Packard's 3000 series) as well as mainframes. In many of these examples, savings in software costs are a significant factor in the decision to go to PC-based client/server systems.

Royal International (a subsidiary of Royal Insurance) quoted savings of over a hundred thousand dollars a year in software costs alone simply by moving from a large Hewlett-Packard machine to a number of PCs. The PCs were able to use an off-the-shelf application which cost $8,000 (a one-off charge). The overall cost of maintaining the system dropped dramatically as well, by over $200,000 per year.

EBC Amro Asset Management, another financial concern, quoted savings of over $400,000 per year by moving from a large DEC VAX to a PC-based local network. Here, the system was not only vastly cheaper, it also was able to provide quicker results to sudden application demands.

An international bank, wishing to remain anonymous, was able to save over three million dollars in its first downsized year by using networked PS/2s for management information instead of upgrading the central mainframe complex to handle that workload. This provides a good example of distributing the information centre away from the traditional monolith toward local systems which are more responsive as well as being infinitely cheaper.

Associated British Ports

A convincing instance of downsizing tied to organizational change occurred when the national port authority of the UK decentralized into largely autonomous units, each based on a major seaport. The existing mainframe system was clearly both expensive and unsuited to this highly distributed mode of operation. The application profile was not a high-volume one, as shipping consists mainly of high-value movements in relatively small numbers. Information handling, accounting and payroll in such a situation are equally suited to small machines close to the end user. Flexibility and responsiveness at local level were very important to the various divisions.

Associated British Ports looked at both UNIX machines and networked PCs as possible solutions to their problems. In this case the PC network won, as it was cheap, easy to use and could clearly handle the basic workloads involved. The DOS workstations were based around Compaq SystemPro servers, the latter using Novell's NetWare for file-server functions. Rather than develop their own software, the installations use packaged accounting and payroll software (SunAccount and Peterborough packages respectively).

Both the speed at which the organization moved and the magnitude of the savings were impressive. The system was installed and live slightly over a year after the initial decision to downsize was made. While a central mainframe facility was retained to coordinate activities across the different locations, the savings over the mainframe alternative for local processing paid for the new system within ten months. The number of people supporting the systems was reduced from 35 to 10, and these remaining people were actually able to spend more time with users than had previously been the case.

Overall lessons from the real world

Earlier in the book, we noted some examples where downsizing had not been successful, and we were able to tie the lack of success to the violation of definite rules. It bears observing that success definitely does come from obeying the rules, and that these rules moreover are based on practicality and not on overly technical issues.

The installations who did things well did not worry much about theories or minor product details, but instead looked at fairly high level at the types of package that would fit their businesses and make their organizations more effective. In all cases, cost was a major factor, as it generally is in the real world. In a number of instances, a new manager had just arrived on the scene, and so was able to provide a fresh view of the situation. In all cases, change was driven by forceful managers who simply wanted to get on with the job as quickly as was feasible.

The cases also illustrate that downsizing in many cases is complementary to mainframe computing, not a direct substitute. The work of the downsized systems was either simple or low in volume, or often both. Large, complex, integrated applications operating at high speed were not attempted, but were left to the mainframe in those situations where such applications were necessary.

25

Downsizing for success

In the preceding pages we have tried to illustrate both the desirability of downsizing and many of its practicalities. To anyone intent on getting the best out of computer technology today, downsizing represents the ideal means of doing so in the vast majority of applications likely to be encountered.

Advocates of downsizing have time on their side. Even if treated with scepticism initially, the high rate of technological change means that one should not have to wait too long before the rightness of downsizing becomes evident to all but the most obtuse.

The issues involved in downsizing are straightforward, as we hope to have shown. Instead of minding one incomprehensible monolith, the new-world IT manager has the more rewarding task of looking after a number of separate but human situations. No one should claim that the new style of management is easy, or that it somehow 'de-professionalizes' people. New-world IT management is in fact much more aligned with management practice elsewhere the organizational world, subject to the same criteria of success and failure as one's colleagues. The competent manager will welcome being judged on overall business effectiveness, whereas the over promoted mainframe technician still common in large organizations will so obviously be out of his element that he will not be able to sustain his position.

Downsizing is here to stay. Those who want to make a success of the remainder of their IT careers must get to grips with it as quickly and as certainly as possible.

The key messages for downsizing success

- Keep it simple
- Watch the application
- Involve the end user
- Don't tolerate time-wasters
- Put business needs before technical details
- Ignore industry fashions
- Don't believe salesmen

Appendix

Benchmarks for small machines

As hardware technology becomes both more powerful and competitive, much publicity has grown around performance benchmarks. Many numbers quoted are misleading or misunderstood, so we will here consider some of the major aspects of the varying claims of suppliers and industry analysts.

Raw central processor performance

With fast microprocessor chips flooding the market, the 'mips' war (for millions of instructions per second) is in full force. Two figures are often cited for a central processor: the clock rate, expressed in MegaHertz (MHz), meaning millions of cycles per second; and the mips rate, the number of millions of instructions per second which the processor is supposed to be able to execute.

In the past, the mips rate used to be much slower than the clock rate, as old style processors used several cycles in order to execute a single instruction (such as an Add or a Move Characters). Lately, the trend has been for mips to overtake the clock or cycle rate, as newer types of processor can execute more than one instruction at a time.

For example, DEC's new Alpha chip claims to run at 200 MHz but be able to execute 400 millions instructions a second – two instructions on average per clock cycle. The fastest current Intel 486 chip runs at 67 MHz and claims around 50 mips, depending partly upon who is doing the claiming.

Raw processor performance for numeric work is also measured in such standard instruction mixes as Whetstones, Dhrystones and SPECmarks. Floating-point operations may be specified in Megaflops or Gigaflops (flop = floating point operations per second). Graphics performance may be measured in 3D vectors per second. Without getting too technical, all of these more basic measures are reasonably trustworthy, so long as the same measure is used between different suppliers. They all measure central processor performance, either in general or for numeric or graphics work, and there is little the truth adjusters (the vendor's marketing staff) can do to alter them.

Commercial benchmarks

When it comes to measuring commercial workloads, life becomes very different very quickly. Part of the problem is that such work does not automatically define itself as do numeric and graphics tasks. Much depends upon how many input/output operations occur per transaction, how they are programmed, and how large or disorderly a database they are accessing. To try to get some even partly accurate measure into the marketplace, various supposedly standard benchmarks have been produced. The best known are the Transaction Processing Council's debit–credit benchmark (based on a banking application) and IBM's RAMP-C.

Like many IT standards, these benchmarks may not run in as standard a fashion as they should. The most standard one is the Transaction Processing Council's (called TPC-A or TPC-B depending upon how the network is emulated). However, a measured result against this benchmark is only meaningful if it has been certified by the Transaction Processing Council itself. Several vendors have been known to quote the benchmark, but to have run it to their own rules and so distorted the results.

IBM's RAMP-C benchmark

Though less 'official' than the TPC benchmarks, IBM's RAMP-C has been around for some time and is widely quoted on that company's mid-range machines as well as on some competitive systems. RAMP-C has a specific objective, and one that is different from that of the Transaction Processing Council. The IBM test is meant to gauge central processor capacity, not overall system capability. In other words, it is meant as a sizing device for a central processing unit so that a prospective customer might know which model to buy. It says nothing about overall system performance, in that it ignores add-ons to the central processor such as disk channels and drives, communications lines and main memory.

To run the benchmark, IBM loads up the central processor until it is virtually 100% full, noting the transaction rate at which this happens. The RAMP-C figure is 70% of this 100% rate, as the corporation feels that this is a reasonable loading for transaction work in a real life environment.

The RAMP-C benchmark is written in COBOL, which is not the best language for all the machines benchmarked (for example, the AS/400 generally runs better in RPG/400). The benchmark consists of four transaction types, as specified below. The transactions arrive at a constant (not random) rate, and no logging or journaling is active. File sizes are relatively small, at approximately 30,000 records each, no matter how many transactions per second are being applied. No particular goals are set on response time, though in general IBM try to keep most of them within two seconds.

Transaction Type	COBOL Statements	Think Time (s)	Percentage of Terminals	Percentage of Load	Number of Files	Number of Logical I/Os
Simple	70	7.5	20	35	2	2
Average	140	10	20	25	3	7
Complex	330	18.2	40	30	3	23
Very Complex	625	26	20	10	5	41

The TPC Debit–Credit benchmark

This benchmark is meant to be a measure of overall system performance, the costings reflecting true cost of ownership over five years, including basic platform costs and maintenance. Files are scaled according to the activity of the system, as would happen in a normal banking environment. Ninety five per cent of the response times must be one second or less.

Debit–Credit is a very simple benchmark, with only four files accessed (one of which is a sequential history file). There are seven input/output operations per transaction, as follows:

- 3 reads
- 3 updates
- 1 sequential write (to the history file)

The files have 20 fields each, with a total of 200 characters per record. Logging is active, as would apply in the real world. The program contains 25 COBOL statements, and the source code is published (which is not the case with IBM's RAMP-C).

Overall issues

The two commercial benchmarks, RAMP-C and Debit–Credit, are useful enough as far as they go, and do provide comparative performance guides so long as vendors stick to the rules. However, both are artificial, though in different respects. RAMP-C would be better if it were a measure of overall system capability, and not just of central processor power. It should also be run with logging or journaling active, as this can make a significant difference in results. Debit-Credit, though realistic enough for its intended application, would not apply to most commercial transactions as the latter are generally far more complex than the very basic banking program used.

With Debit–Credit, there is also a greater danger of inaccurate extrapolation should the prospective user wish to gauge different types of transaction performance from TPC results. In other words, if Debit–Credit shows a result of 200 input-output operations per second (28.6 transactions per second times the seven file I/0s of each), this does *not* mean we can get 200 I/0s per second out of more complex transactions (say, four transactions per second of 50 I/0s each). The reasons for this lack of scalability lie in a combination of queuing theory and the limited architectures of many small machines. In plain language, an item with a long service time (our 50 I/0 transactions) poured into a device of limited capacity can slow it down disproportionately. Products at the smaller end of most suppliers' ranges illustrate this, as they typically have slow, single input/output buses and a very small number of disk drives and controllers (sometimes one of each).

A common question occurs where users are faced with the two different types of benchmark for two different machines. Most usually, this is between an IBM product (say, AS/400) quoting RAMP-C figures and another supplier's system using TPC. Though RAMP-C is clearly a more complex situation, being a mix of four transaction types averaging 14 input/output operations as compared with TPC's seven, other factors (logging, real world system configuration) tip the balance back toward TPC. Industry watchers, Gartner Group, suggests that RAMP-C is 50% more expensive in system resources than TPC's Debit–Credit. In other words, two RAMP-Cs per second would equal three TPC transactions. While such measures are necessarily approximate, this is probably a reasonable ratio to use between the two, so long as only simple transaction work is under consideration.

We mentioned that the TPC benchmark specifies a five-year cost per transaction per second, an item of great interest to many prospective users. The figures vary enormously, depending upon which type of architecture is chosen. As might be expected, client/server wins by a wide margin, with costs of $2,000 or less now common. Minicomputer and AS/400 configurations come in at around four to five times this level (say, $8,000 to $10,000 per transaction per second), and mainframes as expected occupy the financial stratosphere, at several times the mini rate (perhaps $30,000 would be an average figure).

The point worth making from the above is that, as benchmarks are approximate measures anyway, there is no point in worrying about a 20% or so difference between two machines. Other factors such as quality and vendor viability should substantially outweigh such thin margins. The big difference is in the type of solution chosen. Differences of several hundred percent do influence decision makers, as the large savings can be applied to other purposes.

Index